Pelican Books
A History of Modern Ireland

Edward Norman is lecturer in modern British
constitutional and ecclesiastical history at the
University of Cambridge, Dean of Peterhouse,
Cambridge, a Church of England clergyman and an
assistant chaplain to a hospital. His publications
include a book on religion in America and Canada,
The Conscience of the State in North America, *The Early
Development of Irish Society*, *Anti-Catholicism in
Victorian England* and *The Catholic Church and Ireland*.
Edward Norman also contributes articles on
religious topics to the *Spectator*.

Edward Norman

A History of
Modern Ireland

Advisory Editor J. H. Plumb

PENGUIN BOOKS

Penguin Books Ltd, Harmondsworth,
Middlesex, England
Penguin Books Inc., 7110 Ambassador Road,
Baltimore, Maryland 21207, U.S.A.
Penguin Books Australia Ltd, Ringwood,
Victoria, Australia

First published by Allen Lane The Penguin Press 1971
Published in Pelican Books 1973

Copyright © Edward Norman, 1971

Made and printed in Great Britain by
Richard Clay (The Chaucer Press), Ltd,
Bungay, Suffolk
Set in Monotype Garamond

Contents

Preface to the Pelican Edition

This book is intended as an introduction to the political history of Ireland in modern times. It was commissioned – and most of it was actually written – before the present disturbances fell upon the country. It was unfortunate that its publication in 1971 coincided with a moment of extreme controversy, because it was intended to provide a cool look at the unhappy divisions of Ireland. Instead of assuming the structure of interpretation imposed by writers soaked in Irish national feeling, or dependent upon them, the book tried to consider Ireland's political development as a part of the general evolution of British politics in the last two hundred years. To that extent it is a 'British' view of the 'Irish Question'. It was not, however, intended to be a view especially in sympathy with 'British' policies, although those policies receive a reappraisal here. There has never, in fact, been a consistent British view of Irish political questions, and as often as not politicians at Westminster have tended to borrow the analysis of Ireland's problems suggested by Irish polemicism. When the book was published it elicited a hostile reception from the Irish press. The Dublin *Sunday Independent* remarked that parts of it read 'like a Black-and-Tan handout'; the *Irish Times*, on the other hand, wrote that it was 'like a Sunday newspaper reporter hotting up an otherwise dull story'. The *Irish Press*, another Dublin paper, added that the author was the sort of person liable to discount the sufferings of the Jews at Dachau or elsewhere as 'figments of the imagination'. Several papers were good enough to hope that after this aberration the author might return to the excellence of his earlier books about Ireland – evidently forgetting that those earlier works had, in their day, been received with equal hostility, and by the same newspapers. In Ireland time occasionally softens the memory; more often, alas, it does not. The author still hopes that some will find this book a useful introduction; the Irish are too great a people not to be able to bear with an external view of their history.

Peterhouse, 1972   *Edward Norman*

1. Irish Questions and English Answers

It is an extraordinary and unhappy circumstance that the history of Ireland has been conceived as a series of dualisms. Englishmen have often supposed it to be a lamentable chronicle of good intentions frustrated by an ungovernable and ungrateful people; in Ireland, on the contrary, a review of the past has only too readily suggested an unceasing catalogue of usurpation and oppression. But it is through the screen provided by Irishmen themselves, now secure in national independence, that most historical analysis is received. As Sir Charles Gavan Duffy wisely remarked in 1883, his thoughts extending across half a century of political upheaval in which he had himself taken no small part, 'whenever important interests have been in conflict and one has succumbed, the facts are certain to be misjudged by the next generation, who commonly hear only the story of the successful competitor.' The history of modern Ireland has primarily been written in terms of the politics of nationalism. It is a history of agitation. The perspective, as a result, is often wrongly drawn; for Ireland has another history as well. While national politicians exhausted their energies – which were slow to exhaust – in accumulating the evidences of Ireland's misgovernment, a new Ireland was in fact being created. The machinery of modern government and social improvement gave expression, often at first imperceptibly, to something which the nationalists' exposition of Irish history leaves substantially unexplained.

Irish nationalists have so unquestioningly resorted to history in order to reveal what to them has seemed the obvious justification of their beliefs that any critical analysis of Ireland in modern times is obliged to make their assumptions a starting point. But a case which is dependent upon historical interpretation, of course, can be tested by historical analysis. And of that there has been a generous surplus. Irishmen are obsessed by history; as John O'Leary, the Fenian apologist whom Yeats actually honoured with lines of verse, once wrote: 'Most events of the present day have their ultimate roots in the far-away past; most Irish ones being more or less easily traced to the Norman Conquest of Ireland, and by a little ingenuity led back to St Patrick, or even to the Flood.' Irish confidence in historical evidence is such that it has apparently provided the sole justification, on some notable occasions, for some pretty extreme political action. Thomas Meagher told the judges at his trial for treason-felony in 1848 that 'the history of Ireland explains my crime and justifies it.' Lloyd George, himself no stranger to political tautology, found himself outclassed by de Valera in the summer of 1921 when they met in London to discuss an Irish peace settlement. 'When I tried to bring him down to the present day, back he went to Cromwell again,' he recorded afterwards; 'it reminded me of a circus roundabout when I was a boy.' So mystifying was this simple reduction of Ireland's problems to a historical formula that nineteenth-century observers ventured to imagine some defect in Irish character. The matter is an important one, for most Englishmen assumed a racial difference at the very centre of their analysis of the Irish question, just as most Irishmen attributed what they liked to suppose was the brutality of England to the Saxon blood of her inhabitants. There was a 'stage' Englishman as well as a 'stage' Irishman. Thomas Davis, the theorist of Young Ireland nationalism in the 1840s, though he persistently argued for racial cooperation, still assumed the priority of racial distinctions and could not resist an occasional relapse into the normal culture of his countrymen: 'The Saxon plots a vice where the Celt meditates a compliment; and when he falls into habitual immorality he wallows like a hog in the sty of his own moral filth.' There speaks the authentic voice of Irish nationalism. Even the most sympathetic external observers found an explanation of the country's ills in the Irish character. 'The sensuous and excitable nature of the Irish prevents them from undertaking tasks which require sober judgement and tenacity of purpose,' wrote Engels in 1844; 'obviously such a people are not able to engage in industry as it is carried on today.' There were, however, already environmentalists stuffed full of reasons for Irish underdevelopment which, to the modern conscience, sound more agreeable. Thus Goldwin Smith, in *Irish History and Irish Character*, a series of Oxford lectures published in 1861: 'If they are wanting in industry, in regard for the rights of property, in reverence for the law, history furnishes a full explanation of their defects, without supposing in them any inherent depravity or even any inherent weakness.' But it is the people of Ireland who are themselves the most aware of national characteristics, and who secure for them a priority which might otherwise have diminished. Synge was accused of a libel on the Irish character when the *Playboy of the Western World* was produced at the Abbey Theatre in 1907. Yet the dialogue of his characters was carefully copied down by the playwright from real conversations overheard among his servants. The Irish, in the end, are their own most cruel detractors. 'If it rained soup from heaven,' Brendan Behan once remarked, 'they'd be rushing out with forks.'

The Irish, of course, are in reality like any other people –

subject to circumstance. Most of the characteristics which nineteenth-century commentary found less than attractive were in fact ones which could have described any peasant society. The proof of this was actually provided during the century. Emigration dispersed the Irish people across the world, and in their new lands they revealed new qualities. Emigration in significant quantity had actually begun at the end of the eighteenth century, and by the end of the nineteenth there were 5 million Irishmen living outside the British Isles. Over three quarters of these were in the United States, the rest in Canada and Australia. The Irish population of England, Wales, and Scotland must, in addition, have considerably exceeded a million by the end of the century. Three prime ministers – Canning, Wellington, and Palmerston – were Irishmen. The *diaspora* has given the world some distinguished fighting men. Bernardo O'Higgins, the national hero of Chile, was the son of an Irishman who was Spanish governor of the colony. General de Gaulle had an Irish grandmother. And Ernesto 'Che' Guevara's real surname, as it turns out, was Lynch. Emigration became institutionalized in Irish society during the nineteenth century; it became a part of family life. Everyone had relatives overseas. This gave the Irish question an international status, for Irish-Americans did not ignore the fate of their countrymen at home. They simmered with enthusiasm for Irish revolutionary movements, putting up cash and concern with liberality; they managed to squeeze the American administration into periodic exhalations of sympathy. Irish Catholicism went with the emigrants, and there were those who saw in this some compensation for the desolation of the Irish countryside. Ecclesiastical imperialism had much to commend it. 'It was a special dispensation of God to disperse the Irish people over every country of the globe,' said Cardinal Cullen in a sermon of 1864. No doubt the departing multitudes took appropriate consolation from the point. But the most remarkable change occurred among the Irish exiles – they settled in towns rather than in the countryside, both in England and in America. Those who had constituted a rural peasantry became an urban proletariat. Critics who considered the Irish people too idle or too ignorant for a *Gesellschaft* society could have found them, had they eyes to see, by the mere passage out of Ireland, transformed into the working populations of industrial cities. In the United States only two per cent of the immigrants took up rural pursuits. It was a very remarkable change: the result of the most remarkable demographic upheaval in modern times.

To their new lands the emigrants conveyed an antipathy to England which they were not slow in broadcasting. English and American liberals, of course, accepted their version of Saxon brutality at its face value. The 'Irish Question' became the first standing indictment of British maladministration of 'colonial' peoples. When Locker Lampson wrote his influential *Consideration of the State of Ireland in the Nineteenth Century* in 1907, he declared 'a moral purpose': it was 'intended to gibbet the incompetence of Ireland's governors for five centuries, and, in suffusing British cheeks with shame, to evoke better intentions for the future'. To mere incompetence, however, Irish tradition has added the notion that systematic viciousness encompassed the intentions of Englishmen. 'Ireland has suffered at the hands of British administrators,' Casement decided, as if in summary of the entire Irish world-picture, 'a more prolonged series of evils, deliberately inflicted, than any other community of civilized men.' Few Irishmen questioned this conclusion, and testimony to the contrary was so unpalatable as to remain virtually unsampled. Burke had declared that 'the subject is as free in Ireland as he is in England', and in the mid-swell of nineteenth-century liberalism John Stuart Mill allowed himself confirmation: 'No Irishman is now less free than an Anglo-Saxon, nor has he a less share of every benefit.' Yet it has been commonly supposed that the imperial parliament remained ignorant of the real needs and condition of Ireland. If this really was the case, it was not for want of available information. The Irish members saw to that. Between 1810 and 1833, for example, there were 114 Royal Commissions and sixty Select Committees on Irish questions. In 1814 the young Peel, wrapped in the duties of Chief Secretary, was reprimanded by his colleagues for introducing too much Irish legislation to parliament. It is certainly true that many of the owners of Irish land residing in England visited their estates with well-publicized infrequency, and that many of those most concerned with the formulation of Irish policy had no first-hand knowledge of the country. Even Gladstone, the one English statesman conventionally attributed with taking the Irish question seriously, only removed himself and his king-sized conscience to Ireland once, and then extremely briefly. Some excused themselves because of the sea-crossing. Newman, when rector of the Catholic University in Dublin during the 1850s, vowed at the end of every passage never to do it again. It was while recovering from sea-sickness on one such occasion that he fell upon the miraculous truth, as he supposed, that the early saints had crossed the Irish Sea by floating upon the stone tops of altars.

With the feeling that Englishmen were largely ignorant of Irish questions went the assurance, based upon much sounder evidence, that they were insensitive to the prickly national self-consciousness of the Irish people. 'The tactlessness of Englishmen, of men of high order, is the most difficult of the difficulties of the Empire,' as F. H. O'Donnell, the Home Rule politician, wrote of the problem in general. Archbishop Manning, in an open letter to Earl Grey of 1868, was rather more explicit: 'I do not think Englishmen are enough aware of the harm some among us do by a contemptuous, satirical, disrespectful, defiant language in speaking of Ireland and the Irish people.' There can be little doubt that Englishmen were often arrogant; it was the confidence of men from the most advanced society in the world attempting the assimilation of a less developed one. Not everyone had the perspicacity to recognize, as Lord Melbourne did, that despite appearances evidently to the contrary, 'the people of Ireland are not such damned fools as the people of England'. And certainly not everyone could have been correct in the diagnosis of Ireland's troubles. For there was not a single and inflexible English attitude to Ireland in the nineteenth century – there was a conflict of opinion among Englishmen, an aspect of the case which Irishmen were quick to exploit but reluctant to admit. What so few English observers were prepared to see, of course, was that there existed in Ireland a widely diffused belief not only that British administration was imperfectly attending to Irish needs, but that British sovereignty itself was being improperly exercised. When, for example, in his famous 'Pope and potatoes' speech of 1844, Disraeli remarked that 'the Irish question in its integrity' was to effect 'all those changes which a revolution would do by force', he misunderstood the capacity of any Imperial legislation to satisfy the ultimate requirements of Irish agitation. It was to the full exercise of sovereignty in domestic affairs, whether delegated from the Crown or, as more extreme men occasionally hoped, some sort of republicanism, that many Irish politicians aspired. 'I want every Irishman to be convinced of this truth,' O'Connell said in 1842, 'that there is nothing worth looking for, save the power of governing ourselves.' And in 1881 Parnell added, 'the reason the Irish do not succeed in Ireland is because a nation governed by another nation never does succeed.' The government generally supposed that the survival of Irish national feeling was an accident of underdevelopment, and that once the Irish people had been drawn upwards in the scale of civilization their integration within the United Kingdom would eradicate separate national consciousness. Irishmen tended, on the other hand, to vitiate the right of Englishmen to set the values of the scale of civilization at their own definition. The *legitimacy* of British sovereignty was frequently questioned, or, as Tim Healy, the first Governor-General of the Irish Free State claimed, 'the English had no better title to Ireland than that they were better armed some hundreds of years ago than we were.' This resort to distant history in deciding questions of sovereignty was incomprehensible to most Englishmen. It was again Disraeli who, in a House of Commons trembling with approval, issued another example of English logic in reply to Irish sentiment. The occasion was Isaac Butt's Home Rule motion in 1874.

The Irish had a strange passion for calling themselves a conquered people. He failed to perceive when or where they had been conquered. It might be urged that they had been conquered by Cromwell. What of that? Had not Cromwell previously conquered England? Why should his eloquent and imaginative friends [the Irish members] try to extract a peculiar grievance out of a common misfortune?

The incomprehension was not quite joined at all levels, however. During the period of the Union, between 1801 and 1922, Ireland enjoyed considerable stability. It is only when the telescoped vision of nationalist and radical politicians is allowed to assume the authority of orthodoxy that these decades can be represented as ones of ceaseless unrest. Substantial parts of political society found their aspirations about as reasonably accommodated within the existing structure as their counterparts in England did. Many, it is true, were 'Anglo-Irish' Protestants. But it would be a gross error to suppose that they were activists in the 'English' interest. They considered themselves Irishmen first, and attended to Irish interests before Imperial ones. They divided politically between Whig-Liberal and Tory. However much Irish agitators might have tried to represent 'the Ascendancy' as a colonial society given over solely to the exploitation of the Catholic peasantry, the facts are different. Many, it is true, protected landowning interests: so did a majority of the followers of O'Connell and Parnell. The landowning class in Ireland, that is to say, was divided politically. One of the most influential owners of property – the Catholic Church – exercised a political persuasion, usually on behalf of the popular parties, at least equal to that of the Ascendancy landlords.

It was the politics of agitation which most attracted the interest of contemporary and later commentators. Those whose disillusionment with society matures with their education into concepts which they imagine to stand in favourable contrast with the existing order usually create a quite different culture of agitation from those who are born into a society which they are instructed from the beginning to regard as unjust and oppressive. The latter condition, exemplified in Ireland, produces the politics of grievance. They are essentially negative; hence the Irish agitators' obsession with the historical faults of British administration, the lengthy catalogue of English 'crimes', and the absence of realistic alternative models to British constitutionalism. It is the last effect which has resulted in a distinction, employed throughout the present book, between 'radicalism' and 'nationalism' in Ireland. Those Irish agitators who sought merely to redefine the direction of sovereignty, in however drastic terms – men like O'Connell, Parnell, and Griffith – are most usefully described as radicals even though they customarily chose to call themselves nationalists. Those who aspired to replace the existing order with something derived from a quite different concept of sovereignty – as the Fenians, Pearse, and de Valera did – are more properly designated as nationalists, because they actually tried to create new models of social and governmental institutions as the expression of Irish nationality. But politics established in a catalogue of grievances can represent themselves in an extraordinarily fractious guise. To the unfamiliar observer the whole of society appears to have broken up into bickering components. Nassau Senior unkindly remarked that Irishmen 'agitate for the sake of agitation and select for their avowed object an unattainable end because it is unattainable'. Jules de Lasteyrie, writing in the *Revue des Deux Mondes* in 1868, saw the rancour spread with impartiality. Irish discontent, he noted, was likely to be permanent because 'some wish to maintain their supremacy, others their grievances'. One parliamentary candidate in the Dublin election of 1822 promised to enlighten the electors with 'five hundred grievances which they had previously known nothing about'. It was not surprising that government officials were sometimes reduced to inactivity when confronted with demands prefaced by a history of Irish wrongs since the invasion of Strongbow.

It is easy to suppose, as some have supposed, that the chronic disorder of Irish rural society in the nineteenth century was a symptom of political unrest. But this was not usually the case. Rural outrage was politically illiterate; the murders, cattle-maiming, firing of property, and almost universal intimidation were, of course, related to the economic margin at which many of the peasantry subsisted. The poor, however, failed to translate the causes of their privations into political terms. When roused by O'Connell to some measure of political consciousness, the peasantry did not support land legislation but political reforms like Catholic Emancipation and Repeal of the Union – policies whose immediate benefits were scarcely calculated to improve the conditions of peasant society. In 1839 O'Connell emphasized to the House of Commons that the statistics of indictable crime, in proportion to the population, showed a lower incidence in Ireland than in England. During the second half of the century disorder declined sharply in England; in Ireland, sustained by the poverty of the rural population, it continued. To contemporaries, who gave immense publicity to Irish crime, it occasionally seemed as if the whole fabric of society was pulling apart. Radical politicians, like Davitt and the Land Leaguers in the 1880s, exploited the endemic disorders for political purposes. 'Violence,' as William O'Brien announced with typical perspective, 'is the only way of securing a hearing for moderation.' Secret societies absorbed some of the disaffected tenants, but these were concerned almost exclusively with localized and individual cases of eviction and rent. Ribbonism, the most systematic of the rural combinations, had a shadowy national organization but no political influence. The Irish government responded to public disorders by passing coercive legislation and by creating a national and centralized police. By 1845 there were 9,000 men in the Royal Irish Constabulary, and a separate Dublin metropolitan force of over a thousand – a state initiative which was, on balance, popular with the Irish radicals, who wanted protection for their property. It was only in the present century, when republican extremists began a planned attack upon the police, that the R.I.C. came to be represented as the arm of British military imperialism in Ireland.

In addition to rural outrage, Ireland also suffered intermittent afflictions of religious disorder. Especially in Ulster, where Catholics and Protestants were stacked together in comparable numbers, disturbances were easily engendered by demonstrations of denominational loyalty. Casualties were heavy. In many years, the Orange celebrations on 12 July produced quite a bag, but almost any provocation, by either religious group, could start the rioting. In 1864, for example, sectarian disturbances in Belfast resulted in seven deaths, 150 severe injuries, and a Royal Commission of inquiry. Government action was impartial. In 1868 the Orange leader, Johnston of Ballykilbeg, was imprisoned for violating the ban on party processions which was then on the statute book. Both denominations, of course, persistently alleged government discrimination against them.

During the 120 years of the Union between England and Ireland, the government of Ireland was centred in Dublin Castle. There the Chief Secretary's office directed the armed forces and the administrative departments. Although the Castle has conventionally been described by nationalist politicians as a nest of English jobbery, it was, by the standards of the nineteenth century, extraordinarily efficient and uncorrupt. In 1817 and 1824 a lot of surviving sinecures were abolished. Irishmen held prominent appointments at all levels of the public service – especially after O'Connell's compact with the Whig government in 1835, when generous quantities of patronage were placed in the open hands of his political supporters. The employment of Irishmen was not a guarantee of disinterested service: 'it is a well-known fact,' L. Paul Dubois noticed in 1908, 'that they are far more despotic in their tendencies than their English colleagues.' The Irish government was headed by the Lord Lieutenant, as personal representative of the sovereign, and by the Chief Secretary. The latter was usually a politician of cabinet rank. Castlereagh, Wellington, Peel, Melbourne, Derby, Hartington, and Balfour all held the post. The Chief Secretary was responsible to parliament for the conduct of the government of Ireland, and resided half the year in Dublin. There was an Irish office in London, through which he arranged administration for the other six months. The Chief Secretary was assisted by an Under Secretary – a permanent official – and by two Crown law officers, both of whom were political appointments and members of the government. Some of the administrative departments were local extensions from Whitehall, others were exclusively Irish: a dualism chiefly remarkable because it was not ineffective. The only way in which the views of the Irish government could be disseminated was the rather disagreeable one of subsidizing the press. Neither the money nor the will available – for most Chief Secretaries had qualms about the propriety of a state-supported press – were adequate to present a counter-offensive to the offensiveness of the opposition papers.

One of the most advanced features of Irish government was the degree of central control exercised by the Castle over local affairs: the result of the poor finance and the inefficiency of the grand juries in the counties, and of the unreformed borough corporations. Central government intervened with occasional financial grants and by the organization of local effort into public works schemes. The detailed information about actual conditions throughout the countryside which was, as a result, available to the central administration was quite extraordinary in its quality and abundance. The Act of Union transferred the political representation of Ireland to the Westminster parliament, an arrangement which became the centre of grievance in the nineteenth century. Many Irish politicians attributed to an overseas legislature the sort of problems which afflict any country at almost any time. 'The gilded saloons of London,' as John MacHale, the Catholic Archbishop of Tuam, informed Earl Grey in 1831, 'are not the appropriate lecture halls for studying the wretchedness of an Irish cabin.' Electoral machinery revealed an exaggeration of the abuses apparent also in England. The involvement of the Roman Catholic clergy does not seem to have done anything to reduce the appalling frequency of election violence. Deaths were not uncommon. In 1867, at the Tipperary contest (a typical example), a mob carrying bludgeons was led to the hustings by two priests, one of whom carried a whip – presumably, though not necessarily, for political use.

The society presided over by this administrative and political machinery was scarcely at the open end of the British cornucopia in the nineteenth century. Yet the repetition of assertions like Gavan Duffy's, that 'on the face of God's earth there was not a country so miserable and hopeless as Ireland', though an article of every Irishman's creed, did a certain injustice to the conditions of suffering more general among mankind. Ireland's poverty was always set against the relative affluence of England: by the world's standards, the comparison was an unfair one. It was England's well-being which was an exception to the nineteenth-century world; Ireland was a much more typical society. Its population, it is true, increased at a rate which was just about to overtake resources when the great famine, as if in response to some hidden Malthusian device, stimulated the unpleasant solution of depopulation by emigration. The problem was beyond the control of government; and independent Ireland, after 1922, found itself no more competent to cope with its population troubles than the British administrators had been. The population had increased from just over 4 millions in 1791 to 8 millions in 1841. Except in the lower reaches of the Lagan Valley, around Belfast, where industrialization had absorbed and supported the extra inhabitants, this truly phenomenal explosion occurred within a rural society. After the mid-century began the long decline, scarcely interrupted to the present day. In 1961 the population of the Irish Republic was 2¾ millions, that of Northern Ireland nearly 1½ millions. Most of the reduction was due to continued though fluctuating patterns of emigration, but a staggeringly low marriage rate also helped. The 1946 census in southern Ireland revealed that eighty-eight per cent of men between twenty and thirty years of age were unmarried, and that sixty-four per cent of the population as a whole were single: a situation compounded of insecure economic circumstance and Catholic puritanism. The over-population of Ireland in the early nineteenth century was the primary cause of distress. There were simply too many people, living in small subdivided holdings – their existence given a deceptive substance by the potato economy. These conditions produced the misery which visitors to Ireland found so intolerable. In the least fertile western counties, where people had increased most disproportionately to resources, 'the population,' as a government report of 1836 observed, 'exhibits a state of poverty bordering on destitution.'

It was to the question of landholding that most men turned for an explanation of the troubles of Ireland. In the mid nineteenth century, sixty-six per cent of all families derived their living from agriculture. It is a curious fact, though one frequently submerged within the wealth of analysis, that land contract was almost universally upheld in Irish society. The tenants' demands for land reform, when they eventually began, did not question the basic assumption of landed rights: they sought only to secure a greater share of the blessings of landowning for themselves. Projects for land nationalization, which occasionally flipped from the minds of urban intellectual analysts, were always regarded as incurably eccentric by those who actually worked on the land. Doctrinaire nationalists found this truth extremely distasteful. 'So long as they are allowed to possess a certain number of acres,' wrote Charles Kickham, the Fenian journalist, 'they care not what becomes of Ireland.' And James Fintan Lalor, the leading exponent of agrarian socialism in Ireland, was equally realistic: 'The people do not care to subvert the British government,' he wrote in 1848; 'what they want is the land of Ireland for themselves.' The land question was not, therefore, one likely to inspire a revolution. The tenants looked only for modifications of the laws relating to landed contract. The landowners, receiving unsolicited support for their rights from political economists, urged the government to maintain a free-trade in land. But the existing law had produced a situation in which free contract operated to the benefit of the landowners. 'The law as it stands at present is the result of innumerable interferences in favour of the landlord and against the tenant,' as Poulet Scrope wrote in 1848; if the sixty or so statutes protecting the owners were repealed, he continued, 'there would be something to be said for non-interference' by the state.

Irish landowning had marked peculiarities. The owners let land only: the provision of a dwelling and all agricultural improvements were left to the tenants – most of whom, of course, were unable to raise the capital sums required to do more than put up a cabin. Except in parts of Ulster, where 'Tenant Right' enjoyed a customary existence, the outgoing tenants received no compensation for any improvements made during tenure: a state of affairs which placed disincentives in the way of agricultural development. During the Napoleonic Wars increased production had been accompanied by extensive subdivision of holdings. Irish landed society, as a result, became excessively graded, even the humblest tenants subletting small plots to peasant labourers scarcely better off than themselves. There was very little security of tenure, and in the acute deflationary period at the end of the war, when the demand for grain diminished, the more substantial landowners began to clear their estates for conversion to pasture. The effects were passed on down the landed hierarchy. Many landowners were anyway in financial difficulties by the mid-century, and found relief in the Act of 1849, which enabled them to disencumber their properties of legal restrictions on alienation. The land which then fell upon a market anyway depressed by the great famine was bought up, in large measure, by Catholic middle-class Irishmen anxious for quick returns on their investment. Evictions, as a result, increased. The panacea of the political economists – the creation of an Irish class of agricultural capitalists, as in England – appeared to be coming true. Between the Encumbered Estates Act of 1849 and 1882, the year in which Gladstone's second Land Act went into effect, nearly 99,000 families were evicted. Due to the custom of allowing tenants six months' credit on rents, a large number were in permanent arrears, and this, too, featured prominently in the distress of the peasantry. Compensation for improvements, security of tenure, the level of rents, and the removal of arrears formed the content of the land question. A good deal of ill-feeling also surrounded the absentee landowners – perhaps a third of all owners in Ireland – but in economic terms, as the political economists kept insisting, this made very little difference to the national wealth of the country. Irish landowners had a bad reputation in England, and when the Imperial parliament chose to spare them the disturbance of land reform, as it did until 1870, it was not because of sympathy with their conduct, but to avoid creating statutory precedents for state interference with landed contract which might later be applied in England. 'Ireland is the bulwark of the English landed aristocracy,' Marx wrote in 1870; 'the overthrow of the English aristocracy in Ireland has as a necessary consequence its overthrow in England.'

After the land, it was religion which most agitated the agitators of Ireland. In the mid nineteenth century, in the 1861 census, there were $4\frac{1}{2}$ million Roman Catholics and nearly 700,000 members of the Protestant Established Church in Ireland; in twenty-eight counties there was a Catholic majority, and in only four was there a Protestant one. The separation of faiths sliced across society, the Protestants enjoying a substantially more generous quantity of wealth and intelligence. The mutual repulsion was sometimes quite alarming. Protestants imagined the Church of Rome to be submerged in the most dreadful superstitions. 'The chill of death is gathering around the heart of the great Theocracy,' as Goldwin Smith, reflecting the views of many civilized men, remarked in 1861: 'but the pulses of life still beat strongly in the extremities of its frame, and nowhere more strongly than in Ireland.' Catholics responded vigorously to this sort of conclusion. In July 1862, for example, a party of Protestant schoolgirls returning from a dip in Galway Bay were mobbed by local Catholics who alleged that their mere presence in the sea had literally polluted it. Protestants were also accused of unfair proselytism. There were a number of well-supported missions to Catholics, like the 'New Reformation Society'; but Catholics themselves always supposed that the government was attempting to employ the machinery of national education to subvert the faith and morals of their children. Richard Whately, the Protestant Archbishop of Dublin and a man of very liberal persuasion, described how in 1852 an old Catholic woman approached one of his clergy with the words 'I am come to surrender to your Reverence – and I want the leg of mutton and the blanket.' She had been told by her priests that these were the incentives held out by the Protestants to procure conversions among the poor. 'The great instrument of conversion, however,' as Whately observed dourly, 'is the diffusion of Scriptural education.'

The Protestant Church Establishment was easily made to appear anomalous because it floated so unhappily upon a sea of Catholicism. It was also loaded with abuses. The demand for its radical reform, and then for its actual disestablishment, added considerable depths of religious excitement to the agitations of Ireland in the nineteenth century. The right of the Protestant clergy to tithes elicited especial bitterness. 'It is indeed not easy to imagine St Paul seizing for tithe the goods of a famished peasant belonging to a different religion,' as Goldwin Smith said in 1861. The Apostle, presumably, can be imagined even less in the guise of a sinecurist. But it was the difficulty of reconciling the Catholic population to a Protestant state which to most liberal critics of the Irish Church seemed most damaging. 'It destroys among the people reverence for the state' was the true verdict of Aubrey de Vere, the poet-convert to Catholicism. The Catholics, in fact, were still recovering, in both organization and self-esteem, from the penal legislation of the eighteenth century. Its severity had been more injurious to confidence than to faith, and Irishmen, of course, did not forget it. 'The traditions of the penal laws,' the *Freeman's Journal Church Commission* observed in 1868, the year before Irish disestablishment, 'are still fondly and at the same time bitterly cherished.'

By the mid-century, however, Catholic recovery was almost complete, and an incredible number of churches, monastic institutions, charities, and schools had been built across the country; an indication also of considerable wealth in Catholic hands. The political influence of the clergy caused despair to those who find such things improper. It was, in fact, an ascending influence. The voluntary nature of Irish Catholicism – the payment of the clergy from the free-will offerings of their flocks, and the fact that most priests had their social origins among the peasantry – meant that the political opinions of the clergy tended to be derived from those of the tenant-farming class. These opinions were then moulded by O'Connellism. The clergy were often unrestrained in their convictions, and employed intimidation rather lavishly at elections. During the Sligo contest in 1868 Bishop Gillooly stated from his altar that those voting for the Tory candidate would have to 'make reparation before they could be reconciled to God'. The lower clergy used lower language. In the 1852 election in Westmeath, for example, a priest threatened a potential Tory voter with the fate of being turned into an 'amphibious animal'. It was all very stimulating.

The relationship between Catholicism and popular politics projected the question of education as the third major grievance of nineteenth-century agitation in Ireland. As in England, the problems of religious instruction in the schools, and state support for education, were frequently at the centre of the clash between the Established Church and Dissent. The Catholics expected the Irish government to give state financial aid to their denominational schools, and to charter a Catholic university. The government, on the contrary, created a system of national non-sectarian primary schools of its own in the 1830s, and set up secular university colleges in the 1840s: an advanced experiment in state collectivism which, it was hoped, would help to end the social and religious divisions of the country. Only the English language was used in the schools. By 1850 there were 5,000 state schools, and by 1900 the illiteracy rate in Ireland had been reduced to six per cent. In practice, many of the schools became virtually denominational institutions, because the managers reflected the preponderance of religious opinion in each area. By 1880, 2,500 national schools were exclusively Catholic, and only 150 exclusively Protestant. The bold social experiment had, at any rate in that particular, been unsuccessful. But tested by the amount of education given, and the social effects of diffusing a uniform culture, the national system of schools was, as cultural nationalists ruefully confessed, only too effective. At the start of the nineteenth century there were fewer than $1\frac{1}{2}$ million people who could speak English; by the end of the century fewer than 750,000 could speak Irish. The transformation was a huge one, indicating the progressive assimilation of two peoples within a single society. There were, unhappily, reasons to explain why this assimilation did not find a stable political expression. They began, in so far as anything in Irish history is allowed a beginning, with the Act of Union in 1800.

2. The Union

The development of Ireland was so strikingly redirected by the Union of the country with England that it is possible to assign to 1800 a real significance which rarely attaches to a particular year in the history of most societies. Institutional and political tendencies, which for reasons of close proximity and shared experience were already similar, were, by the Act of Union, suddenly confirmed and reinforced just at a time when the transformation of English society was able to carry them into new dimensions. The enlarging responsibilities of government, which in the nineteenth century produced so many changes in the function of parliament, were also reproduced in Ireland as a result of the Union. A modern nation was created; the contrast with the preceding century, which nineteenth-century men themselves were often pleased to declare, was a real one.

The Constitution which was dismembered by the Act of Union in 1800 was one which had enjoyed fewer than twenty years of autonomous existence. The Tudor Poyning's Law, and the Declaratory Act of 1719, had left the Irish parliament almost entirely subservient to Westminster, and it was only the fortuitous outbreak of the War of Independence in the American colonies which suggested the practicality of a general constitutional revision. With sections of the army shipped off to fight across the Atlantic, and with the American commander John Paul Jones demonstrating on the seas off the northern coastline of Ireland, the need to defend the country declared itself vigorously to the Protestant gentry and urban professional men. The result, in 1778, was the formation on a territorial basis of a Volunteer force of armed Protestants. Catholics, who were still prohibited by law from equipping themselves with arms, were progressively admitted to the movement, and within a year an army of 30,000 men was in existence, under the command of the Earl of Charlemont. They were not slow in turning their potential political weight to account.

In 1779 the Irish parliament addressed itself to London on the need for equal trading rights between Ireland and the British dominions; a claim whose obvious affinity with the grievances of the American colonists was as clearly apparent in London as it was in Dublin and Belfast. The Imperial parliament, on the motion of Lord North, gave way. The Volunteers, with the momentum of expectancy, resorted to a convention at Dungannon in February 1782, where they deliberated upon their constitutional liberties. The ensuing claim, that 'any body of men, other than the King, Lords, and Commons of Ireland, to make laws to bind this Kingdom, is unconstitutional, illegal, and a grievance', amounted to a sharp enough definition of legislative autonomy. The executive in London conceded the point: Poyning's Law and the Declaratory Act were repealed in 1782, and Henry Grattan declared – prematurely, as it turned out – that Ireland was now a nation. The Volunteers disbanded voluntarily, and the next eighteen years were given over to lengthy and barren discussions, between divergent groups, about the reform of the Irish parliament. The only significant exception to this extenuated deadlock was the enfranchisement of the Catholic forty-shilling freeholders in 1793 – and this was achieved only with the exercise of pressure from Westmorland, the Viceroy, on the instruction of the British government.

The political connexions and reformist groups who together constituted the 'Protestant Nation' found their mutual discord interrupted by another external event. The impact of the revolution in France had the effect of widening the spectrum of disagreement, for it offered a ready-made political alternative, in the form of republicanism, to the more extreme radicals. And as England's difficulty was already preached as Ireland's opportunity, the chance of a French invasion of 'liberation' during Britain's continental involvement imparted such additional reasons as were still necessary for the Imperial parliament to scrutinize the internal affairs of Ireland. Reforming groups were wobbling to the left. The Society of United Irishmen – a minority alliance of extreme radicals – had been founded in 1791 in order to foster cooperation between the Ulster radicals, most of whom were Presbyterians, and the southern radicals, whose leaders, like those of the American revolution, were largely Episcopalians or Deists. The alliance of interests was primarily propagated as a union of Protestant and Catholic; 'that Religion,' as Arthur O'Connor wrote, 'shall no longer be made the instrument by which the Irish nation shall be divided, enslaved, and debased.' But there was, of course, no real political interest common to both the extreme radical Protestants and the Catholic merchants and tenantry. Wolfe Tone might declaim that as the French Revolution unfolded itself 'the public spirit of Ireland rose with a rapid acceleration', but in fact he described an excitement which was quite narrowly contained within easily definable sections of the doctrinaire disaffected.

In 1794 the United Irishmen were dissolved by law, and in transforming themselves into a secret society they advanced into ideological dimensions even more remote from the commonly acceptable political alternatives conceivable to most Irishmen. The new policies of republicanism and disestablishment were not liked by most of the Catholic clergy, who saw with an easy clarity the disagreeable results for religion of those policies in France. Many, indeed, looked to a union with England as a guarantee of religious and institutional stability. Dr Francis Moylan, the Catholic Bishop of Cork, for example, said quite frankly that only a union could extinguish the religious feuds of Ireland. Tone, on the other hand, representing Protestant radicalism, described the idea of a union quite simply as 'slavery'. The leadership of the United Irishmen, in fact, had passed the point at which its analysis of the troubles of Irish society and government represented any really substantial correspondence with political reality.

The leaders actually came from the Protestant middle class. Arthur O'Connor was descended from an English merchant family. He was the darling of the Foxite Whigs. Like Theobald Wolfe Tone, he was educated at Trinity College, Dublin. Tone's youthful passion for military bric-à-brac was brought to actuality after an unsuccessful venture into the legal profession. His antipathy to England appears to have originated in the frustration of a proposal he made in 1787 that Britain should establish a military colony on one of the South Sea islands which had just been discovered by Cook. When Pitt totally ignored the scheme Tone was furious. 'In my anger,' he later wrote, 'I made something like a vow that, if ever I had an opportunity, I would make Mr Pitt sorry.' That opportunity was not slow in presenting itself. Lord Edward Fitzgerald, who sat in parliament as a reformer, joined the United Irishmen in 1796 when sheer impatience induced him to add the dignity of his title to the cause of militancy. In the 1797 election the voters of Kildare expressed their opinion of this movement to the left; he was unseated. Thomas Addis Emmet was the son of a physician employed by the government. He became a lawyer. His more famous brother, Robert Emmet, was the leader of the Dublin rising of 1803. William MacNeven, a landowner and physician, subsequently wrote works on chemistry, Irish history, and rambling. He was ultimately an exponent of a federal solution to the relations of England and Ireland; in which he anticipated later constitutional theorists such as Crawford, Butt, and Griffith.

The United Irishmen exchanged fraternal greetings with the French Directory, and the worst fears of the government, and of most Irishmen, were nearly fulfilled in December 1796 when a French expeditionary force, which included Tone, sailed into Bantry Bay. It sailed out again after bad weather had prevented a landing. In the same year the United Irishmen organized themselves into military units, and in 1797 this precipitated prematurely in several insurrectionary outbursts in Ulster. Then, in the spring of 1798, came more substantial risings in both the north-eastern and the south-eastern parts of the country. In Antrim and Down, some 10,000 men were said to have joined the rebels. They were quite easily dispersed. The northern rising was predominantly Protestant; the Catholic people generally sympathized with the government's measures to put down the Presbyterian radicals. In Dublin the projected rising was anticipated by the government, and early arrests prevented disorder. But in Wexford the countryside caught fire. Led by the local priests, the Catholic peasants rose with a savagery and fervour which lent their rebellion the passionate characteristics of a religious crusade. It was only with some difficulty that they were eventually put down in a pitched affray at Vinegar Hill.

The 1798 Rebellion was broadly contained within these two areas: the expectations of the United Irishmen of a general spontaneous rising of the country, and of a union of religions in a common political cause, had proved to be empty. In both north and south, indeed – though especially in the south – the rebels, though fired by the agency of the United Irishmen, were not distinctly sympathetic to the political principles of the Society. Everywhere local grievances predominated, leading to different emphases and intensities, and since the ultimate political arrangements of the United Irishmen remained rather ill-defined, even to the leaders, it is hardly surprising that the cohesive qualities which the Society sought to inject into the disparate elements of local discontent proved inadequate. In most places the question of tithe was more important to the disaffected than the theoretical republicanism of the extreme radicals. The rebellion was also in no sense the work of radicals generally. Most of the Irish reformist groups were horrified by the appeal to arms, and all the doctrinaire leaders of the United Irishmen were able to achieve was an uncertain and temporary presidency over local alliances based on discontent. The French landing at Killala Bay was intended as support, but General Humbert progressively discovered that the peasantry of the west were not in a state of revolutionary excitement, as he had been led to suppose, and only 2,000 resorted to the French tricolor. He surrendered to General Lake.

Government suppression of the rebellion was efficient and at times brutal – although as John Beresford, the leader of the powerful Waterford connexion, remarked, the fury of public opinion against the insurgents considerably exceeded that of the military. 'They actually want to hang every person taken,' he said, 'while the Government certainly move very slow and show the greatest reluctance in punishing any man.' After the cleaning-up, the local and national leaders of militant radicalism had all been removed from the political scene. Tone committed suicide in gaol. O'Connor became a general in the French army, and spent the last fifty years of his life in exile. Emmet and MacNeven disappeared to America. Fitzgerald died in prison. About 150 other revolutionaries were exiled. And during the actual suppression of the risings, of course, the military had managed to rub out quite a number of extreme men.

When the rebellion was at its height, in June 1798, the government in Britain began to work towards the solution of a legislative union between the two countries. The Irish parliament had itself proposed union in 1703 and 1707, at a time when the English union with Scotland was being arranged. During the eighteenth century many viceroys had suggested it. The renewed Castle interest at the time of the rebellion became a matter of public controversy at once; over a hundred pamphlets appeared. The country was vehemently divided. It is quite clear that the resulting struggle over the Union was between two groups of Protestant political interests. The majority against the scheme was composed in some measure of men whose interests were involved with place and patronage, and whose vested stake in the unreformed Irish parliament inhibited their espousal of the sort of drastic diminution of influence which a removal of the legislature to London would necessarily bring about. Many anti-Unionists also feared that the British parliament would pass a measure of Catholic Emancipation, and were therefore additionally out to preserve Protestant Ascendancy. The Orange lodges were discreetly – and in Dublin openly – opposed to the Union. 'Among the many who so violently exclaimed against that measure,' as the Catholic Bishop of Cork noticed, 'very few, I am persuaded, ever considered it under any other point of view but as it affected their private interest or ambition.' Interests, of course, were quite legitimate considerations in the working of eighteenth-century politics, but over the Union the divisions interfered with normal groupings of interests. The lure of government patronage to secure support for the measure did not, as is so often supposed, explain the attitudes adopted. In some cases well-established political families, themselves in control of the means of reward, were deeply divided. Nor was the issue widely canvassed. The absence of any spontaneous public feeling was clear, and county meetings were moved to expressions of opinion only when engineered by agents of the great connexions. In provincial cities Unionist votes were freely secured by the hope of increased trade – and not by the allurement of patronage – especially as most of the commercial classes were Catholic, and were outside the political rewards system anyway. A sizeable majority of Catholics everywhere favoured the Union. Still largely excluded from the political traditions which, for their Protestant fellow-countrymen, imparted a hallowed significance to the Dublin parliament, they also hoped to pick up some government concessions. In 1799 Castlereagh suggested state financial support for the Catholic Church, and the Church, under Archbishop Troy, was ready to accept it in return for a Crown right to veto episcopal appointments. Catholic Emancipation, the subject of so much discussion in the Irish parliament, was also promised. The Union was likely to prove immensely beneficial to Catholic interests, since it was believed that members elected to a legislature in Westminster were less liable to involve themselves in clamours for rewards than might have been the case had they become members of an Irish parliament.

The Union was debated in the Irish parliament in January 1799. 'I never heard such vulgarity and barbarism,' Beresford remarked of the discussions; 'I cannot bring myself to repeat what was said and done.' The proposal, in fact, had to be withdrawn because of the strength of the opposition – led, as usual, by the Ponsonby faction. It was reintroduced in the following year and passed in both the Dublin and the Imperial parliaments. The debates in Dublin were centred principally in the opposition claim that the Irish legislature was incompetent to vote its own demise. Plunket warned that the passage of the Act 'will be a mere nullity, and no man in Ireland will be bound to obey it.' The suppression of 200 parliamentary seats was also certain to upset borough-owners and their nominees, especially as the new schedule for representation at Westminster could be quite fairly criticized for disproportion. Ireland, as Grattan argued in a comparison with England, 'is more than one third in population, in territory, and less than one sixth in representation.' From which he concluded that the proposed Union 'is not an identification of the two nations, it is merely a merger of the Parliament of one nation in that of the other.'

Much of the debate also turned upon economic questions. The Irish parliament had become acutely jealous of its economic independence, and when, in 1785, Pitt had proposed free-trade between the two countries in return for a permanent Irish contribution to Imperial defence, it had been rejected. There had anyway been some opposition from English commercial groups, and it was from the same quarters that slight opposition was raised to the otherwise quiet passage of the Act of Union through the British parliament. The United Irishmen had helped to popularize the idea that England was responsible for the economic disadvantages of Ireland, and variations on the theme were audible within the case of the Irish opponents of the Union. By the end of the 1790s Ireland had anyway been drawn into accumulating financial dependence upon England: large sums had been loaned to meet the military expenses of putting down the rebellion. Hence Castlereagh's emphatic realism about the position of Irish finance when he outlined the actual position in the Union debates. They had, he said, 'a military establishment far beyond our national means to support, and for which we are indebted to Great Britain, who is also obliged to guarantee our public loans. You talk of national pride and independence, but where is the solidity of this boast?' Nor was the country really politically independent. 'It has been said that this measure will reduce Ireland to the state of a colony,' Castlereagh explained: 'If I were called upon to describe a colony I would describe it as something very like the present state of this country, enjoying indeed a local legislature, but without any power entrusted to that legislature.'

Many historians and propagandists, following the charges spattered about by the leading anti-Unionist polemicists too uncritically, have made a great deal out of the corruption said to have been employed by the government to get the Union through the Irish parliament. Lecky is responsible for a lot of it. He declared quite bluntly that the Act was carried 'by gross corruption, in opposition to the majority of the free constituencies and to the great preponderance of the unbribed intellect of Ireland'. The opposition at the time had scarcely drawn breath but to make the same complaint. In May 1799, for example, Plunket had said that the Union was 'to be carried by force or fraud'. But before accepting the language of contemporary polemicists at their own valuation it is as well to remember that in the English, no less than in the Irish parliament at this time, opposition groups credited the government with corrupt practices to secure the passage of any piece of legislation they chanced to dislike. Complaints like Plunket's were recorded against almost every Irish legislative enactment carried during the second half of the eighteenth century. And it is certainly true that ministers did bestow honours, places, and pensions to ease the business of governing. It was expected of them. Both the amount and the implications of the 'corruption' actually used to get the Act of Union passed have been exaggerated, however, and where the price paid for political support did run into large figures the fault lay with those anti-Unionists who, expecting to be compensated anyway, exploited the gravity of the issue to demand sums somewhat in excess of the customary market level.

The practical effects were also not great. Only twelve of those who had voted against the Union in 1799 changed their vote in 1800; the majority required to get the Act through came from those who had remained undecided in the first debate. The numerous modifications which the Irish government accepted to the measure before it eventually passed are largely to be seen in terms of adjustment to the particular aspirations of various regional and national interests. Alterations to the clauses relating to parliamentary representation and to commerce, especially, produced a rally of votes for the Union which were earned, that is to say, by the flexibility of the government's approach, rather than by the allocation of bribes.

The Act of Union comprised eight articles which became effective on the first day of 1801. Both houses of the Irish parliament lapsed, and representation at Westminster was thereafter derived from twenty-eight Irish peers elected for life by the general body of the peerage, plus four Irish bishops, and a hundred members of the House of Commons. Irish franchise qualifications remained separate and, like Scotland's, were treated independently in the parliamentary reforms of 1832 and 1867. The executive remained unchanged, and was still nominated by the Crown. The Churches of England and Ireland were united into a single Protestant Establishment of religion. The proposal to grant state payments to the Catholic clergy was left out of the settlement, together with the question of the Crown veto over appointments. Catholic Emancipation had to be shelved *sine die*: the King declared his opposition to it in January 1801, and in the following month Pitt resigned. Pitt had also contemplated a tithe adjustment as part of the Union, and Castlereagh had actually drawn up a scheme of commutation. This had also to be left for the future. In the religious sphere, therefore, the Union postponed three questions in whose long shadows much political agitation was to foregather in the new century. The clauses relating to commerce had the general effect of removing prohibitions and bounties on Irish exports. As a protection to Irish industry – and especially to the cotton industry of the Lagan Valley – selected protective tariffs were to remain for twenty years. In financial matters, Pitt had declared it his intention to 'assimilate Great Britain and Ireland ultimately'. The Exchequers of the two countries remained separate until 1816; but by the 1830s the customs, post-office, and auditing departments had all been amalgamated. Ireland was to contribute two seventeenths of the total expenditure of the United Kingdom. She retained distinct Crown law-officers in the government, and the legal structures of the two countries remained separate.

The Act of Union should also be seen, in one important respect, as a measure of parliamentary reform. The Irish parliament, despite the enthusiasm of the Volunteers in 1782, had not managed to reform itself. The franchise qualifications and the distribution of representation mirrored those of England in their anomalies and disproportions. The boroughs were hugely over-represented, with 218 of the 300 seats in the Irish Commons. But the reform of representation was linked, as it was in England, with the question of economical reform – the progressive abolition of government patronage.

During the debate on William Ponsonby's Reform Bill in 1793, Grattan expressed the double nature of the problem explicitly. There must be, he argued, an 'external' reform of the Irish parliament in order to procure an assembly elected by 'the people' (and by 'the people' he meant what Grey and Althorp meant in 1832: the respectable middle classes of society), but there must also be provision for an 'internal' reform as well: a hacking-away of the means of political reward, of patronage, and place. 'Do not imagine,' Grattan told the Irish members, 'you have secured to the people an adequate, or any representation, by giving them a fair and adequate right of choice, if you leave to the Ministers the uncontrolled and indefinite right of bribery.'

Ponsonby's Bill was heavily defeated. But the question had been neatly formulated. The issue of economical reform was not quite as straightforward as in England, however. The separation of the executive and the legislature in Ireland imparted to the means of reward a greater significance in political cohesion. If in England economical reform was chiefly aimed at the diminution of what was supposed to be the 'undue' influence of the Crown, in Ireland that influence was constitutionally much more central to the daily conduct of government. The system of direct patronage exercised by a resident viceroy had shuddered and all but broken down during the Regency crisis of 1788, when many Irish placemen had defected to the opposition. But it survived as the only means of holding political interests together in Ireland, and it was a wise instinct, as well as making for vivid propaganda, which led radicals of all complexions to demand a root-and-branch economical reform. 'The Temple of your liberties,' as Wolfe Tone instructed the Irish people in 1796, as part of a characteristic bombast against the unreformed legislature, 'is filled with buyers and sellers, with money-changers and thieves; with placement and pensioners; those unclean and ominous harpies, gorged with the public spoil, and sucking still, like insatiable Vampires, the last drainings of the vital blood of their country.'

The Union, in extinguishing the parliament which had failed to reform itself, provided new arrangements which quite altered the balance of representation. The redistribution required by the abolition of 200 seats, and the absorption of the areas concerned into a hundred new ones, effectively shattered a lot of traditional political influence. The balance of representation moved sharply from the boroughs to the counties, and before the existing Protestant magnates and managers had properly consolidated their control within the boundaries of the new constituencies they began to meet a challenge from outside the traditional political connexions altogether. It was in the county seats that the Catholic forty-shilling voters enfranchised in 1793 were most numerous and potentially most politically conscious – with all their grievances about tithes and the rights of the Protestant Church. An opening had been made for Catholic political organization in the redrawn constituencies by the Act of Union. O'Connell was to appeal first to the county voters in the 1820s. The parliamentary provisions of the Union, therefore, had helped to create a Catholic political nation.

The Union touched less directly on the question of economical reform, but in practice the issue was considerably reduced in scale. The Irish members who turned up at Westminster were as susceptible to political influence as everybody else there: but by the first decade of the nineteenth century economical reform was so advanced in England that a lack of official patronage was beginning to prove a serious embarrassment to ministers. After the Union economical reform was accelerated inside Ireland, too. The earliest Chief Secretaries, especially Peel, were scrupulous in their endeavours to eradicate superfluous expenditure at Dublin Castle. With legislative functions removed to London it was also less necessary for the Irish executive to cement political support with rewards. Irish radicals and local interests, nevertheless, like their English counterparts, expended a lot of energy throughout the nineteenth century in seeking to depict the machinery of central government in Ireland as essentially lubricated with corruption specifically designed to reduce the integrity of the Irish people. At Westminster, after 1801, something like four fifths of the Irish members supported the government. The Irish Whig opposition found their niche among the Foxites.

It is also interesting that the borough-owners who lost their representation because of the Union were compensated with the sum of £15,000. The Act, therefore, had the important effect of perpetuating the old principle that parliamentary seats were a species of property. Pitt had provided for similar compensations in his English reform proposals of 1785. They were absent from the measure of 1832. Some of the Irish opposition to the parliamentary aspects of the Union derived from opposition to the principle of compensation: John Foster consistently urged the point. Opposition to the Act at Westminster was less elevated. 'I do not think,' as Lord Sheffield remarked in the course of his attack upon the measure, 'any of our country gentlemen would venture into Parliament if they were to meet a hundred Paddies.'

The implications of the Union, for both England and Ireland, were immense. Despite the extensive complaints of later Irish nationalists that it had destroyed the constitution and all but extinguished Irish national self-consciousness, the Act in fact inaugurated a national uniformity unknown before. There is a real sense in which it created the modern Irish state, both in the political experience and administrative changes which followed during the nineteenth century, and in its immediate broadening of the scope of political possibilities. The 'nation' which Grattan declared in 1782 had in practice excluded the Catholic population: the Union opened the way to a whole series of reforms which, while often of external origin, had the effect of weakening the influence of the old Ascendancy.

Since the Act of Union itself was to become supreme among the grievances of Irish radical and nationalist politicians during the nineteenth century, it is important to notice the extent to which, paradoxically, they were indebted to the concepts at issue between the Protestant groups who had fought out the Union struggle. A great deal of subsequent Irish national thought translated itself into a series of variations on the anti-

Unionists' case of the 1790s. Constitutional radicals like O'Connell and Parnell were to repeat the language of Grattan and Plunket, and more revolutionary nationalists consistently echoed the voices of Tone and O'Connor. The anti-Unionists' arguments, in fact, became conceptually entrenched within Irish political thinking, and it is of crucial importance to realize that those arguments were solidly grounded in British constitutionalism.

The absence of a native Irish political tradition is nowhere more apparent than in this perpetuation of the Protestant polemicism of the last years of the Irish parliament. Mazzini noticed this in 1847 when he remarked that Ireland did not 'plead for any distinct principle of life or system of legislation derived from native peculiarities, and contrasting radically with English wants and wishes'. When O'Connell first gave Catholic Ireland a taste of political debate it was organized around the same arguments for Emancipation and opposition to Unionism which had their origins in the Constitutional debates of the 1790s. His contribution to Irish experience, therefore, was to prescribe the language and the area of political debate which owed its essence to a Protestant constitutional tradition. From the very start of the nineteenth century, as a result, national and Catholic politics were fixed within terms of reference which assumed the virtues of British constitutionalism, even though an attempt was made to employ those virtues to readjust the actual constitutional relationships and practices which obtained in Ireland. And it is especially important to notice, too, the wide context of the later eighteenth-century debate about the relationship with Britain, for this wide context also passed into the common assumptions of Irish political radicalism. It was a context originally established by the claims of the American colonists to enjoy the same constitutional liberties accorded to British subjects resident in England.

44

The American parallel was an implicit element in the concession of the Irish trading rights in 1779 and of legislative autonomy in 1782. On the former occasion Earl Nugent had argued the case for Ireland in the Imperial parliament by direct reference to the upheaval in America, and Burke had exhaled the view that Irish subjects should be admitted to all the privileges of the British constitution. The latter occasion was even more evidently dependent upon the issues germane to the American debate. 'When the Volunteers claimed Irish independence, and the American colonies renounced connexion with the mother country, similar effects were produced by the same cause,' as Dicey wrote a hundred years afterwards, in 1886. 'In each case English colonists revolted against England's sovereignty, because it meant the privilege of Englishmen who dwelt in Great Britain to curtail the rights and hamper the trade of Englishmen who dwelt abroad.' Reformers in the old Irish parliament were not slow in picking up the chips: every demand referred to the American revolt as an example of what could happen if concessions were unforthcoming. The Protestants in the Irish parliament had, therefore, explicitly recognized that their various claims amounted to a wide redefinition of the relationships between geographically separate areas of British constitutionalism. It was this awareness, indelibly British in origin and conception, which nineteenth-century Irish nationalism inherited.

Equally significant, as a principal result of the Union, was the progressive transformation of Irish society and the machinery of government through the adaptation of British administration solutions to Irish conditions. When the Union became law in 1801, a society of retarded development was incorporated into the most advanced country in the world, with an expanding economy. The Imperial parliament intended to extend to Ireland the leading political benefits of the United Kingdom – the extension of equal laws. But conditions

45

there were unsuitable for their immediate reception, and the problem therefore resolved itself simply: how to govern Ireland effectively when the historical instruments of government and administration there were quite inadequate for the modern functions which the development of Irish society required. At the centre, Dublin Castle remained as it had been moulded by the rewards system, even though patronage had been greatly diminished; in the localities, the parish structure was unsuitable because the Catholic population distrusted administrative units which were inherently Protestant, and which were, anyway, about to shudder beneath the weight of tithe controversies. The grand juries, which governed the counties, were corrupt and also lacked the financial means of extending their functions. The corporate boroughs were as unreformed as their English counterparts.

The solution, if anything was to be done, lay in the creation of new instruments of government especially designed to tackle the huge problems of an underdeveloped country. This was soon borne in upon the minds of Chief Secretaries and their officials, men who shared the contemporary theoretical opposition to state intervention in society, but who, confronted with Irish conditions, acted upon expediency to further it there. So there grew up, early in the nineteenth century, whole new areas of state concern in Ireland, with centralized bureaucratic machinery as the only way of defeating vested interests and by-passing local prejudice. The early machinery of state collectivism in Ireland was, therefore, self-generating and pragmatic. In many things it anticipated similar growths in England, and, as in England, it was largely promoted by the appeals of individuals for public action to improve social conditions. It lacked an ideological basis; indeed the political ideologies of the administrators who extended the machinery of government in Ireland – Peel, for example, or Drummond and Larcom – were almost wholly antipathetic to the general principle of state interference. They singularized each occasion of state advance: had the growth of governmental agencies been inspired by identifiable ideology then it would easily have been checked by the strong forces of local anti-centralization sentiment, and the almost universal currency, among social and official theorists, of the non-interventionist principles of political economy and *laissez-faire*. Neither were the exponents of collectivism in Ireland motivated by Benthamism. In fact the absence of this creed in the advanced Irish experience of state intervention suggests that it was probably largely absent in England too, and tends to confirm the supposition that state interference was everywhere a 'natural' growth.

It is a strange paradox, though one apparent at every corner of Irish history in the nineteenth century, that those who set out to promote the extension of equal laws to the country should have proceeded by the piecemeal creation of exceptional legislation to prepare Ireland to receive them. But, in the event, Ireland's early experience of collectivism was at times frankly accepted. In 1838, for example, the Report of the Royal Commission on Irish railways, written under the influence of Thomas Drummond, and ranging over the whole area of economic and social questions, was quite emphatic about the need for direct state intervention in society. 'The policy of rendering such assistance is unquestionable,' the Commissioners reported. 'It is acknowledged to be necessary towards a colony, and must be considered more so in the case of a part of the United Kingdom.' Ireland, indeed, became a testing-ground for novel experiments in state welfare. As Goldwin Smith remarked in 1862: 'In virtue of her long unsettlement and her special claims to consideration, she is affording a clear field for the discussion of political, ecclesiastical, and social questions which the English nation, satisfied with an early and limited progress, will not suffer to be mooted directly in respect to herself.'

The new structures of Irish administration were in some measure paternalistic. There were frequent comparisons between the governmental problems of Ireland and India in the nineteenth century – John Stuart Mill, Sir George Campbell, and A.K. Connell all contributed widely read and sympathetic commentaries upon the comparison. Connell argued for the reconstruction of Irish government under a system of district commissioners on the Indian model, until 'Ireland is raised in the scale of civilization equal to that of Great Britain', when 'the paternal element in local government can be gradually lessened and the popular element increased'. This suggestion was actually made in 1888, two years after Gladstone's Home Rule proposals.

The new structures of Irish administration were necessarily centralized, as Engels noticed after a visit in 1856: 'The government meddles with everything.' Nor was centralization always unpopular. 'There is a disposition in Ireland,' Peel wrote in 1814, 'to refer everything to Government.' He added, 'I think the majority have the same idea of Government which the natives are said to have of the East India Company.'

Anti-centralization sentiment in Ireland came from urban middle-class men; it is clear that most of the Catholic tenantry were not opposed to it. The Irish administration was also often clothed in neutrality. Peel told the Irish members of parliament in 1834 that England refused to be a partisan: 'she has interposed to protect you from yourselves, and she has met with a fate which is not uncommon to those who interfere in others' domestic feuds – she has drawn upon herself the wrath of the parties she attempted to moderate.'

These characteristics of Irish government – centralization, paternalism, neutrality – all became the subjects of

Irish nationalist complaint. Yet it is useful to notice that British administrators *did* respond to the peculiar requirements of Irish conditions. It is true that administrative solutions had the disadvantage of emanating from an external legislature, but the actual contents of ameliorative measures were typically fashioned explicitly for Ireland's special circumstances. This aspect of social improvement was largely discounted by many Irish radicals. 'It seems to be the fate of Ireland,' Archbishop MacHale wrote to Lord John Russell in 1838, at the height of Drummond's period of reform, 'that no plan can be devised for her improvement . . . that is not conducted by individuals opposed to us by religious and national antipathies.' There were mistakes. And it is arguable that some administrative solutions – the Irish Poor Law, for example – turned out to be inappropriate; but the belief of some Irish polemicists that 'English' administration in Ireland was, almost by definition, disadvantageous to the development of the country can hardly be sustained.

It is true, however, that the sort of development which this level of state activity brought about led to a progressive 'anglicization', and it was the symptoms of this transformation which most nationalists rushed to denounce. Social improvement was, in the nature of things, across the board. It usually turned out that the characteristics of Irish nationality happened to reside in just those pockets of retarded social development which the impact of reform removed from the country. Popular cultural relativism is, on the whole, a modern growth; and whatever the romanticism of nineteenth-century urban nationalists may have suggested about the need to preserve Irish folk customs, the fact is that the ordinary Irish people themselves welcomed the penetration of social improvements – until they were taught otherwise by nationalist politicians – even though they derived from the Imperial parliament. Folk customs are rarely agreeable to those whose primitive circumstances offer them no alternative but to go on practising them.

State intervention, therefore, was a crucial aspect of Irish administration in the decades which followed the Union. A selection of key areas will illustrate this. In 1805 the government created dispensaries for the sick in each county; in 1819 sanitary officers were appointed to supervise and inspect the lunatic asylums which had been set up two years previously. State promotion of undertakings to eliminate unemployment – 'public works' – became a permanent feature of government. In 1800 a Board of Inland Navigation was given a state grant of £500,000 to organize public works; the Board of Works itself promoted a huge number of schemes under centralized direction from Dublin – it was reconstructed in 1831 in recognition of the increasing burden of its responsibilities and given £500,000 to stimulate local effort. After 1843 the Board was receiving £15,000 a quarter for permanent works of improvement. On two occasions, in 1823 and 1825, the government arranged emigrations at the public expense, to relieve the pressure of population in congested areas.

Education affords a clear example of the entry of the state into a field from which it was long excluded in England. In 1831 a National Board of Education set up a system of primary schools, and in 1845 three university colleges were built and endowed by the government. Public order also underwent early transformation. By 1836 Ireland possessed – it is scarcely possible to say enjoyed – what England still does not have: a national police force under centralized control.

State intervention in the largest area of Irish industry, the land, was retarded by the almost universal belief in the inviolability of land contract. But even here the influence of the government was felt after the mid-century, when a succession of statutes interfered to protect the tenants and also to promote, with public financial assistance, the redistribution of land among the occupiers.

To the exacerbated problems of religion the government also brought solutions: it disestablished and disendowed the Protestant Church in 1869. This was a withdrawal of state interference rather than an extension, of course; but it required, merely to bring it about, a sense of governmental responsibility for social questions which was advanced for its day.

After the legacy of anti-Union polemicism and the advances of state intervention, there was a third, broad, long-term result of the Act of Union: the impact of Ireland upon the parliament at Westminster. The Catholic Emancipation question was placed at the centre of political disagreement and immediately succeeded in keeping able men out of office and in contriving the disruption of ministries. There were permanent divisions among British parliamentary parties over Irish questions later in the century – one of the legacies of the Home Rule question. Throughout the whole period an impressive number of administrations owed their demise to the divisive nature of Irish problems. The ordinary conduct of business in parliament was at times hampered by endless Irish debates and by the tactics of Irish members. The organization of Irish political parties, especially by O'Connell and Parnell, offered an example of advanced, systematized radicalism which, in many features, anticipated later political organizations in England. Irish demands for Repeal of the Union, and then for Home Rule, by requiring a departure from the settlement of 1800, implied questions of general constitutional amendment. Thus the effect of the Irish debate was central to the entire structure of the Constitution. This was the real sense in which matters touching the relations of England and Ireland within the Union became involved with far-reaching questions of devolution. By the end of the nineteenth century the future relationship with Ireland had come to be seen by many – by Chamberlain and the colonial federalists, and by Irish national politicians – as but one aspect of a general need to redefine, and perhaps to reconstruct, the entire exercise of sovereignty within the Empire. There could be no wider perspective than that.

3. O'Connell and Radicalism

The radical constitutional ideas dispersed within the 'Protestant nation' at the end of the eighteenth century did not lie dormant for long. The Irish radical movement called into existence by Daniel O'Connell was in reality their reawakening – reorientated to have their basis in Catholicism. O'Connell was a radical rather than a nationalist: it was his genius to direct the Catholic forces which he drew into political association for the first time into the evolving patterns of a general British radicalism. His nationalism is easily overemphasized by those who have listened only to his eloquent references to the nobility of the Irish character. O'Connell, indeed, dwelt at length on his love of Ireland, and much of his popularity with the peasantry was prompted by lingering insistence on the fact. Like many subsequent Irish radicals, he was able to manipulate national antipathy to England as a means of political cohesion. But the politics he espoused, and the reformed Ireland to which he aspired, were not characterized by Irish national culture or social institutions.

O'Connell was born in 1775. He had been brought up in the ancient Celtic custom of fosterage – and had actually lived as a child in a herdsman's cabin, the home of one of his uncle's tenants. He spoke Irish as a native language. But when he became a man he put away Irish things, discouraged the use of the Irish language, and worked to assimilate Irish society to the more advanced model provided by England. Having shared the lot of a rural Irish farmer, he enjoyed no illusions about its quality; he was the only national political leader in the nineteenth century who was, as they say in Ireland, 'racy of the soil'. O'Connell looked to the development of his country, to draw it into the civilized benefits of the English world, and that meant a closer approximation to that most practical of nineteenth-century societies. This was why he applauded the Irish national schools when they were created by the government in 1831; they would teach rural Irishmen to speak the English tongue and so absorb a whole new world of political and social values. Those schools would also, by educating both Protestant and Catholic children in the same classroom, lessen the divisive influences of religious difference. It was left to O'Connell's later critics, the Young Ireland nationalists, to preach up an Irish revival based on language and rural folk-culture. As Protestants and townsmen their romanticism was pardonable: O'Connell had lived in the sort of society which the Young Irelanders had only seen from the windows of their carriages.

O'Connell, then, was a radical. He was also a middle-class radical, the representative of a small but increasingly influential Catholic middle class in Ireland. During the eighteenth century, when statute law restricted the ability of Catholics to contract long leases on landed property, and when they were also excluded from politics and from most offices in the public service, the more enterprising of them had turned to trade and commerce. It was like a reversal of the classic model of 'religion and the rise of capitalism'; the Catholic entrepreneurs accumulated wealth because there was no use to which they could turn their profits apart from reinvestment in their business undertakings. By statutory reforms of 1778 and 1782 they were at last placed on an equality with Protestants in landholding, and after the great reforms of 1793 they were admitted to the Irish bar. By the end of the eighteenth century, therefore, the emergent Catholic middle class was investing in land and depositing its sons in the legal profession. The political results could not be slight.

It was from this class that O'Connell came. His education was under the patronage of an uncle, Maurice O'Connell, who had made himself prosperous by exporting cattle, hides, and wool to France, by manufacturing sea salt for export to England, and by some smuggling on the side. He had also managed to retain his family's landed properties at Derrynane, in Co. Kerry, by a series of legal trusts sponsored by friendly Protestants. Like many of the successful Catholic merchants he craved eventual respectability and got it – as a magistrate and a deputy-lieutenant for the county. He came to disapprove of his nephew's political radicalism. The family also enjoyed connexions with France which were, again, not untypical of their class, and two relatives, Colonel Daniel O'Connell and Eugene McCarthy, were commissioned in the Irish Brigade of the French Royal Army. Young Daniel O'Connell and his brother were sent to school at St Omer and Douay, where they had the privilege of witnessing the start of the French Revolution. O'Connell thereafter became a law student in London and passed into the Irish legal profession. His subsequent political agitations were all inspired by the virtues and prejudices of the middle-class Catholics, and they were all solidly middle class in organization. The leadership of the Irish movement for Catholic Emancipation shows this clearly: in the second half of the eighteenth century the agitation was in the hands of noblemen led by the Earl of Fingall, but in the 1790s leadership passed to John Keogh, a merchant, and finally, under O'Connell, the aristocratic membership slid away altogether, and the Emancipation campaign was transformed into a middle-class agitation backed up by appeals to a massed peasantry. Those who find such categorization either interesting or necessary will perhaps see in O'Connell's radicalism the revolution of the bourgeoisie against feudal aristocracy – here represented by the Protestant Ascendancy.

O'Connellite radicalism was also the equivalent of the 'Manchester' middle-class radicalism of England. It was based, as theirs was, in religious dissent. Where O'Connell spoke of English maladministration in Irish affairs, the English middle-class radicals spoke of aristocratic jobbery contriving the same result inside England; where O'Connell turned back his political vision to an idealized Irish parliament before the Act of Union, the gaze of the English radicals fell upon the seventeenth-century conflict, and even further backwards to the supposedly free institutions of Saxon England. Like his English counterparts, O'Connell was socially conservative. As a landowner himself he was well acquainted with the management of landed wealth, and he was opposed to any violation of land contract by the government. Throughout his political career he remained unconcerned with the land question, and it was not until 1846 that, under pressure from his nationalist critics, he gave vague support to the moderate demand for compensation for improvements. There is some evidence that all was not quite as it might have been on his own estates at Derrynane: at the start of the famine, in 1846, *The Times* revealed the dreadful conditions in which his tenants lived, caused by excessive subdivision of holdings.

O'Connell was always anxiously apprehensive of the peasantry to whom he appealed in his campaigns for Emancipation and Repeal. As Bishop Doyle said about them in 1830, 'it is almost a benefit that they follow O'Connell; for if they did not, they would either rob or plunder, or destroy property.' O'Connell was himself aware of the position. He was always conscious that there existed a series of rural organizations which rivalled his appeal to the peasants – the secret societies formed to stimulate local violence on behalf of individual tenant claims; societies which were politically illiterate, but which attacked just those rights of landowning which the O'Connellite radicals sought to protect; societies which adopted the awful names of 'Whiteboys', 'Rockites', 'Levellers', 'Whitefeet', 'Molly Maguires', 'Ribbonmen', and so on. Several times O'Connell urged the government to bring more troops into Ireland to deal with them. In 1833, in addressing himself to Lord Duncannon on the subject, he went out of his way to show that not a single enfranchised farmer had been known to join a secret agrarian combination. The secret societies, that is to say, were composed of the peasantry, not of the rural middle classes to whom O'Connell made his appeals.

O'Connell assumed the maintenance of the existing fabric of society. The political life of the nation was to be radicalized, numerous changes were to bring equal laws to the Catholic people; but in economic structure and social relationships things were to be left more or less undisturbed. 'I desire no social revolution, no social change,' he wrote to Patrick Fitzpatrick, his financial agent, in 1833. 'In short, salutary restoration without revolution, an Irish parliament, British connexion, one King, two legislatures.' His loyalty to the British throne was vividly demonstrated. When George IV visited Ireland in 1821, O'Connell waded into the waters of Kingstown harbour to greet him. He later presented his no doubt gratified sovereign with a crown of laurels. He sustained a chivalrous affection for the young Queen Victoria – acting as cheer-leader of the London crowd which assembled at St James's in June 1837 to listen to the proclamation of her accession. Every meeting of the Repeal Association ended with cheers for the sovereign, led by O'Connell personally. Although this loyalty to the House of Brunswick no doubt did him credit, it went in some measure beyond the traditional Catholic obligation to obey the legal sovereign. And in spite of the policy of Repeal of the Union, O'Connell held the British Constitution in the sort of deep reverence to which lawyers are sometimes given. It was an Irish hand in its operation that he sought, a reformed Irish version of the British model, not a new instrument. As early as 1814, in his speech in defence of John Magee – who was being prosecuted by the Crown for libelling the outgoing Viceroy in the *Dublin Evening Post* – O'Connell stated a position which he constantly maintained:

What is it we incessantly, and if you please clamorously petition for? Why, to be allowed to partake of the advantages of the Constitution. We are earnestly anxious to share the benefits of the Constitution. We look to the participation in the Constitution as our greatest political blessing. If we desired to destroy it, would we seek to share it? If we desired to overturn it, would we exert ourselves through calumny, and in peril, to obtain a portion of its blessings?

O'Connell was then in pursuit of Catholic Emancipation. Throughout the subsequent Repeal agitation he blew both hot and cold about the intentions of the British government, but beneath all the rhetoric there remained a stable allegiance to the structure of the constitution. In 1837, just before a general election in which his candidates offered themselves at the hustings in the Queen's name, he went to his furthest lengths of loyalism. 'Ireland is now ready to amalgamate with the entire Empire,' he said in June of that year; 'we are prepared for full and perpetual conciliation. . . . Let Ireland and England be identified.'

The constitutionalism which O'Connell espoused was, of course, radical constitutionalism. His radical doctrines were drawn from the mainstream beliefs of British radicalism, both from the fashionable literature he had absorbed in his youth – Godwin, Bentham, Adam Smith – and from the general deposit of radicalism expressed by Irish opponents of the Union in the 1790s. But the latter source was in some particulars ambiguous. Many of those whose polemics against the Union O'Connell inherited were aristocratic placemen whose radicalism resided exclusively in opposition to the Union, and in no other areas. The fiercer radicalism of the United Irishmen O'Connell eschewed: it went beyond constitutionalism and preached the destruction of the rule of law. He frequently referred to those men with scorn. It is crucial to realize, therefore, that most of O'Connell's radicalism was drawn from English sources. At his own valuation he was a Benthamite: so he described himself during the Clare election of 1829. It is true that he corresponded with Bentham, and actually managed to induce the great man to donate £5 in 'Catholic rent'. Like the English radicals, he spoke in favour of a codification of the law, and of reformed bankruptcy legislation. But like them, also, he adopted the Benthamite label loosely. 'Benthamism' provided a diluted solution of opinion in which hugely different particles of radicalism were dissolved.

Yet O'Connell's contribution to radicalism was striking. At various times in his parliamentary career he supported a wide spectrum of conventional radical causes: the admission of Jews to parliament, the abolition of slavery, responsible government in the more developed colonies. In church reform he sought a redistribution of the ecclesiastical wealth of the Established Church, with the appropriation of its surplus revenues by the state for general purposes of public utility. He was opposed to church rates, and in nearly everything, indeed, corresponded to the emergent militant dissenters of England and Scotland in demanding the legislative recognition of religious equality.

O'Connell was also, of course, an exponent of parliamentary

reform. In 1830 he joined Thomas Attwood's Birmingham Political Union and spoke frequently on English platforms in the reform interest. At first he hoped for the enfranchisement of all tax-payers; later he advanced to universal household suffrage, the ballot, triennial (and then annual) parliaments, and the diminution of the property qualifications for members. He believed that representation should be according to numerical units, that persons and not interests should be represented in the legislature. These policies would have the advantage of increasing Irish representation. O'Connell also suggested a reform of the House of Lords. In 1834 he declared 'the reform of that House is essentially necessary to the establishment and security of popular freedom.' He proposed an elected senate in its place. As the Lords continued to obstruct the settlement of Irish tithe and municipal questions in the 1830s, O'Connell did not alter his intentions.

Yet it is important to notice that, like so many British radicals, O'Connell's view of the *function* of a reformed parliament was extremely limited. He was soaked, as they were, in all the free-contract ideals of popular political economy. He was in principle opposed to the intervention of the state in private contractual relationships in society, and this was a vastly limiting conviction, since he also viewed society atomistically. It was simply a nexus of such private contracts, to be assisted, if at all, by public cultivation of the atmosphere in which self-help individualism could operate at its most unhindered.

O'Connell made exceptions in his opposition to state intervention – like many tinged with classical economic theories he nevertheless recognized that in a country so relatively undeveloped as Ireland *some* measure of state activity was required to encourage the conditions in which free-contractualism could establish itself. But this was a limited function. The reform of parliament was essential in order to prevent the influence of the aristocracy – and from the Irish point of view this meant the Protestant Ascendancy – from perpetuating a network of jobbery whose effect was to inhibit individual exertion. Aristocratic control of state machinery could most expeditiously be overthrown by popularizing the basis of the electoral system. Its overthrow would actually produce a parliament which would interfere *less* extensively with the freely operating mechanisms of society. Similarly, O'Connell promoted the reform of municipal corporations in Ireland during the 1830s, not to make them more efficient, or to prepare them to take on new functions, but because he hoped to transfer their considerable powers of local patronage from Protestant Tory hands to those of his own Catholic middle-class followers. O'Connell shared these beliefs in the limited intention of governmental reform with the English radicals. The purged legislature was *not* intended to assume a dynamic new function, in which stacks of statutes would alleviate the conditions of the English working classes or the Irish peasantry. There was to be less, not more legislation. The Smithsonian 'hidden hand' was to do the rest, and economic and social well-being would then trickle down through the social structure as soon as the supposedly vicious self-interest of the landed aristocracy had been eliminated from political supremacy. Such was the middle-class radicalism of which O'Connellism comprised an important segment. It consisted of a series of beliefs which, in the largest view, were inimical to the development of the modern state.

Belief in free-contractualism also explains O'Connell's antipathy to trades unionism. In 1837 he put his objections frankly to a meeting of the Dublin Trades Political Union: 'Will anyone imagine that employers will be induced to lay out their capital, and exert themselves for the improvement of trade, if they are not encouraged, and that a system of intimidation is practised against them?' In the following year he condemned trade combinations in the House of Commons. 'The misfortune of Ireland,' he then said, 'was that workmen, impatient of their present state of suffering, did not wait for a gradual and progressive improvement, but they endeavoured by monopoly to obtain that which ought to arise from the competition of employers.'

In the wider context of his general economic analysis of Ireland's position, O'Connell also supposed, in company with many Irishmen, that English competition was destroying Irish industry. In 1830 he told John O'Brien, 'It is scarcely necessary for me to remind you that the poverty and misery of the operative classes in Ireland is mainly, and I may say exclusively, to be placed to the fatal measure of the Union.' This familiar argument was to some extent in conflict with his sponsorship of free competition in trade. And, indeed, O'Connell was a leading advocate of free-trade, fully in sympathy with the middle-class Anti-Corn Law League in England during the later 1830s. He and thirty-four other Irish members voted for the repeal of the Corn Laws in 1846 – an action by then in direct defiance of his Young Ireland critics, who, following the logic of O'Connell's economic analysis, stood solidly behind the principle of protection. O'Connell's free-contractualism also accounted for his opposition to Factory legislation when the Ten-Hour Day Bill was brought forward in 1836. He opposed the Irish Poor Law in the 1830s, in the belief that state-supported relief, even indoor relief in the workhouses, would deter the offerings of private charity. He also disliked the poor law because a higher burden of local taxation fell, as a result, on landowners.

Primarily, O'Connell was concerned with questions relating to the attainment of what he considered to be political justice: religion, voting, and legal rights. He was always cautious of economic issues, fearing their potential to disrupt society. He diagnosed the Chartist movement (correctly, as it turned out) as being generated by economic grievances, even though its professed solutions were all political. He opposed it vigorously in consequence. 'The revolutionary mania,' he remarked of Chartism in November 1839, 'is now abroad and would wreak its choicest vengeance in Ireland.' Chartists were duly expelled from the Irish Repeal Association. O'Connell later adduced his opposition to Chartism as a point of defence during his state trial in 1844: 'With the influence I possessed, could I not have raised the poverty of Ireland against its property, if I chose, and insisted that all those who were rich should feed all those who were poor?' But seeing the movement as one ultimately directed against property, it was in character for him to throw his not inconsiderable weight against it. 'I do firmly declare,' he told the court on the same occasion, 'that if I had not opposed Chartism it would have passed over and spread from one end of Ireland to the other. . . . I shall ever rejoice that I kept Ireland free from this pollution.' There is no clearer revelation of the middle-class basis of O'Connell's political analysis. O'Connellite radicalism was as incompatible with popularly generated political activity as was its English counterpart, the Anti-Corn Law League.

In one area, O'Connell's political achievement went greatly beyond that of the English radicals. The political party which he created and directed in Ireland was almost the model dreamed of by the disparate elements of English radicalism, yet impossible among them because of the failings of eccentric leadership and thin popular support. O'Connell's Repeal party after 1830 was the immediate result of the Emancipation of the Catholics in the previous year. It was the first organized radical group in the Imperial parliament, incorporating all the favourite radical devices: elections managed by agents – usually the Catholic priests – centralized control, election pledges elicited from candidates by the electorate, a permanent political fund to provide an income for the party leader. It had an effective and popular press at its disposal: the *Pilot*, the *Register*, and the *Freeman's Journal*.

The electoral morality of the party, however, was not especially distinguished. There were elections in which the clergy and the tenantry employed 'undue influence' and intimidation; and on one occasion, in 1830, O'Connell was himself forced into the regrettable necessity of attempting to buy a parliamentary seat. He was saved from this implication in the corrupt practice of borough-mongering when Sir Edward Denny turned down his offer of £3,000 for Tralee.

The success of the Repeal party transcended former political experience. Until 1830, Ireland had ordinarily been represented by around seventy Tory members of parliament, and thirty Whigs. After the 1832 election there were thirty-nine members of O'Connell's party in the Commons, thirty-six Whigs, and twenty-nine Tories. The Repeal group was, therefore, the largest single Irish party. This success was not repeated. Slowly the numerical basis of the party was whittled away, until after the 1841 election there were only eighteen of them left at Westminster. But the alliance between the Whigs and the Repealers in 1835 helped to disguise the decline, and to minimize the effect. O'Connell continued to act as the leader of an Irish group of around seventy, composed of both Whigs and Repealers, with the former gaining over the latter. The integration was close – closer than Parnell's with the Liberals after 1882 – with Repealers attending formal party meetings called by the Whigs, and joining the Reform Club in London. Away from Westminster the distinction was more apparent. At constituency level, the candidates sponsored by the Repeal Association, whatever their fraternization with the Whigs after 1835, remained separate.

English observers were unable to comprehend the Repeal party because political organization on that scale was unknown to them. The main English parties, by comparison, were still mere connexions. The phenomenon of a party leader like O'Connell, with no party affiliations in the traditional sense, was one which had not occurred before, and there was no standard against which it could be measured. This led to easy exaggeration of the real novelty of the Repeal party's structure. In fact O'Connell's party was scarcely different in social composition from sections of the English parties. It was largely made up of landowners; it could not be otherwise, since there was still a property qualification for membership of parliament. And this accorded with O'Connell's own beliefs, anyway. Like Gladstone in the 1880s, he preferred landed influence to predominate in public life. In 1843, O'Neill Daunt, one of O'Connell's secretaries, explained that the plan for a restored Irish parliament 'gives to the landed interest preponderating influence in that assembly'. Nor was the party exclusively Catholic. O'Connell inherited some of the pre-1829 Protestant Emancipationists who were prepared to go along with the Repeal policy. In the 1832 parliament, thirteen of his thirty-nine members were Protestants.

A lot of misunderstanding was caused in England by suspicions about the financial basis of the party. It was clearly not without available resources. In 1833 O'Connell indicated this when he suggested that Irishmen should begin a run on gold in the Bank of England as a way of coercing the government into dropping the allegedly inadequate Irish Corporation Bill – an expedient copied from the London radicals who had proposed it as one way of preventing the Duke of Wellington from forming an administration in the Reform Bill crisis of May 1832. Most suspicions were excited by the O'Connell 'Tribute', a levy on the members and associates of the various repeal bodies in Ireland which provided the Liberator with his personal income. A 'Repeal Rent' was also collected from the peasantry, for general political purposes, though in practice the 'Rent' and the 'Tribute' were

65

usually merged into a single account from which O'Connell drew his salary and made grants to assist other members of the party. The 'Catholic Rent' which had financed the Emancipation campaign before 1829 had allowed O'Connell to perfect the techniques of extraction. That 'Rent' had itself been inspired by the building fund collections of the English Methodists, and by the dues levied in the popular radical clubs which thrived among the discontents of English provincial society in the depressed years which followed the Napoleonic Wars. O'Connell himself endured a fluctuating income; the 'Tribute' easily fell off if political passions were allowed to cool. At its height he was drawing about £13,000 a year. At the peak of his legal practice, after 1813, he had got only £8,000.

So complete was O'Connell's ascendancy over the political movement which he had brought into being that it is possible to define the Irish radicalism of his day simply by reference to his own views. His opinion of political questions – indeed of all questions – soon passed into common orthodoxy. The state of affairs was not altogether a blessing. 'There is no case so trite and unimpressive as a case which no one disputes,' as Gavan Duffy remarked of O'Connellism, half a century later. There was, it is true, opposition to him within the Repeal party, but this usually reflected a divergence over tactical devices rather than a difference of political principle. Over the timing of Repeal motions in parliament, over the degree of compromise to be found tolerable in Whig legislation, there were differences of view. Sharman Crawford split with O'Connell in 1836 by insisting on a total abolition of tithes rather than, as O'Connell was prepared to accept, a mere reform of tithe composition. The party was divided over the Irish Poor Law question, and so, between 1836 and 1838, was the Catholic Church. Here was the seed of a real doctrinal difference: between classical political economy, to which some of the party remained faithful, and those who, like O'Connell, shared the romanticized feeling for rural paternalism which had also led to opposition to the Poor Law in England.

The split between O'Connell and Feargus O'Connor, which opened early in the 1830s, was more serious for its effects upon the Irish immigrant populations in English and Scottish cities, where O'Connor was influential, than it was in Ireland itself. O'Connor had intended to become the Liberator's successor in Ireland. Frustrated in this, he betook himself to England, where he became the leader of provincial Chartism, and an opponent of free-trade. The ensuing rivalries between O'Connorite and O'Connellite factions among the Irish settlers rather confused the Irish contribution to English working-class politics for some years. It is interesting that O'Connor's Chartist Land Plan, which actually operated for a few years after 1845 – by settling urban families back upon rural plantations intended to encourage self-sufficiency – was in effect an Irish solution to the problems of Irish land tenure. It was ludicrously inappropriate in England, but was, in a sense, O'Connor's protest at O'Connell's failure to take up the land question in Ireland. The two men shared a mutual bitterness, originally inspired, it seems, by O'Connell's shocked disapproval of O'Connor's habit of sharpening his razor on the calf-leather binding of his Bible.

It was not to be expected that any political party in Ireland would remain innocent of disputation. O'Connell's control, however, was impressive. The newspapers supported by the Repeal movement were kept under close scrutiny by the leadership and were allowed to print only approved commentary. O'Connell soon built up his own system of patronage and family connexion within the party. In the 1832 parliament, eight of his relatives sat in the Commons. After the Whig alliance in 1835 he became an agent for Whig patronage in Ireland, pressing the claims to office of his family and his political sympathizers, usually in direct approaches to the Under Secretary, Thomas Drummond. A large number of Repealers, as a result, were placed within the administration of the country.

Although given to the labour of diffusing general concepts of British radicalism throughout a country ill prepared to receive them, O'Connell suffered grave disappointment in his personal and professional relationships with English radicals. He was a popular speaker on reform and free-trade platforms in England, but with the parliamentary radicals things never went quite right. On arrival at Westminster in 1830 he had naturally gravitated towards Joseph Hume, Sir Francis Burdett, and Henry Hunt; and it was to this radical spearhead that O'Connell sought to fashion an Irish shaft. His party voted with them with consistency, even after the Whig alliance, when this occasionally meant voting against the ministers. Sometimes the peculiar requirements of his Catholic support and convictions led to differences with the English radical group. O'Connell was attacked by them for opposing the Poor Law and for accepting the compromise tithe settlement in the 1830s; and in the 1840s he attacked the 'godless colleges' and Irish coercive measures, while they welcomed both. But the real differences were personal.

O'Connell was the sort of man known to his contemporaries as a 'swaggerer'. Sensitive and kind in his most private relationships, he was loud-mouthed and abusive in his public controversies. He was boastful and histrionic. He was prickly over criticism and overreacted in defence. His extraordinary vulgarity of dress indicated his feeling for the dramatic. During the Emancipation campaign he wore a gilt button on his shoulder as a sign of his leadership; afterwards, as the Liberator, he customarily appeared enveloped in an immense cloak which was supposed to possess a certain Irish symbolism. He encouraged the cult of his own personality in crude displays of his public influence. In 1845, for example, in celebration of the anniversary of his release from gaol, his supporters staged a gigantic happening, of which the centrepiece was O'Connell himself, seated upon a monstrous throne, surrounded by men in green uniforms and waited upon by deputations from local bodies throughout the country.

No doubt the English politicians had their own views of such goings-on; but it was O'Connell's personal vilification of opponents which really made him unpopular with public men in Britain. The habit, if it ran to excess, was not one expected of a gentleman. O'Connell, of course, was excessive. His differences with Peel were all public, and they began as soon as Peel had become Chief Secretary for Ireland in 1812 – an appointment which ought not to have gone, in O'Connell's view, to a 'raw youth, squeezed out of the workings of I know not what factory in England'. It is interesting that in this definition O'Connell clearly considered the station of gentleman as exclusive to the landed classes. In 1815 Peel and O'Connell would have fought a duel had not O'Connell's wife restrained him in a humiliating resort to the law. On subsequent occasions, far too numerous to describe at any length, O'Connell rattled out public abuse of his opponents. In 1835 he said that Disraeli was descended from the impenitent thief who had died upon the cross next to the Saviour; in 1844, during a mind-evaporating tirade directed against the Duke of Leinster, he remarked that his Grace's very name 'operates like a vomit'. In 1833 he denounced the entire House of Commons as 'six hundred and fifty-eight scoundrels'. It was really rather disagreeable.

The subjects of his displeasure sometimes returned the fire. *The Times*, in 1835, actually allowed itself a verse upon the Liberator which opened with the couplet: 'Scum condensed of Irish bog! Ruffian, coward, demagogue!' O'Connell, characteristically, was deeply hurt. In the same year, as a gesture in disapproval of his attacks upon public men, the radical Burdett, and others, tried to get him expelled from Brooks's. Even the considerable conscience of Richard Cobden was moved with antipathy to O'Connell, with whom, he once observed, he would no sooner think of forming an alliance than with an African chief. O'Connell could never bring himself to realize that his almost universal unpopularity with the political classes in England arose not because of his radical politics, or because he was Irish, but because he was the sort of person that he was.

O'Connellism, above all things, was Catholic. It was this combination of religion and politics which lay at the basis of O'Connell's very considerable reputation abroad. It is true that Havlitcheck in Prague, and Seward and Greely in New York, might have looked to O'Connell for an inspiration in nationalism, but it was as a Liberal Catholic that he was known to most European intellectuals. In the 1840s, biographies of him were written in France, Germany, and Italy. The king of Bavaria once asked for his autograph, and the young Montalembert used to pray for his success. O'Connell's Liberal Catholicism, indeed, was the quintessence of his political analysis. The Irish Catholic Church was in alarming disarray at the start of the nineteenth century. The penal laws of the previous century had denuded the country of bishops, and the vicars-general who administered the Church in their absence had been hindered by the affliction of local rivalries and the regrettable necessity of admitting poorly educated men to holy orders. After the first few decades of the eighteenth century the penal code was allowed to remain unenforced, but the restrictions remained on the statute book as a safeguard for the rights of the Protestant Church and State. Except for some irritating particulars – of which the most grievous was the parliamentary oath – most of these legal restrictions had been removed by the time of the Act of Union. But the Church was by then in a condition of lamentable disorganization. Irregularities of discipline were present in many forms. In parts of the country, and especially in Galway, episcopal government had virtually been replaced by popularly elected 'wardens'; and in the north-eastern areas of Ulster many parishes had adopted lay participation from their Presbyterian neighbours. Everywhere clerical discipline was informal: priests took to the hunting field like the Protestant parsons, many speculated in land, and still others – and this was most displeasing to the hierarchy – attended places of public amusement. Irish Catholicism has a strong puritanical fissure, and it was the last defect which the episcopate sought to correct first. In 1819 Dr Doyle, the Bishop of Kildare and Leighlin, began a campaign to tighten up discipline in the Church. He revived the practice of holding periodic conferences of the clergy. His new regulations were widely adopted in other dioceses. But huge diversities remained to trouble the Church until well into the mid-century, and it was not really until the 1850s, when Cardinal Cullen imposed a strict ultramontane discipline, all hot from Rome, that ecclesiastical government was fully regularized in Ireland.

Now the importance of O'Connell is that he gave the Catholic Church a national existence for the first time, by organizing it through the agency of the bishops and parish priests, in the Emancipation campaign. And he organized it for political purposes. In 1840 he declared: 'The Catholic Church is a national Church, and if the people rally with me they will have a nation for that church.' The Union of Catholicism and political radicalism was a crucial development for the future of Ireland. O'Connell brought it about at all levels of Catholic society. The rural peasantry were excited by the parish clergy to look for salvation in a radicalism which was, in inspiration and social analysis, essentially urban. The Catholic middle class, unable to ape the manners of the gentry because the gentry were Protestant, turned to ape the Catholic clergy as a substitute. It was all very refined.

There were, of course, as in Europe, problems with Liberal Catholicism. Tension with the Vatican was not the least of these. Early in the nineteenth century, Rome was quite ready to do a deal with the British government over the Emancipation question. So was O'Connell, but his terms were different. The problem recurred in 1844, when the Vatican censured the Irish clergy for taking part in the Repeal agitation. The Catholics had always to be especially careful to avoid the imputation that they were subject to the temporal sovereignty of the papacy – during the Emancipation campaign they scrambled to show that the jurisdiction of Rome was purely spiritual. O'Connell himself had a very simple attitude to the Temporal Power. He did not believe in it. 'I deny,' he said in 1814, 'the doctrine that the Pope has any temporal authority, directly or indirectly, in Ireland.' O'Connellite radicalism was always as uniformly explicit. In 1844 the *Pilot*, commenting on the Vatican's censure of the Repeal movement, observed: 'We have discernment enough to distinguish between the spiritual and the temporal authority of His Holiness; and while we bow reverently to the one, we spurn with indignation the exercise of the other.'

The same attitudes were to recur in later episodes of the century, when Rome and popular politics came into collision – at the time of the papal condemnation of the Plan of Campaign in 1888, for example. O'Connell, similarly, always exercised his abilities to point out that Catholics sought no ascendancy in Ireland. He always hoped that Protestants would adhere to his various political schemes. Straining after toleration was at times too much, however, and on one occasion in the House of Commons he denounced a series of appointments of Irish Protestants to the administration on the grounds that 'they are foreigners to us since they are of a different religion'.

There was a further difficulty. O'Connell attacked the Protestant Established Church in Ireland on ordinary utilitarian grounds: because it was an unreformed institution propped up at the public expense. He also attacked it because he was a Catholic; to whom the legal privileges of the Establishment were a national badge of superiority. The maintenance of the state Church, he remarked in 1840, was 'the first and greatest of our grievances'. John MacHale, the O'Connellite Archbishop of Tuam, wrote in 1833 to advise the Bishop of Exeter that the Irish Establishment was 'the prolific womb from which all the misfortunes of Ireland teemed in fearful succession'. O'Connell's problem was how to pursue the radical reform, and eventually the disestablishment of the state Church, without allowing himself or his supporters to slide into religious bigotry. It was especially difficult because the Irish Catholics had inherited a ghetto mentality from the penal days – a mentality which they were busy, during the first decades of the nineteenth century, in developing into a national paranoia. The formal savagery of the penal code was remembered; the fact that it was rarely enforced was not. In O'Connell's day the Catholic Church saw itself as under perpetual and insidious persecution. 'We are arrived,' as MacHale said, 'at one of those perilous periods in the annals of the Church of God, at which, under the treacherous guise of peace, the most deadly hostility is aimed at our holy religion.'

The Catholic Church was also revealing signs of revivalistic fervour. There were, in the middle years of the nineteenth century, two great religious revivals in Ireland, which demonstrated all the characteristics of personal salvationism and the sectarian consciousness of 'churches of the disinherited'. One began during 1859 in Ulster, among the Presbyterians, when thousands received conversion in somewhat hysterical circumstances at mass meetings. As in contemporary American 'frontier' revivals, a lot of men and women were subject to bodily jerkings. Unhappily there were also many whose religious excitement was founded, as Archdeacon Edward Stopford curtly put it, 'on delusions by which it is very difficult to avoid being deluded'.

The other revival was slightly earlier, in the later 1830s and in the 1840s, and it was among the Catholics. Father Theobald Matthew was a Capuchin friar who had been attracted to temperance by the example of three Protestant philanthropists working among the poor of Cork City: Nicholas Dunscombe, a parson, Richard Dowden, a Unitarian, and William Martin, a Quaker. It was Martin who persuaded Father Matthew to grasp the temperance banner in 1838. Within the next few years the movement covered the country, and over two million persons were pledged to total abstinence. The accompanying mass meetings and personal commitments produced all the symptoms of revivalism. The friar himself was actually credited with miraculous powers – people touched him in the hope of a cure. He was widely recognized as 'the moral regenerator of Ireland'. His appeal was to all classes; public gatherings in his honour were filled with Protestant dignitaries as well as Catholics.

But it was among the Catholic peasantry and urban working classes that the temperance movement disclosed its most acute revivalistic qualities. The people flocked to offer their testimonies; the Catholic middle classes toasted the cause at 'Water-parties'. It was left to Lord John Russell, in 1844, to summarize the reaction of public men: 'We all know the extraordinary eloquence, the untiring energy, the disinterested forgetfulness of all selfish objects, which did enable Mr Matthew to accomplish this moral miracle, and, by his exertions, to effect a change in Ireland which was surprising to the whole civilized world.' It must have seemed no less. In the year of Emancipation, 1829, Ireland had spent £6 millions on proof spirits. By 1842 the Exchequer was losing nearly £1 million in excise duties as a result of temperance. Crime statistics also showed a beneficial, although temporary, slump. The liquor trade suffered a recession. O'Connell's Repeal agitation was just passing into its most critical phase, early in the 1840s, when Father Matthew's movement was also at its zenith.

O'Connell recognized in it both a potential rival to his own influence over the people, and a splendidly fashioned moral instrument for keeping the peasantry from rushing to excesses. An alliance with the temperance movement was therefore essential. O'Connell, it is true, had invested in a Dublin brewery in the 1830s, and the resulting enterprise was actually known as 'O'Connell's Brewery'. But this contradiction was not allowed to stand in his way, and, as a sign of his adhesion to the cause of abstinence, O'Connell gave up drinking wine for a short period – resuming consumption, indeed, only at the urgent insistence of his doctor. Father Matthew was anxious to preserve his movement from political involvement, but after 1842, the year in which O'Connell joined the temperance procession in Cork, his followers easily slid into the Repeal agitation. It became, thereafter, difficult to distinguish repeal and temperance themes in the speeches heard at public meetings. O'Connell had successfully added a new dimension to his political movement: the moral fervour of religious revivalism. The parallel with the Anti-Corn Law League in England became even more apparent. Father Matthew himself travelled in England, Scotland, and America speaking the word. He supported the United Kingdom Alliance – the English temperance movement – at its formation in 1853, and died in 1856, the recipient of an annual royal pension.

4. Radicalism and Reform

It was, of course, through his leadership of the movement for Catholic Emancipation that O'Connell achieved his greatest influence in Ireland. The question was not, as is so frequently supposed, one of giving the vote to Catholics – they had enjoyed that privilege since 1793. Catholics could also stand for election to parliament: the difficulty lay in the parliamentary oath which had to be subscribed by elected members. This happened to describe the Catholic religion as 'superstitious' and 'idolatrous'. Clearly no conscientious Catholic could swear to those opinions, and the Emancipation question therefore revolved around the formula to be substituted for them.

It is also important to notice that in England the Whig exponents and the Tory opponents of Emancipation shared the same views about Catholicism. Both saw it as potentially, and at times actually, destructive of civil liberty. At its most common expression anti-Catholicism was a popular culture which enjoyed a multi-class appeal during most of the nineteenth century. Catholicism was held to be, of its very nature, essentially illiberal and inherently intolerant. Catholics were supposedly engineering the subversion of Protestant kingdoms; the universal monarchy of the papacy demanded a 'double allegiance' which was itself prejudiced by 'Jesuitical' constructions proving that heretic sovereigns could be deposed by their subjects. The 'medievalism' of Catholic dogma, in the words of Lord John Russell, 'enslaved the intellect'. The Catholic priesthood was sunk in moral depravity and employed the device of the confessional to propagate treasonable doctrines as well as to derive perverted sensations for their own gratification. Reference was frequently made to a long tradition of Catholic persecution – the Reformation martyrs and the victims of the Inquisition were popular heroes in nineteenth-century English culture.

Furthermore, this interpretation of Catholicism did not diminish. It was reinforced in the mid-century by the pontificate of Pius IX; with that insistence on the central direction of the Church's affairs from Rome known as ultramontanism; by the Syllabus of Errors, the Vatican Council, and the struggle of Catholicism and the state in Germany – the *Kulturkampf*. Whigs and Tories both spoke of Catholicism in a vocabulary of vituperation drawn from this sturdy tradition during every debate on the Emancipation question. The Act of Union had projected the question into the centre of British parliamentary life.

Popular prejudices against Rome were reinforced by constitutional theory. The wide acceptance of the notion of the 'Protestant Constitution' was the centrepiece obstacle to Emancipation, especially as it was a theory which corresponded to the facts: the organic union of Church and nation described by Hooker. The Established Church of England and Ireland was an integral part of the Constitution, protected by the coronation oath of the sovereign. Since this Erastianism required an exclusively Anglican legislature for its logical operation it was necessary to exclude dissenters from parliament. The system was not operated very logically, however. Annual acts of indemnity had, in the eighteenth century, protected Protestant dissenters who sat in parliament; yet when the Test and Corporation Acts were repealed in 1828 safeguards for the state Church were incorporated into the reform as a legal reminder that public confessionalism was still the orthodoxy of government.

Protestant dissent was one thing, however; Catholicism quite another. Both Whigs and Tories, both pro- and anti-Emancipationists in England accepted the maintenance of the state Church as the highest political duty. Only a handful of radicals disagreed. The real differences arose in matters of expediency. The Whigs and 'trimming' Tories who favoured Emancipation did so precisely because they believed that timely concessions to the Catholics would in fact operate to preserve the Protestant Constitution by giving the leading enemies to its existence a stake in its operation. The opponents of Emancipation differed on this point. Many Tories like Peel argued that by conceding a great constitutional principle a whole series of piecemeal reforms would be inaugurated, and an accumulating series of precedents would in the fullness of time bring down the entire fabric of the Protestant state. Public life would no longer be in a position to profess a religious creed: first Jews, and then freethinkers would be lined up for Emancipation, and the public conscience would be rendered ineradicably ambiguous. In this diagnosis the Tories were broadly correct. Their opposition to Catholic Emancipation, therefore, resided not in some special viciousness of their natures, or in antipathy to Ireland – for after 1800 Emancipation was largely an Irish question: they were simply unable to conceive a state which did not profess a single and well-defined religious conscience.

Serious attempts to redeem Pitt's pledge that Emancipation would follow the Act of Union turned upon the nature of the safeguards to be provided for the Protestant Establishment. Two devices provided the nucleus of the discussion: the payment by the state of the Catholic clergy, and the concession of a Crown veto over unsuitable episcopal appointments. The first was intended to adhere the priests to the government, and to offer them the chance of independence from the political prejudices of their flocks. The notion recurred frequently during the first two thirds of the century, although after the mid-century the clergy themselves began to show an increasing unwillingness to accept what could only too easily be represented as government bribery. The second device came near to reality early in the century. The veto had first been accepted by Pius VII in 1808, although the Irish hierarchy, with three dissentients, were opposed to it. In 1814 Mgr Quarantotti of the Propaganda gave theological justification for a veto, and in 1815, following the good relations established between Cardinal Consalvi and Castlereagh at the Paris and Vienna peace negotiations at the conclusion of the continental wars, Cardinal Lita declared that the Pope was ready to submit episcopal appointments for the scrutiny of the British Crown. In 1816 the Pope wrote to assure the Irish bishops that their reservations were unnecessary; that the Vatican had 'acted according to the invariable rule of the Holy See, that is, never to promote to vacant sees persons who were known to be displeasing to the powers under whom the dioceses to be administered were situated.' But by that time O'Connell had already moved in to oppose the veto. He seems to have believed that it would, in his own words, 'have the effect, if passed into law, of placing in the hands of the Minister a new and extensive source of patronage'. He also feared a schism. In 1817 he noticed that the people were siding with anti-veto priests. 'I really think they will go near to desert all such clergymen as do not now take an active part in the question,' he wrote. The question also divided the hierarchy, and it separated the hostile majority of anti-vetoists from the Protestant pro-Emancipationists in Ireland, led, still, by Henry Grattan. It tended, as well, to divide the Irish from the English Catholics, most of whom were quite happy to accept the veto.

O'Connell therefore entered the political scene at a moment of depressing disunity. He had managed to take over leadership of the various Catholic boards and committees which had endured a continuous existence since the middle of the eighteenth century. The government periodically suppressed these agencies by exercising the powers of the Convention Act, passed by the Irish Parliament in 1793 as a blanket measure against the United Irishmen. O'Connell's legal acumen always found a way around the law.

In 1820 the death of Grattan removed the only political figure who could still rival O'Connell's influence in Ireland. In 1821 Lord Wellesley became not only the first Irishman to take office as Viceroy since the seventeenth century, but the first Emancipationist too. In 1821, also, Plunket's Emancipation Bill passed the Commons by a narrow margin, only to go down to defeat in the Lords. This Bill, incidentally, was the last occasion on which Catholic relief was linked with the veto, and O'Connell had opposed it for that reason. But after Plunket's Bill, the issue became practical politics, even with an administration like Lord Liverpool's, itself so divided on the Catholic question that the government was only held together by sterilizing it as an 'open' question in the cabinet. In 1823, therefore, and at the age of forty-eight, O'Connell founded the celebrated Catholic Association in cooperation with Richard Sheil.

This body was centralized in Dublin but had a large provincial organization with the Catholic priesthood – all of whom were ex-officio members – directing local effort in every parish. It was they who collected the 'Catholic Rent', a voluntary tax of 1d. a month paid by the half-million associate members. Bishop Doyle was the first member of the hierarchy to join the Association; the rest soon followed. As a sophisticated and successful mobilization of the massed peasantry for political purposes, the Association was without precedent.

English radicals learned plenty of lessons from the example, and the government was duly alarmed by the implicit threat to political stability. Goulburn's Act, in 1825, which suppressed the Association, was supported by most sections of parliamentary opinion: in Ireland O'Connell avoided the law by changing the name of his society to 'New Catholic Association'. In 1825 Sir Francis Burdett introduced another relief Bill to the Commons. Determined to soften the opposition of those men who feared that once concessions had been made O'Connell would fill the hundred Irish seats with his own nominees, Burdett proposed two main safeguards. First, the payment of the Catholic clergy; secondly, the disfranchisement of the forty-shilling freehold voter in Ireland – a strange proposal to come from a radical otherwise committed to the extension of the franchise. O'Connell, furthermore, accepted both these provisions. The Bill, like its predecessor, was lost in the Lords.

It was during the 1826 general election that the value of the forty-shilling voter became clear to O'Connell. In Waterford the revolt of the Catholic electorate against the traditional political influence of the Beresford family was organized by the priests according to a plan devised by Sir Thomas Wyse – who was later to become British ambassador in Greece. O'Connell had taken no part in the astounding Waterford success; indeed, until the very eve of polling he considered the whole scheme of the utmost lunacy. However, he was quick to realize a good thing when he saw it, and immediately the Association scrambled to influence the vote in Louth, Monaghan, and Westmeath. As at Waterford, the Catholics were directed to support Protestant Emancipationist candidates. Nothing like this had ever happened before. It seemed as if the influence of the landlords was about to be disregarded everywhere. Then, in 1828, came the unexpected catastrophe for the Wellington administration. When Canning resigned from the ministry over the Penryn and East Retford disfranchisements, a rearrangement of the government resulted in a number of new appointments. One of these was of Vesey Fitzgerald to the Board of Trade. He was a liberal, pro-Emancipationist Tory; he had now to seek re-election in his Co. Clare seat on accepting office. Following the pattern established in the 1826 elections, the Catholic Association decided to sponsor a Protestant candidate of their own. They were unable to find one, however, and only eight days before the election O'Connell was prevailed upon to stand himself. He was extremely reluctant, especially as the expenses of the contest were likely to be huge. This sensational election, therefore, was not designed by O'Connell to blackmail the government by threatening to wreck the Constitution. It happened by chance. Fitzgerald withdrew in the face of a clerical opposition which amounted at times to quite open intimidation. Even his own tenants were led out by the priests to vote for O'Connell, whose successful return left the government in an intolerable fix. O'Connell refused to take the existing parliamentary oath.

During the autumn of 1828 Wellington made the first intimations of his conversion to Emancipation during a number of audiences with George IV. There was much background noise about a possible civil war in Ireland unless concessions were made. These fears were in fact groundless, because both O'Connell and his clerical agents were ideologically opposed to the use of force for political purposes. But disturbances on a large scale were likely. Irish and English ultra-Protestants, sensing the drift of the ministry towards surrender, found in the Orange lodges, and in the newly formed Brunswick Clubs, suitable vehicles for their opposition.

But a popular movement, nurtured in traditional No-Popery, somehow failed to take fire. There was no repetition of the Gordon Riots of 1780. Reaction came mostly from Tory political interests, from the Church of England and from the universities. Peel's conversion resulted in his being sacked from the representation of the University of Oxford. 'Orange' Peel became 'turncoat' Peel. Finally, in January 1829, the King at last so overcame his scruples about his coronation oath as to allow the cabinet to draft a Bill.

In its first version the proposed legislation included payment of the priests as one of the safeguards. This was dropped in order to avoid the difficult precedent of establishing a formal connexion between the state and the Catholic Church. But the Act as finally passed still retained important securities. The parliamentary oath was duly altered to remove the offensive phrases, though it still required an explicit undertaking not to subvert the Protestant Establishment and to offer full allegiance to the House of Brunswick. A number of clauses contained lesser restrictions. The Catholic clergy were forbidden to wear ecclesiastical dress in public; bishops were not to assume territorial titles; and religious orders of men, but not of women, were banished from the realm. This last item remained a dead-letter. The exclusion of women from the banishment did not reflect the refined susceptibilities of a parliament of gentlemen towards the honour of ladies: the fact is that they did not have a vote.

The leading securities came in two separate legislative provisions – the 'wings' of the Emancipation Act. The first outlawed the Catholic Association, thus seeking to remove the threat of continued interference with the traditional operation of political influence in Ireland. The second disfranchised the forty-shilling freehold voter by raising the qualification to £10. Emancipation, therefore, was a measure of parliamentary reform not only in the sense that it admitted a new category of

83

persons to the legislature, the Catholics, but because it also involved an adjustment of the franchise – even though it was an adjustment in an upward direction.

The Emancipation debate had also clarified much broader parliamentary views on the whole question of the relationship of church and state. In this it both hastened and articulated the arguments, on each side, which were deployed in the great church reform discussions of the 1830s. Hurrell Froude wrote his *Remarks on the Interference of the State in Matters Spiritual*, which pointed to the implications of Emancipation for the future conduct of a mixed legislature in its future dealings with the state Church. A great constitutional debate was given clarity and edge. O'Connell was buoyant. 'I will stake my existence,' he said of Emancipation, 'that I will run a coach-and-six three times told through this Act.'

But in 1830 his enthusiasm was instead directed towards the repeal of the Act of Union. This had always been his long-term intention. In 1810 he had said, 'I abandon all wish for Emancipation if it delays that Repeal'; and on another occasion, 'I have an ulterior motive – the Repeal of the Union.' His announcement in 1830 that a new political campaign for Repeal was about to begin was not as widely acclaimed as he supposed it would be, however. Many of those who had supported him over the Catholic claims – especially the Protestant Emancipationists – now stood aside. The Church was divided. A large number of parish priests passed straight into the new agitation, but the hierarchy exhibited more caution. In 1830 the bishops published a joint pastoral letter, drafted by Doyle, which instructed the clergy to avoid political organizations; a policy reinforced by resolutions of the bishops in 1834. No mention was made of Repeal, but the implications were clear enough. A few prelates, like MacHale, ignored these injunctions and joined O'Connell's cause quite openly. The new Repeal movement incorporated all the favourite items of O'Connell's radicalism. In August 1831 he declared his priorities: 'a domestic parliament, an absentee rate, an arrangement of church property.' This order was never particularly stable, and the dozen or so radical societies which the Liberator floated in the next decade revealed far wider objectives. By Repeal itself, he seems to have meant a simple removal of the Union. The ambiguities germane to such a course were soon to declare themselves.

From the Whig administration which took office under Lord Grey in 1830, O'Connell at first expected little. They were, it was true, an improvement on the Tories in his view. But the beginning was scarcely encouraging. The Whigs undertook the coercion of Ireland as their first task, and in January 1831 O'Connell was arrested for sedition. He was released, but the indignity offered to him was inauspicious. Then, in 1833, the government passed a tight measure of coercion aimed at the containment of the tithe war in the Irish countryside. O'Connell's opposition was bitter. It is curious that although the 1832 election had returned thirty-nine Repeal members to parliament O'Connell's political influence with the ministry was at this time slight. The Irish reforms of the administration cannot therefore be adequately explained, as they so frequently are, as concessions to successfully presented agitation, nor were they wrung from a reluctant parliament. The outgoing Tory ministry under Wellington had in fact prepared a number of Irish Bills, especially concerning police reform and land improvement. The reform proposals continued under the Whigs and, after 1841, under Peel. In reality the Irish ameliorative measures form a continuous sequence from 1829 to 1847, when the exceptional conditions of the great famine interrupted them. Most Irish reforms were suggested to the government from within the public service. Parliament was quite willing – even anxious – to do something about the chronic conditions which

85

manifested themselves in rural outrages and in the general state of underdevelopment. Reform came, at this time, only secondarily as a concession to organized agitation. Both Melbourne and Peel sought to conciliate O'Connell, but the measures they proposed had all been more or less in the pipe-line anyway. O'Connell always liked to imagine that Irish reforms had to be squeezed out of parliament; in fact the behaviour of parliament in relation to Irish reforming pressures scarcely differed from its relation to English ones. The legislature which ignored the clamours of the Anti-Corn Law League up to 1846, and which refused even to debate the Charter, can hardly be accused of partiality in its unpreparedness to govern at the behest of organized opinion, whether it came from England or Ireland.

The Whigs tried first to do something about Irish local government. Stanley, as Chief Secretary, attempted a reform of the grand juries by transferring the chief incidence of county cess (rate) from the tenants to the landowners. O'Connell objected to this as an unwarranted increase in the burden of taxation which fell upon the landed classes. Stanley's plan lapsed. The grand juries remained encumbered and exclusive for the next half-century as a result. The government did achieve, however, a consolidation of the Board of Works. In 1831 the Board was reconstituted with a permanent staff of officials, and empowered to advance £500,000 in loans to promote public works as well as to distribute £50,000 in outright gifts to stimulate local effort. Land drainage schemes, road building, river navigation, and fisheries were, under the direction of the grand juries, assisted by these means. A centralized agency had thus been consolidated in Ireland to supervise the development of public utilities. It soon extended its activities and its staff.

Central direction was also the leading feature of the National System of primary schools established in 1831. A commission of 1812 had suggested the creation of a government department to supervise a public system of education. The idea was extremely novel, not only because of the principle of centralized control, but because men did not look naturally to the state as the proper agency for education. In 1831, in his famous letter to the Duke of Leinster, Stanley outlined a scheme of primary schools conducted by local boards of managers and under the direction of a central board in Dublin. The existing educational grant made by parliament – £30,000 a year, divided between the Kildare Place Society and the Society for Discountenancing Vice – was to be turned over to the new board.

This plan was far in advance of English experience, where there was no direct state sponsorship of education until 1870. The Irish primary schools, furthermore, were non-sectarian: religious instruction was according to a carefully constructed formula which extracted the doctrinal points thought essential to both Protestant and Catholic traditions. The device allowed one great benefit – the education of children of all denominations in the same classroom. As such, the national schools were intended to soften the religious rivalries of the Irish people. The experiment was very original.

'Common Christianity' worked for a time, and its first critics were not, in fact, the Catholic prelates – who accepted the scheme in the realistic awareness that the government would not support denominational Catholic schools – but groups of Protestants who managed to believe that Catholic dogmas were sliding into the curricula. During the 1840s the Catholic hierarchy gradually moved over into opposition to the National System, which they finally censured at the Synod of Thurles in 1850. Archbishop MacHale, as usual, had anticipated the trend. 'Our "common Christianity" – the fashionable and favourite phrase of the day,' he wrote to Lord John Russell in 1839, 'is represented as a sort of commonage in

87

which the legitimate inheritors of the true faith, as well as the roving hordes who are the followers of every error, may be squatted down together.' The changing Catholic position over the state schools reflected both a rising confidence prompted by awareness of the strength resident in their numerical superiority over the Protestants, and the new ultramontane exclusiveness spreading out from Rome. The National System survived the withering assaults of the hierarchy, but it was to become one of their leading grievances in the second half of the nineteenth century.

The Irish Reform Bill of 1832 was moderate. The forty-shilling freehold franchise was not restored, the ministers maintaining that as part of the bargain struck to secure Emancipation the disfranchisement must continue. Five new borough seats were added to the Irish representation, which scarcely did much to alter the political circumstances of Ireland. But in 1833 the Whigs decided to reform the Protestant Established Church, and the sky was really set on fire.

The case for general church reform presented itself quite forcibly in the 1830s, in England as well as in Ireland. The Whigs decided to deal with Ireland first, since the huge Catholic majority projected the issues with a clarity which was much less easily discernible in England. Both Irish Catholics and English radicals had ideological objections to the ecclesiastical establishment. Reform was promoted by the Whigs, and supported by Peel and many Tories, on grounds of expediency, however. They sought to prop up the Irish Church by removing the most obvious abuses with which it was afflicted. As Lord Grey told the Lords in July 1833, 'the Bill did not seek to weaken, but only to avert dangers, and thus to strengthen that Church.' The Irish Establishment was not in fact as loaded with riches as its opponents always believed. Certainly it shared to a quite gross degree all the anomalies which characterized the English branch of the Church, too; but it was not supremely wealthy. The trouble was that ecclesiastical revenues were disproportionately distributed, so that the dignitaries had far too much, and the inferior clergy not enough. The Whig reform Bill had at first – in its notorious clause 147 – provided for the appropriation, to secular use, of surplus revenues. This was withdrawn due to the massive opposition of those in parliament who denounced any 'spoliation' of sacred property and who also objected to a violation of the scarcely less sacred rights of corporations. Four ministers resigned from the government in opposition to appropriation. O'Connell attacked the Bill when it was removed. The question was, as it turned out, hypothetical; a complete investigation of the Church's revenues after 1833 quite soon revealed that there was no surplus to appropriate.

The Irish Church Temporalities Act of 1833 set up a permanent ecclesiastical commission to administer revenues. In this, as in so many other features, the Act proved a precedent for English Church reform. Church cess was abolished, to the immense delight of English dissenters, who were themselves seeking a precedent for their own campaign to abolish Church rate. Six Irish bishoprics were abolished. This aspect of the reform especially alarmed English churchmen, who regarded it as an unpardonable disturbance of spiritualities. It was while the Bill was passing through the Lords that Keble preached his celebrated Assize sermon at Oxford on 'National Apostasy'. Newman, hurrying home from Italy, was becalmed in the Straits of Messina, and suppressed his impatience by composing the hymn 'Lead Kindly Light' – of which the 'encircling gloom' referred to the Irish Act. Those appealing against the right of the state to interfere with the discipline of the Church found material for their opinions in the early fathers: the Oxford movement was the result. The Whigs had not, of course, foreseen such a portentous outcome to their Irish scheme.

O'Connell, meanwhile, was beginning to recognize the disadvantages of enmity with the Whigs. Although he introduced his first Repeal motion to the Commons in April 1834, he was, as early as 1833, preparing for some sort of *modus operandi* with the ministry. 'As long as I could see the utility of the British Parliament – and an immense utility may exist,' he wrote in 1833, 'I should prefer seeing the House doing justice to my countrymen rather than that it should be done by a local legislature.' By May of the following year he was already beginning to shelve the immediacy of Repeal and offer it only as a sword of Damocles above the heads of the government. 'I will get what I can,' he then declared, 'and use the Repeal *in terrorem* merely until it is wise and necessary to recommence the agitation.' That was the background to the Whig alliance.

In February 1835, during Peel's interregnum administration following William IV's dismissal of the Whigs for sustained attacks on the Irish Church, he drew up what he called his 'terms of support'. These conditions included a new reform of the franchise in Ireland, the appropriation of the 'surplus' revenues of the Irish Protestant Church, and a reform of municipal corporations. With the addition of a tithe settlement, they formed the basis of the Lichfield House 'Compact' of March 1835 – a gentlemen's agreement reached when Melbourne undertook to take all these questions into consideration. In the new Whig administration, Mulgrave became Viceroy, Morpeth Chief Secretary, and Drummond the Under Secretary. O'Connell's expectancy of a place in the cabinet was disappointed. Furthermore the official Irish appointments, though of persons to whom he was not averse, were made without consulting him. Ten of the Repealers got either office or title. O'Connell himself turned down the

Mastership of the Rolls when it was offered in 1838, correctly foreseeing that its acceptance would diminish his popular influence in Ireland.

So there began what in 1837 O'Connell was to describe as 'the only bearable government Ireland ever experienced since the fatal day when the followers of the murderers of Becket polluted our shores'. The Whigs, in fact, resumed their reform programme, but now with the additional advantage of Irish sympathy. In Thomas Drummond, especially, they had a good public relations man. He was from an aristocratic Scottish family, trained in the Royal Engineers, and then, after 1833, he had become Lord Althorp's secretary. When he died in 1840 the *Dublin Evening Post* remarked that 'no Irishman that ever lived was more thoroughly, more cordially Irish than he.' Drummond, in fact, was a 'scientific administrator'; a trained engineer, a practical man. He was one of that distinguished corps of British officials who, while opposed to state interference with social relationships on principle, yet did much in practice to bring it about, convinced of the need for public action by the immensity of the social evils which work in the field brought to light. In 1836 he consolidated the Irish police and centralized the force under the direct control of Dublin Castle, so completing the earlier pioneering reforms initiated by Peel when he was Chief Secretary in 1814. Drummond was also responsible for admitting Catholics to the force, and for appointing Catholics to stipendiary magistracies.

Catholics were admitted to many other offices, too. Three of the six Whig appointments to the bench were of Catholics, and so was one of the two Crown law officers. It was also Drummond who, in May 1838, addressed the famous open letter to the Tipperary magistrates who had asked the government for more coercive measures to put down agrarian crime. In refusing their petition, he established a maxim which endeared him to the peasantry for all time: 'Property has its duties as well as its rights; to the neglect of those duties in times past is mainly to be ascribed that diseased state of society in which such crimes take their rise.'

Drummond also took a leading part on the Royal Commission into Irish Railways, appointed in 1836. Its Report, of 1838, dwelt extensively, and in nice detail, upon the prevailing social and economic ills of the country, and provided ammunition for reformers. It also outlined the case for a rearrangement of land tenure, to eliminate subdivision of holdings, for state-aided land drainage, agricultural improvements, and public utilities; for assisted emigration and for state construction of railways. Drummond's proposal to implement the last of these was defeated in parliament during 1838. But above all, Drummond won golden opinions among the Irish Catholics by encouraging the dissolution of the Orange Order. In view of its recurrent appearances in modern Irish history, it is necessary to describe the early development of Orangeism in brief outline.

Founded by northern Protestant peasants and small-farmers in 1795 to create a counter-balance to the Catholic 'Defender' movement, the Orange lodges expanded impressively in both numbers and political influence during their first three years. When the Defenders merged with the republican United Irishmen, the Orangemen formed a providential link between the Castle administration and the Protestant yeomanry. In 1798 the Grand Lodge was moved from the north to Dublin so that, with the outbreak of rebellion in that year, a framework of centralized loyalist organization was already in existence. The actual part taken by the Orangemen in suppressing the rebels is obscure; in most accounts of the rebellion the terms 'Orangeman' and 'loyalist' are used interchangeably. These events did not promote an enduring Orange influence, however. In 1799 the movement was split over the Union question, and its influence evaporated. From this point the fortunes of Orangeism vacillated and its composition changed. Irish noblemen patronized the lodges during the Protestant rally to the Union prompted by the Emmet rebellion of 1803, and in the 1820s clergymen of the Established religion added the benefit of their presence, too.

But at no time did the governments of the day, Whig or Tory, regard the movement with anything but the most profound distrust. To the Whigs, Orange opposition to Catholic Emancipation and to the Reform Bill of 1832 seemed sufficient evidence of unworthiness; to many Tories the lodges, despite their overflowing loyalism, were scarcely to be distinguished from the other sinister manifestations of 'club government'. Yet Orangeism did spread in England among the military and among groups of ultra peers. One of the constables at the Peterloo disturbance in 1819 was an Orangeman. The Duke of York was Grand Master of the English lodges until obliged to resign in 1821, when questions were asked in parliament about the political reliability of the movement.

In 1825, in fact, the Irish lodges were dissolved under the law passed to extinguish O'Connell's Catholic Association. They were not revived until that legislation lapsed in 1828. Orange recovery was then slow, and its practical influence negligible: even the Wellington administration did not for a moment contemplate the promotion of Orangeism as a counterbalance to O'Connell's influence in Ireland. And in 1836, following a parliamentary inquiry ordered by Melbourne, and suggested by sensational (and untrue) rumours about an Orange conspiracy to set up a Regency under the Duke of Cumberland, the lodges were again suppressed. There were then 1,600 of them in Ireland, with a membership of around 150,000 men. Between thirty and forty regiments had their own lodges. Their objects embraced the general maintenance of the Protestant throne and altar. Members were expelled if they attended a Catholic Church or voted Whig. The order re-established itself in 1845.

The other reforming measures of the Whig ministry all concerned aggravated matters which had been the subjects of O'Connell's agitation. This was because both he and the ministry shared a similar view of the type of reforms required for Ireland: both looked essentially to the settlement of questions touching political justice in the realms of religion, education, and administration. The same was true of Peel after 1841. Neither the English ministries nor O'Connell looked to social reforms, or to reforms which might, as far as they could see, involve too great a degree of economic adjustment.

Early in the 1830s resistance to the payment of tithe had attained epidemic proportions in the Irish countryside. The question had always been a leading grievance, and had loomed gigantic in the rebellions of 1798. It also irritated the peasantry into joining the Whiteboys and other rural secret societies. It covered the Protestant parsons with odium. Dr Montgomery noticed, in his evidence to the Commons' Select Committee on tithes in 1832, that the peasantry 'knew little of the Protestant Episcopalian parson, save in the character of tithe-proctor.' The clergy themselves were awkwardly dependent on tithes for income, and the non-payment movement of the 1830s left many of them in extreme distress. It was conventional for them to exempt the local Catholic priest from payment, and it was a breach of this custom in 1830 when a Father Doyle of Graigue, Co. Carlow, had his horse impounded by the parson in reprisal for non-payment of tithe, which set the anti-tithe movement alight. The resulting 'tithe war' was bitter. Disturbances and petty rioting occurred throughout the country, with troops brought in to break down the resistance of the tenants – a resistance organized in most places by the Catholic clergy. At Newtownbarry twelve men were killed when the yeomanry opened fire on a tithe demonstration in June 1831. In December of the same year there was a battle between police and tenants at Carrickshock in which eleven policemen were killed.

The social composition of the anti-tithe movement is interesting. It was not dominated by the peasantry but by the more substantial Catholic tenants – the rural middle class who were the hard core of O'Connell's supporters, and as a class normally characterized by a deep respect for landed property. In Carlow and Kilkenny especially, the centres of the movement, the larger tenants were clearly in control, and some Protestant tenants joined in, too. They demanded an adjustment of tithe payment, to lift the heaviest burden into the higher reaches of landowning society. They did not, on the whole, seek the abolition of tithe altogether – a solution which seemed to many a violation of property rights. During the period of the tithe war this class was allied with the peasantry, on whom the burden of payment fell lightly if at all. To them, the tithe question was simply an aspect of the general grievance of Irish land tenure, and in many places the peasantry pushed the tithe movement into a wider demand for reductions of rent.

In 1832 the Whigs passed a Tithe Composition Act, compensating the parsons for lost revenue and providing for government collection of arrears. The cost of collection, it was soon discovered, substantially exceeded the actual receipts. After the Lichfield House Compact the Whigs were obliged to try again. They were unwise enough to attempt to relate a tithe settlement to the principle of appropriation. Just as in the Church Temporalities Act this induced the severest qualms in the consciences of all those who watched over the rights of sacred and of secular property. After failing with several measures through the promotion of this principle, and with O'Connell dragging along on their coat-tails, the Whigs finally managed legislation in 1838. Their Tithe Act substituted a rent-charge for the old system, and the principle of appropriation was dropped. O'Connell supported the Bill, and was criticized by some of his followers for doing so. The new Act exempted the largest class of Irish tenants, the tenants-at-will, from payment of any tithe at all. As this was the class also most liable to agrarian disturbance, the 1838 Act brought some measure of tranquillity to the Irish countryside.

The question of an Irish Poor Law was also complicated. The government had settled the problem of the rising cost of poor relief in England by the legislation of 1834 which had established the 'less-eligibility' principle according to the vision of Edwin Chadwick. Poor relief was to be made so unattractive – by the creation of residential workhouses – that only the really destitute would seek it. Able-bodied pauperism would, theoretically, disappear. The problems of poverty in Ireland were even more urgent than in England. Information had piled up which revealed the horrifying dimensions of Irish poverty: there had been parliamentary Select Committees in 1819, 1823, 1827, and 1830. The post-war depression had led, as it had in England, to a partial collapse of existing machinery of poor relief. This operated at the parish level, and additional assistance came mainly from philanthropic and religious charities, from occasional state grants for areas of extreme distress, and from as much beneficial local employment as the inefficiency of the grand juries might allow to exist.

In 1833 the government appointed a Royal Commission under the chairmanship of Richard Whately, Protestant Archbishop of Dublin, to inquire into the relief of poverty in Ireland. Its reports, in 1835 and 1836, rejected the general principles of the new English system on the grounds that there were simply too many able-bodied paupers for indoor relief to work in Ireland. In this they were correct – there were even too many for the workhouse system to operate felicitously in England. Whately's report therefore recommended state-sponsored public works, to be used to employ the poor, and assisted emigration.

At this point the Whigs demonstrated an obtuseness which did them no credit. George Nicholls, one of the English Poor Law Commissioners, was dispatched to Ireland to report on conditions as he saw them. After a visit of scarcely nine weeks he was back in London bubbling with enthusiasm for the adoption of the English system. The government agreed, and it was Nicholls who actually framed the Irish Bill of 1837. By 1841, 130 Poor Law Unions had been set up in Ireland, and a network of workhouses was under construction. The 1838 Act was scarcely in operation when, in the mid-forties, the famine intervened to bring about a total collapse of the system in the most distressed parts of the country.

The Repeal party had been divided over the Poor Law question. O'Connell supported the Act in 1838, though he was himself opposed to legislation on principle, believing that poverty was best left to stimulate private charity. In this he differed from Bishop Doyle and most of the Catholic clergy, who tended to favour state promotion of public works, and it was in deference to their views that O'Connell supported a legislative solution at all. Fifty-six of the Irish members of parliament voted for the Act, including O'Connell; only sixteen voted against it. It is a curious irony that the weight of Irish parliamentary opinion should have been so broadly favourable to legislation which was so plainly unsuited to Irish conditions. Political economy had won again. In Ireland, popular opposition to the law was not as great as in the experience of England. It came from similar sources, however; from gentry and clergymen who objected to the centralization of the new system, and who were jealous of their own traditional paternalism in local government.

The question of Irish municipal reform had a much more cogently political edge. It, too, was one of the conditions of the Whig alliance. Like the Poor Law, the issue was related to English experience. The Irish corporations were characterized by the same sort of corruptions, only in Ireland the religious exclusiveness was much more complete. If the English dissenters were upset by the Church of England's close relations with the corporations before the 1835 reform, in Ireland the same sort of relationships appeared even more anomalous. By the 1830s, some sixty corporations existed in Ireland; two thirds of these were self-electing oligarchies, and only four had Catholic members. At the apex was Dublin, exclusively Protestant, and like most of these bodies, sunk in debt yet magnificent in pecuniary rewards. As in England, the radical attack on the corporations – here led by O'Connell – was largely unconcerned with the question of their efficiency. The attack was upon the ramparts of 'aristocratic' and religious monopoly; the reforms demanded were for political justice, not for better machinery of local government. In 1833 the Whigs had appointed a Royal Commission on the Irish Corporations which sat concurrently with the English one. Its composition was evenly balanced between Protestant and Catholic, but radicals dominated its proceedings. The Commission was chaired by Louis Perrin, a liberal-radical Irish equivalent of Joseph Parkes. Its Report, which was extremely partisan, condemned almost everything. Legislation, however, was held up by the House of Lords, and the Bill which finally got through in 1840, though it still abolished fifty-eight corporations and reconstituted ten new ones upon a £10 franchise, was a good deal less radical than the proposals of 1835. O'Connell's objections to the moderation of the measure – and especially to the limit of the franchise compared with

England's – were largely formal. He became Lord Mayor of Dublin in 1841. The symbolic change in Irish urban government was immense. The Protestant and Tory oligarchs were swept away at one stroke, and O'Connell's supporters took their places and possessed themselves of their regalia. O'Connell had also won new bases of political influence.

The 1837 general election had shown clear signs of apathy among the Catholic electorate; the collection of the 'Tribute' was also falling off. In 1838, therefore, O'Connell decided to remind the Whigs that he still held Repeal *in terrorem*. He founded the 'Precursor Society', designed to 'precede' Repeal unless satisfactory reforms were forthcoming. The less gifted of his followers, as it happened, supposed that its object was to 'curse' the government. It was accordingly popular. 'A real effectual Union, or no Union – such is the alternative,' O'Connell had declared during the election campaign. After the establishment of the Precursor Society, however, he continued his adhesion to the Whig administration. At times, it is true, even his spirit seemed to weary within him; in 1839 he contemplated retiring to a monastery. But his tasks were too urgent, so it seemed, and the injustices too galling. In 1840, instead, he set up the Loyal National Repeal Association. By this time incipient divisions within the Irish radical camp were becoming apparent. In 1840, also, Sharman Crawford and the northern Protestant radicals founded their own Ulster Constitutional Association, which aimed at securing Irish reforms within the Union. Cooperation between their new venture and O'Connell's proved impossible; the personal antagonism of O'Connell for Crawford was too openly paraded.

And at this point a further antagonism smote the Liberator. In 1841 the Tories returned to office, and he had to face his old adversary, Peel. The Whig alliance, though it was maintained in opposition, was now of little service. O'Connell was obliged to activate the machinery for Repeal which he had created as an insurance against such a contingency. There was a slight stillness before the earthquake, while O'Connell fulfilled his duties as Lord Mayor of Dublin, between 1841 and 1842. But in 1842 the economic slump and its associated distress added an urgency to the case for renewed agitation. The Chartist campaign in England and the new Repeal agitation in Ireland took their life from the years of hunger.

The new campaign was explicitly intended to repeat, in both shape and outcome, the victory of 1829. But on this occasion the peasantry and the priests were slow to respond, and O'Connell was left thrashing round in pursuit of ever more daring stimulants. It was unfortunate for his credibility that he should have declared 1843 'Repeal Year'. The moment was very unlike 1829. There was no substantial opinion in England ready to countenance Repeal. O'Connell was deceived. Perhaps he was carried away by a success in February 1843, when, as the first fruit of municipal reform, he induced the Dublin Corporation to resolve in favour of Repeal. The debate was sensational, and the issues emerged with clarity. O'Connell rested his case on the belief that as the old Irish parliament had been incompetent to end its own existence it was, in a sense, still in existence and needed only the issuance of the Queen's writs to be reassembled. In constitution and function, and in its relations with the executive, parliament would be essentially as Grattan had left it. The opposition case was presented for the Tory rump on the Corporation by Isaac Butt, the future Home Ruler, then a young lawyer. Butt exploited the ambiguities in O'Connell's simple proposal. He pointed out that the constitutional rights to which the Repealers looked were of British origin anyway. He then listed the radical doctrines to which O'Connell had always subscribed, insisting that those doctrines would have, if the revived parliament was to prove satisfactory to the Repealers, to become incorporated in the structure of the legislature. 'It was not a proposal to return to any state of things which had previously existed in Ireland,' Butt argued, 'but to enter on an untried and wild system of democracy.' O'Connell's motion was nevertheless carried by forty-five votes to fifteen.

The effect was staggering. Middle-class men who had previously remained aloof now joined the Repeal Association. Radicalized town councils petitioned in favour of Repeal. Most of the Catholic bishops became friendly. In fact the partiality of the clergy was such that in 1844 the Vatican, under discreet pressure from Metternich, acting for the British government, actually instructed Cardinal Fransoni to tell Archbishop Crolly of Armagh to restrain the political enthusiasm of the priests.

Government response to the renewed appearance of an Irish mass movement was swift. In May 1843 troops were reinforced and an Arms Act was passed. Twenty-four magistrates, including O'Connell, were relieved of their commissions for attending Repeal meetings. 'There is no influence, no power, no authority,' Peel told the Commons, 'which the prerogatives of the Crown and the existing law gave to the Government, which will not be exercised for the purpose of maintaining the Union.' It looked rather as if the ministry was prepared to use force to put down mere opinion, and a number of prominent Irish liberals, including Smith O'Brien, joined the Repeal movement to express their disapproval. O'Connell, meanwhile, had a vision of the distant heights. During the summer months of 1843 he addressed mass meetings in places especially selected because of their association with creditable events in Irish history. He managed to organize as many as forty of these. At the same time the Association set up 'arbitration courts' – a sort of private enterprise justice to enable sympathizers to avoid resorting to the Crown courts. O'Connell also allowed himself – for the only time in his career – to hint at the possibility of violence. At Mallow in June he told his audience that they might 'soon have the alternative to live as slaves or die as free men'. It is true that he afterwards went to some lengths to deny the logical implications of this outburst, but it is hardly surprising that the government looked to its defences. In August O'Connell proposed a 'Council of Three Hundred', who were to constitute a national assembly and arrange the details of Repeal.

Then, in October, this escalating mysticism vanished overnight. The largest and most impressive of all the monster meetings, to be held in the fields of Clontarf, was cancelled by O'Connell after the government had decided to ban it. The evening mists of O'Connell's political life were lifted; the Repealers saw a barren land beneath. To some extent the Liberator's authority was sustained by the excitement surrounding his state trial for conspiracy at the start of 1844. The indictment, printed on a roll of paper produced in court, was a hundred yards long. O'Connell was convicted, got a year's detention, and a fine of £2,000. During his stay in Richmond Gaol in Dublin his health and his confidence began to seep away. Things were not exactly uncomfortable. He was lodged in the Governor's own residence, attended by his two daughters and his own servants. He received vast numbers of visitors in a large tent especially put up on the lawn. He was eventually released on a writ of error issued by the House of Lords. But his leadership did not recover.

Peel's administration followed up its coercive measures with a resumption of Irish reform. This was in the pattern of the previous decade, although its timing was much more clearly dictated by events in Ireland, and the need to conciliate O'Connell's followers. The government was full of collected experience; it contained five former Chief Secretaries for Ireland. A start was made in November 1843 by appointing the Devon Commission to inquire into 'the state of law and practice in respect to the occupation of land in Ireland'. Evidence was heard from O'Connell and other Repealers, and from both tenants and landowners. The Report and evidence, which appeared in 1845, provided an extensive source of information about the exact nature of the land question. It recommended a programme of governmental action which included legislation to free encumbered estates, to assist emigration, to reclaim waste land, to undertake public works, to reform the grand juries, and to extend and legalize the practice of 'Ulster Custom' – the payment of compensation to outgoing tenants for improvements to their holdings made during their occupancy. For the administration, Lord Stanley introduced a Bill to give limited compensation in 1845. This was intended as the first of a series of measures to implement aspects of the Report. The Bill was dropped after running into heavy opposition in the Lords, and the government had left office – defeated in 1846 over the Irish Coercion Act – before further measures could be brought forward.

Stanley had also tried to pass a Registration Bill in 1844, intended to increase the numbers of those enfranchised in Ireland by introducing a £5 household suffrage in the counties. This had been withdrawn because of opposition from the Whigs, and the government decided instead to press on with a series of measures designed to eliminate a number of Catholic grievances. The first of these was the Charitable Donations and Bequests Act of 1844. This created new machinery to administer existing law, with equal representation of both Catholics and Protestants on the board. It was intended as a safeguard to Catholic Charities, and it incidentally gave legal recognition to the existence of Catholic prelates for the first time. Despite its easy passage through parliament, the Act was extravagantly denounced by sections of Irish opinion as tending to allow state interference with the discipline of the Church. Special exception was taken to the clause – copied from the corresponding English statute – which invalidated wills conveying property to religious use if made within three months of the testator's demise. This was represented as a slur on the integrity of the priesthood. Archbishop MacHale wrote to inform Peel that the Act had characteristics 'surpassing, in its odious provisions, the worst enactments of the penal times, and developing a maturity of wicked refinement in legislation which the more clumsy artifices of the anti-Catholic code would, in vain, attempt to rival'. O'Connell expressed the same view, in less mannered style, from prison. The government elicited a vague approval of the Act from the Vatican, but its good intentions were not, on the whole, accorded recognition. The Act proved to be an immense benefit to the Irish Catholics.

The administration then turned to another question: the endowment of Maynooth. The Royal College of St Patrick at Maynooth, in Co. Kildare, had been established by the government in 1795 in an attempt to provide a domestic training for Catholic priests who would otherwise have resorted to French seminaries – where they were liable to imbibe revolutionary political doctrines. It was supported by annual votes of money from parliament, and in 1845 Peel proposed that there should be, instead, a permanent grant from the Consolidated Fund. He had two motives. One was to dispose of the annual display of ultra-Protestant opposition each time the appropriation was brought forward; to remove the Maynooth question from politics. The other was to offer a symbol of conciliation to the Irish hierarchy, who had requested an increased grant in 1842 and 1844. The proposal was well received in Ireland. But in England popular and parliamentary objection swelled into a gigantic national fiesta of No-Popery.

The question, however, had important constitutional

implications. The *permanent* endowment of Maynooth in fact inaugurated a clear species of state concurrent endowment, and although parliamentary grants were already made to support Catholics in some colonial territories the settlement of that principle within the United Kingdom was fraught – as the opponents believed – with dangers to the survival of the Protestant Constitution. Certainly state sponsorship of the training of Catholic priests did compromise the religious conscience of the state: like Catholic Emancipation in 1829, the Maynooth endowment marked a milestone on the road which led to the dissolution of the connexion between public life and religious exclusiveness. Despite the religious bigotry of some of the opponents of Peel's measure, therefore, the leading objections to the Bill were constitutional and they were, within their terms of reference, quite understandable ones. After a summer of clamorous popular upheaval – and there was no doubt that English feeling was overwhelmingly against the Bill – the Maynooth Act received the royal assent in June 1845. The annual grant was raised from £9,000 to £26,000, and an additional sum of £30,000 was voted for outstanding repairs to the fabric of the College. More Conservatives voted against the Second Reading of the Bill than voted for it. The price of Irish conciliation was turning out to be the division of the party.

It was one of the leading Tory opponents of the Maynooth Act who also led the assault upon the last of Peel's great Irish measures. Sir Robert Inglis, in a memorable phrase which O'Connell then made his own, described the Irish University Bill of 1845 as the creation of 'godless colleges'. The problem of higher education in Ireland was simple – how to provide institutions to which the Catholics could resort without danger to their faith and morals. The government was firmly against the endowment or chartering of a Catholic denominational university, although this was what the bishops ultimately sought. The logical alternative was to set up university colleges in which there was no religious instruction at all, and no religious tests for matriculation. In 1845 the government therefore made a grant of £100,000 to build three Queen's Colleges, at Belfast, Cork, and Galway. There was to be an annual endowment of £30,000. The plan was an advanced one, as there were few, apart from doctrinaire philosophical radicals, who were yet prepared to favour the notion of higher education divorced from religion. As in England, indeed, higher education was seen as the exclusive preserve of clergymen. It was also the first time the state had built a university in Britain. The Irish bishops were divided over the Queen's Colleges, with rather over a half of them following MacHale's denunciation of the whole system. Archbishop Crolly of Armagh and Archbishop Murray of Dublin were prepared to give the Colleges a trial.

Into the twilight of the government's legislative programme stepped O'Connell after his release. First he tried to revive the Whig alliance, and then, this seeming ineffectual, he flirted with federalism in October 1844. A federal solution to the Irish question was currently being preached by Sharman Crawford and the Ulster radicals. O'Connell's abortive conversion was in part a late overture to these men, and in some measure it was also an attempt to garner at least some crumb of local autonomy to show the Irish people that he was still in command of the situation. He also hoped, in vain, to get Whig support. In his new scheme, Ireland was to receive more representation at Westminster and an Irish legislative council with local fiscal powers. Gavan Duffy compared this council to an inflated grand jury. Even O'Connell's closest advisors, like O'Neill Daunt, disapproved, and O'Connell himself had to admit that he was 'opposed by one half of his friends and deserted by the other half'. The northern federalists were unsympathetic. By this time also, the young critics of O'Connellism were in open disagreement with the old man. The bright minds which had projected the *Nation* newspaper in 1842 – Dillon, Davis, and Duffy – had prepared the intellectual basis for a revolt within the Repeal Association. The first open breach had occurred in 1845 when the young men supported the Queen's Colleges against O'Connell's declared opposition. Progressively as the Liberator's charismatic qualities seemed to fade, they saw in him no more than a broken has-been clinging to power for its own sake. During his frequent absences his son John O'Connell was left in charge of the Association. He proved to be a slight and unauthoritative substitute; he was like Richard Cromwell compared to the Protector. The young men were also impatient with the Whig alliance and, as many of them were Protestants, distrustful of O'Connell's reliance on the Catholic priesthood. Eventually most of 'Young Ireland' seceded from the Repeal Association, and in December 1846 they turned deaf ears to O'Connell's grandiose instructions for them to return.

With the genesis of a new nationalism on the one side, and the enveloping disaster of the great famine on the other, O'Connell set off, ill and tired, on a pilgrimage to Rome. He died at Genoa, *en route*, in May 1847. His heart was sent on to the Irish College in Rome, where it still is; his body was returned to Dublin and laid to rest beneath a commemorative round-tower in Glasnevin cemetery. He was a very great man.

5. The Genesis of Modern Irish Nationalism

Young Ireland nationalism was nurtured in hopeful opposition to O'Connell's policies and influence: it ended in the general burial of hopes during the great famine. It is as well, therefore, to turn first to the appalling national crisis of the second half of the 1840s before attempting to examine the movements of opinion which were eclipsed by it. There had been, in the previous hundred years, several bad failures of the potato crop: famine was endemic in Ireland. In many parts of the country something over seventy-five per cent of the population was entirely dependent on agriculture, and it was the cultivation of potatoes on small subdivided plots which allowed that intensive congestion of population which excited the remark of so many visitors to the south and the west of the country. In the autumn of 1845 a partial failure of the crop produced a partial famine in many areas. In Ireland, this was not extraordinary. Then in 1846 came a complete failure with people dying of actual starvation in the frightful winter of 1846-7. In 1847 the blight was less severe, but conditions were scarcely improved; many of the seed potatoes had been eaten, and in some places the disheartened peasantry, anticipating another failure, had not even bothered to plant the fields. Thereafter the incidence of blight diminished, but recovery was slow because of a disastrous grain harvest in 1848.

Almost no part of the country escaped the blight. The constant precipitation provided perfect conditions for the germination of the fatal spores: it started raining in May 1845 and went on until March 1846. The result was evident from the stench of fields blackened with decayed potato plants. Tubers dug up and apparently unaffected turned rotten within weeks. Those parts of the country which sustained a relatively mixed rural economy – notably some Ulster counties – were able to absorb much of the loss. In parts of south and west Cork, in mid-Limerick, Galway, Mayo, and Donegal, however, the effect was catastrophic. It was from these areas, and especially from the small town of Skibbereen in Co. Cork, that the harrowing scenes of death by starvation, widely canvassed in the English press, were reported. Although the conditions in these places were exceptional, and were contained, they were sufficient to prick the consciences of observers at the time and to pass, afterwards, into searing tableaux of folk memory. Here there were corpses at the roadside – many of people overtaken as they sought to reach a plot of consecrated ground in which to expire. From here, reports were broadcast of incredible and macabre conditions: of people taken for dead accidentally buried alive; of coffins with false bottoms which were used repeatedly; of coffinless bodies which were rooted up and eaten by pigs and dogs; of blood extracted from living cattle and consumed as food; and even of cannibalism – one woman was seen to eat the flesh of her dead daughter. In the wake of the famine, fever and dysentery easily attacked the reduced physical condition of the people.

Special local boards of health were set up by the government in 1846 to deal with the epidemics. Of the 473 medical officers appointed by the Central Board, one in thirteen died of the fever. Despite these visitations of calamity the peasantry were on the whole tranquil, and crime actually went down in the famine years. It seemed as though some dreadful eschatology was impending. Many attributed the famine to the inscrutable machinations of Providence, but there were some who believed they knew the hidden Will with greater accuracy. The famine, as the Revd Hugh McNeil, later Dean of Ripon, remarked, was a rod 'to scourge England for tolerating Popery'. Even Peel had not imagined so devastating a return for the endowment of Maynooth.

'The total failure of the food of a nation,' as the Revd John O'Rourke remarked in his account of the famine, with only slight exaggeration, was 'a fact new in history; such being the case, no machinery existed extensive enough to neutralize its effects, nor was there extant any plan upon which such machinery could be modelled.' The government had, during earlier periods of distress, taken exceptional measures. In 1817 Peel, as Chief Secretary, had authorized the expenditure of £250,000 on relief public works. Between 1821 and 1822 the government had responded to further distress by providing £300,000. Much smaller sums were frequently made available to individual parishes to enable them to bear the financial burden of relief. Now, in the autumn of 1845, Peel was ready to meet the situation with similar expedients. In October he sent a special scientific mission to Ireland to report on the causes of the blight. In November he procured the appointment of a Royal Commission to conduct relief measures. Indian corn was imported from America to the cost of £100,000, and the Commissioners set up local food depots in February of the New Year to sell the stuff to the people at nominal prices. Local relief committees collected contributions from landowners to finance public works undertaken to provide employment for the destitute. These came under the central control of the Board of Works in Dublin, which, by the second half of 1846, was employing 12,000 subordinate officials to organize relief.

In January the government had also introduced a number of Irish measures intended to help alleviate the distress. There were two Public Works Bills, a Bill to assist the development of harbour installations, and a drainage Bill intended to encourage the introduction of the techniques of improved agricultural productivity known in England as 'high farming'. These palliatives were all, on the whole, well received in Ireland – even the *Nation*, in August 1846, admitted that the government had done well. Peel had also, in January, introduced a measure to repeal the Corn Laws. This auspicious legislation had only proceeded after a lengthy governmental crisis, in which it had become apparent that Peel's 'conversion' to the case for removing exceptional protection to British agriculture was permanent. The distress in Ireland had occurred at just that moment when Peel was anyway worried about the possibility that a general increase in the British population was likely to outstrip food supply. He was quite aware, from diplomatic dispatches, of the general European scarcity of corn. The Irish Repealers were not particularly interested in the Corn Law question: their chief concern lay in opposing the administration's Irish Coercion Bill. This had been brought forward in anticipation of agrarian disorders engendered by the distress. In this the ministers were mistaken. Disorder did not increase, but the Coercion Bill was defeated. The government fell as a result – on the same night in July on which the repeal of the Corn Laws was finally carried.

The new Whig administration, headed by Lord John Russell, received the seals of office in July 1846. In its earliest spasm of enthusiasm, it projected landlord and tenant legislation for Ireland, and a land reclamation Bill. The general principle of state-sponsored food supply for famine relief, as espoused by the late government, was to be abandoned, however. The new Whig policy, embodied in the Poor Employment Act of August, threw the obligation of relief upon the local Poor Law machinery instead. This in some measure reflected the government's conviction that food supply was no fit occupation for a *laissez-faire* state, but in some part it also revealed the general feeling in London that the Irish landlords, who paid the bulk of the poor rate, should be obliged to do more. Not everyone, however, was out to get the landlords. 'As a general rule,' O'Connell said in January 1847, 'no man can find fault with the conduct of the Irish landlords since the awful calamity came upon us.' Now, in August 1846, the Board of Works was reconstructed in order to coordinate the new programme of relief works. These were entirely unproductive undertakings – mostly the construction or repair of superfluous roads and bridges. Indeed, the extensive road system from which the Irish Tourist Board now derives such agreeable advertising copy owes its existence largely to the nineteenth-century famine relief. Some in Ireland expressed extreme dissatisfaction with the unproductive nature of many of the public works: both landowners, who paid the local taxes and therefore felt entitled to benefits like land drainage or fencing on their estates, and nationalists like Mitchel, who rightly pointed to the need for land development. The government, in fact, ordered unproductive works simply to prevent the use of public funds from adding to the value and amenity of private landed property.

In the spring of 1847, after the terrifying destitution of the winter months, the Whigs were forced to renew food distribution. By then three quarters of a million people, in a population of some eight millions, were receiving state wages on the public works schemes. By mid July three million people were getting free state food rations daily. Soup kitchens had first been opened by Quaker philanthropists in 1846. In January 1847 the government joined in. A Commission was appointed to set up the soup kitchens, and M. Soyer, the chef of the Reform Club, was sent off to Ireland to exercise his art in the contrivance of soups of the utmost piquancy and maximum economy. As Sir Charles Trevelyan remarked from the Treasury: 'Neither ancient nor modern history can furnish a parallel to the fact that upwards of three million of persons were fed every day in the neighbourhood of their own homes, by administrative arrangements emanating from, and controlled by, one central office.' It was, indeed, truly impressive. So was the cost.

By May 1847 the government had closed down the relief works, and in June the Poor Law was amended. The existing Act had, anyway, proved hopelessly inadequate in the face of the famine conditions. Under the new arrangements the Irish was separated from the English Poor Law Board, permanent salaried officials were introduced to the most distressed unions, and, in 1850, the Treasury provided £300,000 to wipe out the debts incurred by many of the Irish Poor Law Guardians. The amended Act also allowed outdoor relief to be organized, and even provided for limited public assistance for the emigration of tenants whose land was below £5 in rateable value. The Gregory 'Quarter-Acre clause' prohibited the allowance of poor relief to anyone with a holding larger than a quarter of an acre in extent. Some gave up their land to qualify for relief. The clause therefore had the unhappy result of stimulating evictions. A Land Improvement Act of 1847 made £1½ millions available in loans to landowners requiring financial assistance for agricultural improvements. This completed Russell's Irish legislation; his early inspiration of landlord and tenant legislation had faded from sight.

The great famine left a bitter legacy, and recriminations against the supposed inadequacies of government policy are still heard to this day. It is certainly true that the relief measures proved insufficient in many places. It is also difficult to imagine how a government and a public opinion soaked in *laissez-faire* economics could have stretched its principles further than

113

it did. Administrators at all levels recognized that they had a national disaster on their hands and treated it accordingly. The state *was* forced to intervene throughout the economic order. Altogether the government spent £9½ millions on relief. Some of this was in the form of loans, but even of these loans slightly over a half were converted into gifts when, in 1853, as a balancing measure, Gladstone extended the spirit duty and the income tax to Ireland. In addition, extraordinary funds for relief were raised out of local taxation of landowners; and still more aid came from private philanthropic agencies like the Central Committee of the Society of Friends, and the British Association for the Relief of Extreme Distress in Ireland and Scotland. In some parishes, unfortunately, the agents of philanthropy were Protestant parsons who managed to associate the distribution of food with the dissemination of the Reformed religion. These 'soupers', though small in number compared with the huge body of altruistic clerical workers for relief, have passed into folk memory. Although there were those in England who purported to believe that money donated for relief in Ireland was immediately used by the peasantry to purchase weapons, the public subscriptions attained sums impressive by any standard.

Both during the famine and afterwards, much incomprehension was expressed at the continued export of foodstuffs from Ireland. It was, of course, distressing to see vessels laden with provisions leaving the shores of a land speckled with areas of extreme destitution. Governments committed to free-trade found it impossible to interfere, although, ever since the formation of the Mansion House Committee in October 1845, Irish politicians had been suggesting a prohibition of food export as a necessary measure of emergency control. But both Peel and Russell were determined to make orthodox political economy serve their ends, rather than to tamper with the laws of supply. The government imports of American corn were not essentially to feed the starving, but to help keep the price of other foodstuffs on the competitive market at a reasonable level by unloading cheap state food when prices began to rise. Russell objected even to that extent of state interference with the market.

In fact both Peel and Russell failed to realize that because of the prevailing potato economy there was no organized food trade outside the towns. The tenantry fed themselves off their own potato crop; they grew cereals to pay the rent. To have stopped the export of cereals during the famine would have led to non-payments of rent and increased eviction. Many landlords were unable to reduce rents during the years of distress, and there were a large number who were unable even to afford poor-rate payments. The Irish landowning class were frequently on the edge of insolvency. The Russell administration, attributing their reluctance to finance local relief to their self-interest, was in error when it made the landowners and the Poor Law the basis of its policy. There were, however, many landlords fully cognisant of the position of their tenants, who were in a position either to reduce rents or to suspend payments altogether. Thus the amount of corn available for export went down because those tenants who had got reductions of rent were consuming more of it at home. During 1846 and 1847, wheat imports into Ireland were five times as great as the amounts exported, and this was at a time of exceptional general European shortage. Where landowners were unable to afford a reduction of rent, the tenants were forced on to the public works schemes. These were also unsatisfactory for local reasons: a lot of the money paid out in wages vanished – it was saved up to buy land. The money in Irish savings banks actually went up in the famine years. Before the famine, many labourers had not been paid in cash anyway, and relief given in exchangeable value was to some extent meaningless to them. The only beneficiaries of these years were the village usurers or 'gombeen men', and the food merchants. Both belonged typically to the Catholic middle class, and their exploitation of the peasantry in the favourable circumstances so providentially sent to them appears to have been extensive.

The social and economic effects of the famine years were very considerable. Fintan Lalor exaggerated in 1847 when he remarked that it was 'one of those events which came now and then to do the work of ages in a day, and to change the very nature of an entire nation at once'. But the disruption was still remarkable. The class of agricultural small-holders was reduced by fifty per cent. Massive emigration to England, Scotland, America, Canada, and Australia vacated land which, together with the continuing sequence of ordinary eviction, accelerated the conversion from tillage to pasture; 'clearances' had been stimulated. Emigration also produced an overseas population of embittered Irishmen straining to assist their fellow-countrymen at home in acts of revenge against England. The Encumbered Estates Act of 1849 was intended to create a freer market in landed property by enabling the breaking of entail. It had been recommended by the Devon Commissioners in their 1845 Report. Land prices at the end of the famine years were depressed, and in the decade after the 1849 Act a huge amount of land changed hands. Unhappily the new owners were frequently land speculators out to make quick profits from improved agricultural undertakings, and that meant larger farms, increased evictions, and more conversions to livestock. The new landowners were Irishmen, and many were Catholics. It is likely that the merchants and usurers who had accumulated capital during the famine sank it into the land put on the market by the Act. Only 314 of the 7,216 purchasers in the first eight years of the Act were English.

The most noticeable result of the famine, however, was the numerical decline of the population. There were 2 million fewer people in 1851 than there had been in 1841. Most of the decline was due to emigration. In this, the famine offered a dramatic encouragement to existing trends. Nevertheless, 20,000 persons died of starvation between 1846 and 1851, and 339,000 more of fever, dysentery, and dropsy. This frightful death rate must be set against the normal losses familiar to British society through epidemic diseases in the mid nineteenth century. During the distressed years of the 'Hungry Forties' in England and Scotland almost nobody died of actual starvation, but the low level of nutrition then prevalent carried off huge numbers through infectious diseases. Those who read Engels's description of the Lancashire working classes in 1844 will clear their minds of any supposition that conditions for the inhabitants of English industrial cities were much more agreeable than those in which the Irish peasantry had to live. The worst years of the English depression were passed by 1846; but Gavan Duffy was scarcely fair when he wrote, in 1847, that 'England at this hour is teeming with wealth and plenty.' Between June and October 1848 no fewer than 72,000 persons died in England and Wales of cholera. The English mortality from diseases which owed their tenacity to the evil effects of a bad environment was probably just about equal to Ireland's in these years. 'It appears to us to be of the very first importance to all classes of Irish society to impress on them that there is nothing so peculiar, so exceptional, in the conditions which they look on as the pit of utter despair,' remarked *The Times* in September 1846, with brutal moralism but with a balance of perspective which remained true even after the worst effects of the disaster had revealed themselves in the following year. 'Why is that so terrible in Ireland,' *The Times* continued, 'which in England does not create perplexity and hardly moves compassion?'

English opinion had, anyway, scarcely been soothed by some of the outpourings of Young Ireland nationalists, and it is to these men, whose dissentient voices had so disturbed O'Connell's declining years, and who turned out to be the harbingers of a new nationalism, that it is now appropriate to turn. It is, perhaps, useful to examine their social contexts before attempting to describe their ideas. Their ideas were not static; they moved fumblingly towards the left during the 1840s, and in 1846, with the infusion of a second wave of young men, the movement lurched towards revolution. The Young Irelanders really were young: most were under thirty. They came mostly from the urban professional classes, and many of them were Protestants. The earlier group, the original critics of O'Connellism, were centred around the newspaper which they founded: the *Nation* gave shape and momentum to their cooperation. Thomas Davis was the son of a British army officer. He was called to the Irish bar in 1836, and first appeared as a theorist of Irish nationality through the Trinity College Historical Society. He was a member of the Church of Ireland. Charles Gavan Duffy was a northern Catholic who had turned to journalism by editing the *Belfast Vindicator*. John Blake Dillon, also a Catholic, came from a middle-class commercial background. His earliest political opinions were typical expressions of O'Connellite radicalism. He had also read Bentham, and attacked the principle of aristocracy in government. At Maynooth, where he studied for the priesthood, he discovered that his vocation had evaporated; so he defected to Trinity College and became a barrister instead.

The second wing of Young Ireland, who adhered to the group after the split with O'Connell's Repeal Association in 1846, were essentially similar in social origin. John Mitchel was the son of a northern Unitarian minister who had sympathized with the rebellion of 1798. Mitchel was especially remarkable for the force with which he expressed himself, and of all of these men he was the one who most systematically argued the case of immediate armed revolution. He also argued for the retention of Negro slavery in America, denounced the emancipation of Jews, and advocated the death penalty for theft and forgery. He was invited by Duffy to take over Davis's work for the *Nation* after the latter's sudden death in 1845.

William Smith O'Brien was the old man of the party. He had sat in parliament for twenty years as a follower of O'Connell, and it was only in 1846 that he was finally induced to throw in his lot with Young Ireland. He was a Protestant gentleman.

Thomas Francis Meagher came from a Waterford family which had waxed fat on trade. He was a Catholic, and had been sent off to Stonyhurst for his schooling. Like Smith O'Brien, therefore, his manners and accent were English.

Thomas Reilly was the son of a country lawyer, and was drawn into political discussion while at Trinity College.

Thomas d'Arcy Magee had received no formal education at all. He came from the Catholic gentry and had, before joining the Young Irelanders, worked as a journalist for a brief interlude in America. He offered his opinions vigorously, and due to what Gavan Duffy discreetly referred to as 'an unaccountable Negro cast of features' was known to his detractors, who were numerous, as 'Darky' Magee.

John Martin came from a Co. Down farming family, with interests in linen manufacture. He went to Trinity College. It was only after Smith O'Brien had joined the Young Irelanders in 1846 that Martin joined them too. He became the proprietor of the *Irish Felon* in 1848, although the views expressed in that journal at times went in some measure rather beyond his own.

The party also enjoyed the support of a Tipperary priest, Father John Kenyon of Templederry. He was a man of violent and unreliable opinion, infamous for declaring, in 1847, that O'Connell's death was no loss to Ireland, and for urging the Catholic priesthood to arm themselves. He maintained a close friendship with John Martin, which the latter's biographer (P. A. Sillard) has compared to the friendships described by Plato.

Finally there was James Fintan Lalor, the son of an O'Connellite member of parliament who had been a local leader in the tithe war. Lalor developed advanced ideas about land redistribution and the sovereignty of the people which were in part inspired by his reading of Louis Blanc. He was as much the theorist of Young Ireland in its militancy after 1846 as Davis had been the theorist of cultural nationalism in the earlier phases. Lalor was a bitter man, who had given up apprenticeship to a chemist in order to devote himself to the vocation of thinking.

Lalor also demonstrated one curious bond which linked so many of the Young Irelanders. There was something wrong with them: they suffered ill-health. Davis and Lalor had both been too frail as children to participate in the games and exercises of normal children. Davis remained weak as an adult, the doyen of valetudinarians. Lalor was permanently afflicted with a spinal disorder and was actually deformed. Both men died young. Reilly suffered from nervous pains in the head. Mitchel was a chronic asthmatic. These were a strange group of men to find glorying in the military virtues of the Irish race, and inciting to physical force as the only way to get their ideas advanced. And yet the paradox is not an unfamiliar one. Young intellectuals of advanced political and cultural theories, 'alienated' from a society unprepared to hand itself over to their direction, and impatient with their own numerical and physical weakness, quite often attach themselves to romantic cults of violence. There are many contemporary parallels.

It is also useful to emphasize that, disruptive as the Young Irelanders proved to be for O'Connell and the Repeal Association, they were at no time a significant political force in

Ireland. The *Nation* successfully propagated national ideals which quite effectively percolated down into Irish society, but the people were largely ignorant of the young men themselves, and when they became aware of their advanced political opinions they turned them down flat. It is interesting that the mother of Oscar Wilde, who happened to arrive in Dublin on the day of Davis's funeral in 1845 – having travelled up from the country – had to inquire who the dead man was. The Young Irelanders found out just how unknown they were in the heady days of 1847 and 1848, when they uselessly appealed to the people. As Meagher said in 1847, 'the people of Munster knew as little of Mitchel as of Mahomet.' The masses, of course, in the control of the Catholic clergy, remained loyal to O'Connellism. Young Ireland was indelibly urban in its orientation; the intellectuals and the poets who occupied its vanguard had little notion of the peasantry to whom they looked for the salvation of Ireland's national and cultural identity.

It was in the spring of 1842 that Davis, Duffy and Dillon repaired to the shade of an elm tree in Phoenix Park and decided to establish a new weekly newspaper. There is some discrepancy about the actual author of the idea; both Duffy and Davis claimed that it was theirs. 'But Davis,' as Duffy later generously remarked, 'was our true leader.' The *Nation* first appeared in October 1842, and its success was immediate. Before long it enjoyed a circulation of some 9,000 to 10,000 copies, and was estimated, by its editors, to reach a readership of about a quarter of a million. The 300 Repeal reading-rooms all took it. In the initial publicity hand-out, the founders of the *Nation* had declared their intention of fostering 'a Nationality of the Spirit as well as the letter – a Nationality which may come to be stamped upon our manners, our literature, and our deeds'.

The method of contriving this result was carefully planned.

As Gavan Duffy later remarked, 'Passion and imagination have won victories which reason and self-interest would have attempted in vain, and it was upon these subtle forces the young men mainly counted.' Articles and poems – endless poems – duly appeared which ransacked Irish experience to present a sense of national cultural coherence. Inevitably Irish history was reinterpreted in the process, with lives of the early Irish saints rolling off the presses; lists of Irishmen who had fought in foreign armies; details of the Irish heroes who had participated in the liberation of the Latin-American Spanish colonies. A sense of literary revival was also fostered – early Irish literature was translated, and in 1845 a 'Library of Ireland' began: the publication of a series of works of Irish national interest. Davis began to write a life of Wolfe Tone. A choral society for the middle classes was set up – to sing the stirring ballads published in the *Nation*'s columns. An actual revival of the Irish language was projected. Davis had written that English was the tongue of 'the alien, the invader, the Sassenach tyrant'. Unhappily, however, he was compelled to stick to it: he went off to stay with the Dillons in Mayo in order to learn Irish, but failed to grasp even its essentials. Yet these new stirrings provided an exciting diversion from the arid radicalism of O'Connell. A new, romantic nationalism was being created.

The historic names dimly remembered by the people as of men upon whom the law had left the stain of blood or banishment, and who had been generally ignored by later writers, or named only as unwise enthusiasts, were reinstated on their pedestals. . . . Foreign affairs were considered primarily as they affected the interests of Ireland, not as they affected the interests of England. . . . And week after week songs were published full of passionate longing for the revival of an Irish nation, uttered in language which the timid called sedition, but which was merely the long silenced voice of national self-respect.

Gavan Duffy's later summary exactly describes the mood of the paper. A model had been provided which made the Ireland of their day appear excessively dull.

For the country which had been conjured up before their young imagination was as little the Ireland of the hour, whining complaints or framing petitions for some scanty crumb of relief, as the Ireland of English burlesque; it was the old historic island, the mother of soldiers and scholars, whose name was heard in the roar of onset on a thousand battlefields, for whose dear love the poor home-sick exile in the garret or cloister of some foreign city toiled and plotted. . . .

Conjured, indeed, it had been. O'Connell could not understand this sort of thing at all. 'They dreamed,' Duffy also said of the young men, 'not of becoming Repeal Wardens, but of becoming martyrs and confessors.' This elevated ambition lifted the new political movement into realms where it lost touch completely with the real aspirations of the Irish peasantry. The young Irelanders did not realize it. 'It was the duty of the political teachers of the people,' as Davis plainly remarked, 'to spiritualize and nationalize them with higher and nobler aims.' The hostility to O'Connellism was clearly latent here; as Davis wrote on another occasion – 'A lower form of Nationhood was before the minds of those who saw in it nothing but a parliament in College Green.' That was all O'Connell saw in it. There is, however, no compromise with piety, and the Young Irelanders forged ahead with still more novel interpretations of Irish realities.

Their language also tended to advance beyond their immediate intentions. There was, as with the old United Irishmen, to be a union of creeds for national purposes, but since these purposes went rather beyond the intentions of the British government, some new tactics had to be envisaged. Constant dwelling upon the military capacities of the Celtic peoples soon suggested the cult of violence to their young minds. Davis and the original *Nation* writers declared their theoretical support for physical force: after 1846 the new wave of Young Irelanders began to translate theory into practice. 'Arms are the badges of freedom,' Davis had declared. Mitchel was a good deal more explicit: 'All the constitutional rubbish must be swept away and the ground cleared for the trial of the final issue.' In 1846, O'Connell was even moved to quote numerous British judicial decisions to show that the young men were guilty of high treason. But romanticized musings upon the use of violence for noble ends soon passes beyond the point where common ground can be occupied by different parties contending for similar objects. The analysis of the more extreme Young Irelanders advanced to a species of mysticism. In 1848 Mitchel did not even bother to lay plans for a revolution: they were unnecessary, for the people would rise spontaneously in response to a call upon the soul of the nation. Charles Kickham's observation of Smith O'Brien upon the barricades of Ballingarry in 1848 is interesting – he was 'like a man in a dream'.

It was a hatred of England which furnished the culture upon which the resort to violence grew. Dillon said that the *Nation* writers and their followers were 'not animated by any malignant hatred of England', but the facts would appear to vitiate his conclusion. The *Nation* was itself crammed with articles bearing such suggestive titles as 'English Aggression' and 'The Latest English Crime' (both by Davis). Reilly provided the motivation for many subsequent writers when he remarked that 'in fact the history of Ireland may be written as English crimes'. The famine, of course, was easily represented as offering the British government the chance to attempt something like a 'final solution' of the Irish question. 'I had watched the progress of the famine policy of the Government,' Mitchel wrote in 1847, 'and could see nothing in it but machinery deliberately devised and skilfully worked for the entire subjugation of the island – the slaughter of a portion of its people, and the pauperization of the rest.' Even the gentle John Martin allowed himself strong language to describe the whole system of British administration. It was a 'foreign tyranny', 'the reign of fraud, perjury, corruption, and Government butchery', and a 'monstrous system of base and murderous tyranny'. There was nothing for it but to appeal to 'the God of whose righteous decrees British rule in Ireland is a dire violation'.

Yet there is an ironic sense in which the protestations of the Young Irelanders reveal just how effectively the assimilation of Ireland to England was proceeding. In many particulars, the forces found at work in one country were also to be found in the other; but the Irish counterparts of English movements of opinion were usually disguised in nationalist language, and this has been misleading. For one of the more important aspects of the government of their society to which the Young Irelanders were reacting was centralization. All the anti-centralization sentiments, so strong in nineteenth-century England, were also to be found in Ireland. In Ireland, indeed, they were stronger; for there the growth of state collectivist machinery was relatively more advanced. Whereas in England, Toulmin Smith and his Anti-Centralization League, and all those men who opposed public health legislation, factory reform, or other evidences of state interference, emphasized local institutions as a counter-balance to central boards, in Ireland the central government had already secured effective control over local organs of government, because in Ireland they were too inefficient, or insufficiently financed, to undertake the works of social improvement. Lacking a local basis for their opposition, therefore, the opponents of centralized collectivism in Ireland lashed out at the whole structure and authority of government. That it could also be represented as an instrument of English oppression was in a sense a minor feature – though one liable to win popular sympathy – of an indictment of a system whose chief characteristic was that it was oppressive simply because it was *governmental*. Gladstone had the perspicacity to notice this, while discussing a possible reform of Irish local government in December 1882: 'As long as the portentous centralization of the present system continues, Government will be to the common Irishman, I am afraid, an exotic, a foreign thing, and he may for long look upon it with a consequent aversion, which will extend to the simplest and most needful beneficial acts.'

An examination of the thought of the leading Young Ireland nationalists brings this out. When attention is diverted from their exciting polemics against the historical 'crimes' of the British connexion, and turned instead to what they actually said about *government*, a wholly new perspective emerges from their protestations. It is a familiar one, because it is precisely the same as that enveloping English opponents of state activity in the nineteenth century. Both Davis and Fintan Lalor, the two leading theoreticians of the new nationalism, were consistent in their denunciations of state activity. Lalor opposed what he called 'that vile and vicious political philosophy which looks alone to public wealth'. But in the writings of Davis the point is given much purer expression. His thought is littered with direct assaults on the centralization principle, and on what he called 'utilitarianism' – by which he meant all nineteenth-century attempts to apply science to government, a blanket condemnation of 'scientific administrators'. In 1842 he wrote,

Utilitarianism, the creed of Russell and Peel, as well as of the Radicals . . . which measures prosperity by exchangeable value, measures duty by gain, and limits desire to clothes, food, and respectability – this damned thing has come into Ireland under the

Whigs, and is equally the favourite of the 'Peel' Tories. It . . . threatens to corrupt the lower classes, who are still faithful and romantic. . . . To use every literary and political engine against this seems to me the first duty of an Irish patriot. . . .

These forces for social improvement, of course, were making for the assimilation of Ireland to England, and as such were supported by O'Connell and formed the reform cement in the Whig alliance. They were working to eliminate the atrocious conditions of the peasantry. But Davis correctly saw that they were also forces which operated by destroying the surviving traces of peasant 'culture', that is, Irish culture. The Young Irelanders, it must be remembered, enjoyed a town-dweller's rural romanticism. 'Since my boyhood,' Mitchel wrote in his *Jail Journal*, 'I have always looked with a sort of veneration upon an independent farmer cultivating his small demesne.' Fintan Lalor's elaborate agrarian theories had the same simple proposition as their basis: 'A productive and prosperous husbandry is the *sole* groundwork of a solid social economy.' The thought forms a consistent thread for most of the Young Irelanders. With it went an unconcealed distaste for industrial society. 'A manufacturing system such as it exists at this day in England,' as Lalor wrote, 'is far from being a gratifying subject of contemplation, whether as regards moral or material results.' O'Connell, on the other hand, had sought to foster Irish industry as a necessary accompaniment of advance in Irish society. The centralization of government was also assailed by Davis pretty forthrightly:

Centralization was a Tory practice; but the Whigs believed in it, professed it and carried it into every detail of [Irish] government. Some central machinery to prevent the growth of civil feuds and to make military power more actively defensive seems desirable to every nation. But the utter absence of such machinery is preferable to systematic centralization. Centralization obscures the history, dilutes the original tastes and peculiar faculties, weakens the patriotism, corrupts the ambition, and misapplies the resources of the provinces subject to it. . . . Chiming as it does with the low material philosophy of English and French Liberals . . . it has been peculiarly dangerous in our days. . . .

And perhaps even more explicitly:

The 'Useful Knowledge Society' period arrived in Britain, and flooded that island with cheap tracts on algebra and geometry, chemistry, theology and physiology. Penny magazines told every man how his stockings were wove, how many drunkards were taken up per hour in Southwark. . . . Unluckily for us, there was no great popular passion in Ireland at the time, and our communication with England had been greatly increased by steamers and railways, by the Whig alliance, by democratic sympathy, and by the transference of our political capital to Westminster. Tracts, periodicals, and the whole horde of Benthamy rushed in . . . we were proclaimed converts to utilitarianism. . . . At the same time the National Schools were spreading the elements of science and the means of study through the poorer classes, and their books were merely intellectual. . . .

It is therefore clear that almost all the progressive elements making for social improvement were to be swept away by the Young Irelanders. At their most coherent, they seem to have supposed that the mere existence of a society of small independent farmers would be regenerating. But the peasantry were not to be so mistaken: they preferred the prospect of material social improvement, and the loss of folk 'culture', to the elevating sensations of nationalism.

The men who founded the *Nation* in 1842, and their immediate following, had, of course, no intention of a break with O'Connell. To his policy of Repeal – to which they remained loyal – they sought merely to add a revival of distinct Irish nationality. But it will have become obvious, from a glance at the theories which their renaissance threw up, that the common ground with O'Connellite radicalism was slipping away. The young men were also disappointed that their own section of the Repeal Association never managed to get its hands on any of the funds. They were impatient with O'Connell, who regarded them with jealousy, and disgusted by the sycophancy of his adherents. With O'Connell's slow retirement and the succession, even before the great man's demise, of his son John – the 'Vice-Tribune' – the differences between 'Young' and 'Old' Ireland were laid bare for the world to look upon. The row in the Repeal Association over the Queen's Colleges in 1845 was a wound whose fatality was proved within a year. O'Connell had then accused Davis of sneering at Catholicism. Davis had replied that some of his best friends were Catholics, but O'Connell had dismissed the young agitators with contempt: 'Young Ireland may play what pranks they please.' Davis had wept. Shortly afterwards, in September 1845, he had died at the age of thirty-one. Early in 1846 the new adherents of Young Ireland had appeared: Meagher, Mitchel, d'Arcy Magee, Reilly, and Fintan Lalor. Their sense of outrage exceeded that of the earlier *Nation* group, and the occasion for a final split with O'Connellism was provided by the renewal of the Whig alliance when Lord John Russell came into office in 1846. O'Connell attacked the Young Irelanders for advocating physical force, and this was the formal cause of the rupture. The Young Irelanders, on the other hand, regarded this as a mere pretext, and believed the real question in dispute was the nature of the Whig alliance. Four members of the Repeal party had got jobs in the new ministry, and when O'Connell allowed the unopposed re-election of one of them, Sheil, at Dungarven, scales fell from eyes on both sides. Smith O'Brien elected to join the party of youth.

The secession of the Young Ireland party from the Repeal Association in July 1846 was not catastrophic. The Catholic clergy and the peasantry remained loyal to O'Connell, as did almost everyone else. The young men were more isolated than ever. The priests, in fact, were relieved. The *Nation* had purported to unite Protestants and Catholics, but the clergy suspected its 'indifferentism', and expected, under the shadow of O'Connell, some sort of priority. Bishop Higgins of Ardagh was loud in his scorn of the 'schoolboy philosophers' and 'Voltairian newspapers'. 'Are we to listen to Young Ireland?' asked Bishop Browne of Elphin in November 1846. 'Can we, for one instant, allow amongst us those principles that led to Jacobinism and other monstrous evils?' In the same month also, O'Connell had predicted that the young men 'will be led on perhaps further than they intend.' He was proved correct.

O'Connell died, and events moved Young Ireland progressively towards revolutionary excess against the background of the sad desiccation of the country during the famine. The young also quarrelled among themselves. First, those who had seceded from the Repeal Association established a society of their own – the Irish Confederation, set up in January 1847 under the leadership of Gavan Duffy and Smith O'Brien. It had a Dublin headquarters, and about 150 local clubs; but it was never a large or effective movement, and its policy of Repeal was scarcely distinguishable from John O'Connell's Association. As soon as the Confederation began to define its nationalist content, the thing fell apart because of differences of emphasis among the members.

The influence of James Fintan Lalor was the ultimate cause of the trouble. He had impressed Duffy with a letter he sent for publication in the *Nation* just about the time that the Confederation was being set up. He remained, until 1848 (when he tried an unfortunate excursion into activism), an isolated theorist whose influence was felt entirely through his writings. He believed that the famine had dissolved the social contract in Ireland. The right to reconstitute it lay through the armed force of the people – the peasantry. 'My principle is this,' Lalor told d'Arcy Magee in March 1847, 'that the entire ownership of Ireland, moral and material, up to the sun and down to the centre, is vested by right in the people of Ireland – that they and none but they are landowners and lawmakers of this island; that all laws not made by them are null and void.' In April 1847, in his *Letter to the Landowners of Ireland*, this simple principle was elaborated into a scheme for peasant propriety. 'Political rights are but paper and parchment,' he explained to the trembling recipients of the forthcoming blessings; 'it is the *social constitution* that determines the condition and character of a people, that makes and moulds the life of man.'

Attempts have been made to depict Lalor as an advanced social theorist. In fact his agrarian vision was romantic and backward-looking; it was at once Lockian and populist; it looked to a sort of Jeffersonian farmers' republic rather than to rural socialism. But Lalor made two important converts: John Mitchel and Father Kenyon, both of whom were also leading advocates of immediate physical force revolutionism. Smith O'Brien was not attracted to Lalor's ideas; they would frighten off the gentry, whose support was essential for any transformation of Irish society. In fact, he was one himself. Gavan Duffy was also left unmoved by the new learning. 'To me Lalor's theory seemed a fantastic dream,' he wrote later; 'his angry peasants, chafing like chained tigers, were creatures of the imagination.'

Their differences of emphasis were translated into schism. With all the prissy insistence on 'correct' tactics to which revolutionaries are given, both Mitchel and Reilly retired from the *Nation* in January 1848, and from the Confederation in the following month. Both now looked to an immediate rising, and founded a paper of their own, the *United Irishman*, to teach the people what their own best interests were. The revolution in France, in the same month, produced a sensation in Ireland from which the new journal profited. It also offered a timely example of that political device for which the *United Irishman* was now contending: a Republic. The *Nation* group, in contrast, were still hoping for a simple Repeal which would revive the Irish parliament and Constitution of 1782; but their language, too, though still holding the possibility of armed rebellion in theoretical reserve, was gradually giving way to advanced militancy. The last tenuous hold on political reality was weakening for both groups of Young Irelanders, as the early months of 1848, the year of revolutions, gave way to summer.

At this point also, the government intervened to stop the flow of revolutionary propaganda. Additional troops were sent into the country to reinforce the garrisons, and the prosecutions of Smith O'Brien, Meagher, and Mitchel were begun. The potential revolutionaries were not disheartened. O'Brien and Meagher, released on bail pending their trial, betook themselves to Paris in March to solicit sympathy from Lamartine, Ledru Rollin, and Louis Blanc. Lamartine, who had been nobbled by the British government, declared that he could not interfere with the internal affairs of the British Empire. His speech was printed by the government and posted in every police station in Ireland. Back in Dublin, O'Brien pressed on with the preparation of the Confederation for an armed rising, to be attempted in the autumn. There was to be a Council of Three Hundred, and the clubs were to transform themselves into a National Guard. In May, the state prosecutions of O'Brien and Meagher for seditious speeches failed. The Crown pressed on with the case against Mitchel, who was charged with the more serious crime of treason-felony. He was convicted and transported. The moment was a decisive one: the Confederation was finally pushed into the ultimate militancy; the search for arms and money to begin the revolution took on priority. Agents were dispatched to America and France, and the Council of the Confederation converted itself into a Directory. Martin began to publish the *Irish Felon* as the replacement of Mitchel's *United Irishman*, which the government had suppressed. It preached immediate armed rebellion.

Then, in June 1848, the hopes of the revolutionaries for any measure of public support were overtaken by events. The French Republic was overthrown by the Paris working men, and the Archbishop of Paris was shot on the barricades. The effects in Catholic Ireland were scarcely calculated to inspire the clergy and peasantry, or the urban middle classes, with much confidence in revolutions. They were inexpressibly shocked. The government moved in to exploit the situation. In July, Gavan Duffy, Martin, and Magee were arrested, and *habeas corpus* was suspended. A large slice of the leadership of the projected revolution was removed to Newgate prison in Dublin, where they wasted away on food brought in from a local hotel, received numerous visitors – including Father Croke, the future Archbishop of Cashel, who offered journalistic aid – and planned to escape through a window with a ladder knitted out of silk. Meanwhile, Dillon, O'Brien, and Meagher met at Wexford to begin the revolution. A provisional government was to be set up at Kilkenny, and the people were to lay down their lives for it. At Kilkenny, however, and at Cashel, the people turned out in only modest crowds to listen to the young men; they applauded their jibes against England – and, incidentally, cursed the red flag of Paris – but they refused to take to the streets. The Young Irelanders were unknown to them; they had never heard of Smith O'Brien. They were, it is true, latently hostile to England, but such portions of the young men's political ideas as they were able to grasp they rejected.

The revolutionaries themselves later believed that the people were so reduced by the prevailing famine destitution that they were too dispirited to join them. In this they were mistaken. The towns had turned them down flat. In November 1847, when a deputation from the Confederation had gone to convert the people of Belfast, they had been shouted down and mobbed: the people, loyal to the Repeal Association, had greeted them as 'murderers of O'Connell'. At Limerick they had been burned in effigy, and when the deputation held an evening tea-party to explain their ideas to the ladies of the city, a dissenting crowd had tried to burn the house down. The Confederate leaders had to be rescued by a troop of soldiers. When Father Kenyon had proposed a Confederate candidate to the citizens of Limerick in the 1847 general election, even he had been assaulted by a mob and had to be saved by the police. When Meagher had contested the Waterford seat, his own father had campaigned against him. And now, in July 1848, the towns failed the young men once again. So they turned instead to the countryside, and began a hopeful progression through the lush county of Tipperary searching for 'the people'. They were joined by a few local organizers of the clubs – men who formed the later leadership of the Fenians: John O'Mahony, James Stephens, and Charles Kickham, all of whom were Protestant gentlemen. They were ill prepared for revolution, but by now it was clear that they looked only for a rising, a gesture to declare their beliefs. O'Brien was convinced that he was going to his death. Father Kenyon was no doubt overcome with similar forebodings. He stayed at home.

At Boulagh Common, in Co. Tipperary, Smith O'Brien gathered a band of 500 peasants. He sent them home overnight to get rest and provisions, but they never returned. So he sought out some local coal-miners, drilled them, and prepared them to fight with their mining tools. When the police arrived, they withdrew to the farm of the widow MacCormack at Ballingarry, and there, in a vegetable patch, they threw up barricades. 'The cabbage-garden revolution', as *The Times* unkindly called the adventure, had begun. The rebels had a drum, eighteen pikes, twenty firearms and enough ammunition for one shot each. A small force of police moved in to occupy the farmhouse. Mrs MacCormack was extremely cross, and abused O'Brien for messing up her land. As her five children were in the farmhouse, the rebels felt unable to attack it. A column of troops turned up, and the rebels dispersed into the hills. Shortly afterwards O'Brien was arrested at Thurles railway station by a guard. This man, it transpired, was English, and, of course, was said to have drunk himself to death on the reward money.

In August the trials of the revolutionaries began, in what many Irishmen supposed was an orgy of jury packing. This largely meant the exclusion of Catholics from the juries on the grounds that their inherent sympathies were likely to be prejudicial to the Crown. The point is difficult to argue either way. Certainly some of the panels from which jurymen were chosen were scarcely representative. The panel for Duffy's trial contained the Viceroy's hairdresser and shoemaker, and two vicars-choral from St Patrick's Cathedral. At Mitchel's trial, earlier, the accused had remarked that the names of the panel 'read like the muster-roll of one of Cromwell's regiments.' But whatever the circumstances, the fact remains that the juries did not always convict, as O'Brien and Meagher had discovered in May. And after August 1848 Duffy went through five trials before he was finally acquitted in April 1849. After the Ballingarry rising, the prisoners still in Newgate were duly convicted of treason-felony and transported. At Clonmel, O'Brien and Meagher, with their leading supporters, were similarly condemned. They were shipped off to Van Diemen's Land, where they were reunited with Mitchel, who, after a sojourn at Ireland Island in Bermuda, had been sent to join them. There they lived in 'ticket-of-leave' conditions, as private gentlemen in their own houses. Mitchel cursed the civility of British justice which had, by this treatment, deprived them of the crown of thorns. A few escaped to America; the rest were released by an amnesty in 1854. Martin returned to Ireland and eventually espoused Liberal politics. Meagher and Mitchel remained in America, the latter having the opportunity of sampling American justice as well: he was imprisoned for supporting the Confederacy in the Civil War. Smith O'Brien retired to private life in Ireland. Of those who had escaped the law in 1848, Dillon and d'Arcy Magee both managed to flee to America disguised as priests. Dillon returned in 1855 to become member of parliament for Tipperary in 1866, and a founder of the National Association in 1864. Magee gave himself up to journalism in New York, then entered Canadian politics where his opposition to the attempted Fenian invasions led to his assassination, no doubt at the hands of another Irishman. Gavan Duffy entered parliament in 1852 as an Independent Oppositionist, emigrated to Australia in 1855, and became, complete with knighthood, Prime Minister of Victoria. Fintan Lalor had taken some part in the 1848 rising. He had rushed down to the country to incite the peasantry, but had been ignored. He was tried, imprisoned, and released after a couple of months due to ill-health. He died shortly afterwards. Father Kenyon remained at Templederry.

So ended the extraordinary political venturings of the Young Irelanders. Early in 1849 the rump of the movement plotted another rising, but it came to no issue. At its centre lay a plan to kidnap Queen Victoria during her visit to Ireland, and hide her away in the mountains of County Dublin. In fact, the Queen's visit was an immense success, eliciting national sentiments of loyalty to the throne which were as moving for the young Queen as they were unexpected by her ministers.

But the Young Irelanders did not sink without a trace. They had propagated a vision of Irish cultural nationalism; they had gazed upon a promised land. Ireland was not unaltered by the experience. They had made available, in a form capable of easy popularization by men more in sympathy with the real aspirations of the country than they were, a national alternative to the assimilation of Irish society to that of the United Kingdom. Their ideals lay ready to be ransacked by later nationalists. As Arthur Griffith said in 1916, 'when the Irish read and reflect with Davis, their day of redemption will be at hand.' Davis would have agreed.

6. Experiment and Rebellion

The period of the great famine proved to be a political, no less than a social and economic divide. The O'Connellite Repeal programme had rattled towards its demise; after a vain attempt to revive the Repeal Association in 1849, John O'Connell allowed it to lapse in the following year. He then retired to private life. The Young Ireland leaders were in exile or in detention. The moment was not unlike that which succeeded the defeat of the United Irishmen in 1798. In the twenty years after 1849, however, there were two notable attempts by Irish radical and liberal politicians to make the Union work by concentrating popular pressures for reform upon the Imperial parliament. It was, therefore, a period of experiment and even, at times, of optimism.

The first of the new political expedients is associated with the Independent Opposition party of the 1850s – itself a logical development of O'Connell's parliamentary group before the Lichfield House Compact. The second matured with the 1860s, and was in part a conscious attempt to fashion a constitutional alternative to Fenian revolution: the National Association of Ireland and the renewed Liberal alliance turned out to be the last attempt by Irish radicalism to secure a solution to the grievances of the country within the structure

of Unionism. The triple failures of the Independent Oppositionists, of the Fenians, and of the Irish Gladstonians resulted
in the renewal of the old Repeal policy. Isaac Butt founded
the Home Rule movement in 1870.

There is something misleading about describing the politics
of these twenty years – as of other periods of Irish history –
wholly in terms of radicalism. The political innovators, to be
sure, were important for the dissemination of devices and
theories which eventually served as crucial catalysts in the
formation of the modern Irish state. They have also been
acclaimed as the progenitors of the winning side. These are
conditions which are hazardous to a sense of proportion, and
it must therefore be emphasized that for most of the time Irish
political interests remained largely integrated within the
British parliamentary party structures. The Irish Conservatives have a history which has usually been remarked upon
merely as a foil to show up the virtues of the radicals and the
nationalists. They were written off to such an extent by those
who referred to them simply as the political agency of the
landlords as to make their genuine existence as a political interest
difficult to conceive. But the Irish Liberals were no less the
agency of the landlords, as reference to the personnel of
O'Connell's or Parnell's following will establish. It is rather
that the landowners on the Liberal side found themselves in
strange alliance with urban radicalism – just like the landed
Whigs in England. The normal parliamentary integration of
Irish political interests is the most marked feature (though
one absent from history books) of Irish politics. Attempts at
independent or 'third party' activity were generally short-
lived. Thus O'Connell's group slid quite easily into the Whig
interest after 1834, and the Independent Opposition Party of
the 1850s were progressively drawn into the parliamentary
Liberals.

Irish political commentators always viewed these

'defections' to the British parties as monstrous deviations purchased by corrupt patronage. In reality, however, they were a reversion to a normal state. Despite the tactical expediency of O'Connell or even of Parnell, and despite the sophisticated organization to which they advanced their supporters, even these men continued to espouse a rather limited view of the nature of political parties. By the general standards prevailing among all but the most advanced English radicalism, they were innovators indeed. Nevertheless, their conception of the scope of parliamentary politics did not vary so much from the currently rather circumscribed practice as to suggest a condition of permanent Irish party independence. Attempts at Irish 'third parties' were generally tactical – for the attainment of specific legislative proposals. They were not really intended, at this period, to survive the achievement of those particular reforms. It was the originality of Parnell, in fact, to have created a political party which, though through an accident of policy increasingly dependent on the English Liberals, managed to retain a formally independent existence for nearly forty years.

The culture in which the independent party of the 1850s was matured demonstrated another constant element of Irish political experiment. This was the attempt to combine agrarian and urban radicalism. O'Connell had achieved some success here through the priests, but he had been more anxious to enlist the rural areas into the cause of a radicalism which was uncompromisingly urban in conception. He ignored agrarian questions if they appeared to interfere with the *status quo*. The 'New Departure' of 1879, O'Brien's United Irish League of 1898, and subsequent nationalist ventures were all attempts to unite town and country. The movement of the early 1850s had a disguised importance in this respect, too. Historians of the Tenant League of 1850 have been impressed by its character as a 'League of north and south', a Union of Creeds stimulating to national consciousness because it was suggestive of the leading feature of the United Irishmen of the 1790s. The Tenant League was, indeed, for a short time a vehicle in which both Protestants and Catholics found themselves passengers. But it was much more. It was an attempt to interest the urban radicals in tenant grievances. Tenant societies had appeared sporadically from 1847; but in October 1849 the first successful Tenant Protection Society was founded by two Catholic curates at Callan, in Co. Kilkenny. Now it is important to notice that the society of Father O'Shea and Father Keeffe had an urban membership: it consisted of shop-keepers and professional men. The Callan movement extended itself during 1850 to many parts of Ireland, and everywhere the new tenant protection societies were full of urban men prepared to agitate for amelioration of the conditions of the rural tenants. The great famine had aroused their awareness of the problems. It is interesting that Connaught, where the new movement was unsuccessful, had the fewest urban centres and the largest rural population in Ireland.

The tenant protection societies lifted the land question to the centre of Irish radical politics for the first time. They relied for publicity upon the excruciating suffering associated with the sudden leap forward in evictions during the last years of the famine. The Callan society had been inspired by the Earl of Desart's eviction of 442 of his tenants. In 1850 the number of evictions in Ireland reached the astonishing figure of 104,000. Removal of the tenants had become quite a minor industry in its own right, and in Tipperary a Catholic landlord called Scully had actually expedited matters by invent-ing a machine to demolish tenants' houses at a low cost. There was a very real feeling prevalent in the country that the tenant question was about to be solved by depopulation and a scorched-earth policy. 'Ireland was fast dissolving before the landlord,' the *Nation* remarked in 1852, 'as the Jewish nation dissolved before the curse of God.' By 1849 evictions had spread to the north and had revealed the cardinal weakness of 'Ulster Custom'. It was to this varying and limited recognition by landowners of the value of improvements made by their tenants that most men looked for an explanation of the greater prosperity and quiescence of the northern counties. But these benfits were purely customary; they lacked a basis in law; and in 1849, as evictions increased, tenant-right societies appeared throughout the northern province too. They were essentially concerned to give the organized support of public opinion to the efforts of Sharman Crawford – himself a large landowner – to squeeze tenant-right legislation through parliament. The ground was already littered with the remains of previous attempts at adjustment of the Irish land code. Bills to secure compensation for tenants' improvements had been brought forward and defeated almost annually since the Devon Report had recommended it in 1845. In 1847 Sharman Crawford framed another luckless Bill: this became the model adopted by the tenant societies as the basis of their agitation.

The collapse of the O'Connellite and nationalist parties meant that the Irish Liberals had inherited the earth. They had soon realized that it was scarcely worth possessing. But the sudden appearance, in both north and south, among Protestants and Catholics, of a large tenant-right movement was not to be left unexploited. In April 1850 a group of Liberal politicians signed a circular letter calling upon tenant societies from all parts of the country to send delegates to a central conference in Dublin. John O'Connell was one of the signatories, but he soon dropped out of the new movement. Charles Gavan Duffy, the only Young Ireland leader remaining in Ireland, was another. He now turned all his energies, which were considerable, upon the tenant question. Dr John Gray, the Protestant proprietor of the *Freeman's Journal* (a paper beginning to emerge as the central agency of Liberal propaganda) also signed. The delegates duly assembled in Dublin during August. The sight of southern Catholic and northern Presbyterian clergymen sinking their sectarian disagreements in a common political crusade prompted some observers to emphasize too emphatically the real extent of the reconciliation which had taken place. Dr M'Knight, the founder of both the Ulster Tenant-Right Association and the *Banner of Ulster*, the paper of northern Liberalism, headed a block of enthusiastic Presbyterian ministers at the conference. Not all of their northern brethren were sympathetic. Although a large majority of the Synod of Ulster had in May voted to petition parliament in support of tenant-right, those who followed Dr Cooke's condemnation of the entire policy as 'socialism' were by no means uninfluential. The Catholic clergy at the conference included Father O'Shea, of Callan, and Dr Spratt, the chief lieutenant of Father Matthew in the Temperance movement. The clergy of the Established Church were absent. So, too, were the landlords, many of whom were anyway agitating for a different solution to Ireland's rural problems, under the guidance of Isaac Butt: a return to agricultural protection. The abundance of priests at the conference was soon picked off by the opposition press. The *Morning Herald* unkindly referred to the 'hungry, half-fed, and wholly untaught dogs of Maynooth, who longed not only for power and preponderance, but for the pleasant enjoyments of a material and sensuous life'.

Gavan Duffy was the most advanced, as well as the most experienced, of the new leaders, even at his own valuation. He did not view the conference and its outcome as the exclusive passage to salvation, and in 1851 became involved with John Sadlier and his Tipperary Bank in a 'Freehold Land Society'. This piece of land redistribution by private enterprise was reminiscent of the Chartist Land plan – which had just gone out of business. The Society was to buy up large tracts of land and resell them, after subdivision, to the tenantry. The scheme was under-capitalized and folded after Duffy and Sadlier had allowed themselves several sharp quarrels over its management. Duffy also wanted the 1850 conference to resort to direct action – to support the tenants should they withhold the payment of 'unfair' rents, the principle later adopted by the Land League in the 1880s. The preparatory committee had rejected this suggestion since it was likely to encourage agrarian disturbances.

The conference established the Irish Tenant League. It had a three-pointed programme. There was to be parliamentary action to secure compensation for tenants' improvements; security of tenure ('perpetuity'); and fair rents regulated by impartial valuation. The last point, described by Duffy as 'the main principle', and acknowledged by him as being regarded by most sections of public opinion as outrageous, was clearly the most potentially divisive. John O'Connell declared it to be a ridiculous impossibility. In reality, it was a demand for direct state intervention; to place the valuation of land occupied through private contract on the same basis as, for example, the valuation of poor rate. 'Never,' *The Times* remarked of the conference, 'were fatal mistakes so eagerly insisted on.' The three points were to be presented for parliamentary attention by the organization of an articulate public agitation in Ireland. The question of direct support in parliament was also raised, and an agreement was reached, sufficiently inexplicit as to prevent disharmony, pledging the new League to offer support only to those parliamentarians willing to sponsor its programme and to decline office under any administration unprepared to take it into consideration. The League then proceeded to set up local societies throughout the country, and to organize county meetings which were to be so moved by the justice of the tenants' cause as to subscribe £10,000 to the League's expenses. The meetings were duly called, usually by the priests, and in all slightly more than one tenth of the required sum was collected. Enthusiasm, however, was freely given, and Father O'Shea, with brimming exaggeration, felt called upon to announce that the Tenant League was 'as just a cause as that which was preached by Peter the Apostle'. The cause actually preached by the Apostle, as expounded by the Catholic hierarchy in Ireland, was not unsympathetic to the League, and several bishops gave in their adherence. From his exile in New York, John Mitchel, representing the nationalist doctrine that no good could be expected of parliament, condemned the entire venture. Most of the sixty-four Irish Liberals in parliament regarded the League's demands as too extreme, and only two were prepared to support them. The thirty-seven Irish Conservatives and four Irish Peelite members of parliament were even more intensely unsympathetic.

But the parliamentary situation was quite suddenly transformed, *deus ex machina*, by a plethora of No-Popery. The white heat of the Protestant movement against the Maynooth grant had scarcely cooled when, within five years, two events of a type particularly calculated to inflame Protestant susceptibilities were passed into the political currency of the day. In 1850 the new Papal Legate in Ireland, Archbishop Paul Cullen, convened the Synod of Thurles and elicited the condemnation of Sir Robert Peel's Queen's Colleges – on the grounds that they encouraged 'indifferentism' and infidelity since they were not confessional institutions under the control of the Church. There was a great deal of talk about 'ultramontanism'. It is difficult, at this distance of time, to imagine the sensation which then ensued when, in the autumn of 1850, Pius IX announced the restoration of a Catholic hierarchy in England. The very innards of Protestantism pulsated with disapproval. And when Cardinal Wiseman duly arrived to 'govern' his specified counties the country shuddered with protest.

Lord John Russell's administration decided to save the Reformation by passing an Ecclesiastical Titles Act in 1851. This reinforced the prohibition on the assumption of territorial titles already used by Protestant dignitaries by any other ecclesiastics, and voided any bequests made to such persons under illegal designations. In Ireland, of course, the measure was vigorously denounced by the Catholics as penal legislation. Offending bishops were to suffer the indignity of a £100 fine. Cullen predicted that the Act would 'recommence the war of intolerance and bigotry'. In fact the legislation, apart from causing some inconvenience in the matter of bequests, was a dead-letter and Cullen's extreme forebodings were unfulfilled. But in the short term the tide of indignation which lapped over Ireland proved an immense service to those seeking to generate a popular support for the new political movement sponsored by the Tenant League. The Catholic clergy plunged themselves into the agitation; a few experienced a militancy which knew no bounds. One priest in Dublin declared that he was ready to raise a battalion of 2,000 men to defeat the Titles Act by force of arms. The government was unmoved.

In this new enthusiasm, however, there were dangers. A too distinctly Catholic agitation against the Ecclesiastical Titles Act might offend the Presbyterian ministers who had thrown their support behind the Tenant League. The Catholic Defence Association, when it was founded in August 1851, was therefore explicitly opposed by Duffy in the *Nation*. The Association, for its part, admitted no members of the Tenant League to its committee. But the Association did enjoy some parliamentary support; in fact its creation was in large measure the work of those Irish members who had led the opposition to Russell's Titles Act. Forty-four Irish Liberals had voted against the Act, thirty-four of whom were Catholics. This group was soon identified by the public as the 'Pope's Brass Band' or the 'Irish Brigade'. Their leading spokesmen were G.H. Moore, a landowner, a litterateur, and a steeple-chasing champion; John Reynolds, a Dublin merchant; John Sadlier, a Catholic financier and landowner; and William Keogh, a barrister and former Peelite.

The Catholic Defence Association was generous in its field of interests. It was intended to promote Catholic charitable and educational institutions as well as seeking to contrive the repeal of the Titles Act and the disestablishment of the Church. The essentially parliamentary nature of its objectives and support was its most useful feature. It was just such an outlet that the Tenant League most required, and now it made greedy approaches to the Association. The popular following of the tenant movement was evaporating rapidly, and when it managed to bring about an alliance with the Defence Association the decline was disguised and compensated.

Irish public opinion had predictably shown itself to be more extensively moved by religious affront than by tenant grievances. The arrangement between the League and the Association, however, meant that the Irish Brigade in parliament obliged themselves to add the land question to their programme in a form explicitly agreeable to the League. It was at this point that the principle of Independent Opposition was injected into the marriage. Those Irish Liberals adhering to the united programme were to pledge themselves not to tender support to any administration unless it should adopt Irish legislation suited to meet their demands. The simple purity of this device was not so easily operated: many Irish Liberals belonged to Whig connexions and anyway felt too comfortably integrated into the existing parliamentary groups to sacrifice the expectancies of patronage and influence for what some correctly diagnosed as a temporary political alignment precariously balanced upon unlikely policies.

The Independent Oppositionists looked to the general election of 1852 with hope only slightly deflated by three unsuccessful interventions at by-elections in 1851. The Derby administration which had succeeded Russell's did have good things about it, too. It contained Napier as Attorney-General for Ireland, and it was widely broadcast that he was preparing land legislation said to incorporate fairly advanced principles. But such dulcet overtures as might have been imminent between the Irish party and the Conservatives were abruptly silenced in June 1852, when a Royal Proclamation reminded Catholics that the statutory prohibition of public religious ceremonies was liable to enforcement. Apparently this was enough to excite a disagreeable militancy in the breasts of some of the sturdier Protestants. At Stockport there was serious rioting in the Irish quarter of the town in which a lot of Catholic property was destroyed and two Catholic chapels were sacked and desecrated. The resulting uproar in Ireland robbed the Conservatives of any chance of significantly increasing their representation in the elections. During the polling, in the following month, the frenzied scenes rivalled any which even the lush texture of Irish electoral disturbance might afford. The returns revealed one striking feature: the defeat of twenty-three of the thirty-six Whig followers of Russell; a punishment for the Titles Act. The Conservatives actually got three extra seats. As far as the Independent Oppositionist party is concerned, the election is less easily assessed. Twenty of the Irish Brigade were returned as Independents, together with a slightly larger number of Liberals inclined in varying cadences of enthusiasm to give the new alignment a trial. Gavan Duffy entered parliament for New Ross, and John Francis Maguire, the proprietor of the *Cork Examiner*, for Dungarvan. A conference of parliamentary

148

followers called by the Tenant League after the election spelled out the principle of Independent Opposition and asked for allegiance to it. There was a good deal of critical dissatisfaction at this procedure, and finally a diluted and equivocal formula was subscribed by forty-two Liberal members of parliament.

It is easy to exaggerate the potential strength of the new political group. In reality, the period immediately after the election saw the disintegration of organizations which never had much substance anyway. The Catholic Defence Association passed into a terminal coma. The league of north and south broke apart within the tenant movement. Northern separatism, indeed, had been well indicated in the elections: the Independent Oppositionists had failed to get a single member elected in Ulster. Sharman Crawford had lost his seat in Co. Down. The Independent party, in fact, was quite insubstantial, and it was only the chance that it enjoyed a balance in the new House of Commons which temporarily afforded it an influence greater than its real cohesion warranted. The resumed Derby administration scarcely fell over itself, all the same, to seek the goodwill of the Irish Independent members. When Sergeant Shee declared that he would gladly support the Conservatives on such matters in which he might agree with them, the government chief whip (Hayter) was unenthusiastic. 'You are very obliging,' he said, 'but we want men who will be glad to support the government when they don't agree with them.' Napier produced four land Bills. Two of these related to land improvement, one was a consolidating measure, and the fourth conceded the principle of compensation for improvements. This last got a Second Reading and was in its committee stage when the Prime Minister, only too conscious of the menacing disapproval of both English and Irish landowners, declared that the administration was not pledged to carry it. The Irish party retaliated by defeating the budget, and the government resigned.

The immediate effects were to lay bare the ephemeral structure of the Independent Party. Two leaders of the group accepted appointments in the succeeding Aberdeen coalition. John Sadlier became a Lord of the Treasury, and William Keogh was appointed Solicitor-General for Ireland. The incoming administration was clearly uncommitted to the policy of the Tenant League, and both men were therefore caught out in the most blatant violation of their pledges. They were abused and disowned by their colleagues. Sadlier, in seeking re-election at Carlow, was actually defeated by a Tory – the result of intervention against him by the League – and had to get himself accepted at Sligo instead. Both men were easily represented as unprincipled place-hunters by their opponents. They actually were. Sadler's financial empire had been frankly employed for political ends: four of his relatives were endowed with parliamentary seats in the 1852 elections. The use of influence in this way was, of course, a widely accepted aspect of public life and went uncriticized by the Independent party while Sadler was still in it. After his 'defection', the political employment of his riches was immediately denounced. A. M. Sullivan, the assistant editor of the *Nation*, depicted the subsequent Sligo election as a positive festival of 'shameless bribery and terrorism'. The moral rectitude of Sadler's opponents received an unexpected confirmation when in 1856 his fraudulent transactions to the value of £1¼ millions were rumbled, and he poisoned himself on Hampstead Heath. William Keogh owed his seat at Athlone to financial backing supplied by Attwood and his Birmingham radical circle. Keogh, in fact, was the informal leader of the Irish party, and it was only after he had accepted public office that his earlier contemptuous dismissals of Irish nationalism were held against him. Gavan Duffy then remarked that he 'belonged to the gay, exhuberant class of Irish adventurers who are fatal to weak women and credulous men'. But in Ireland, where the wicked were always expected to prosper under English influence, Keogh became successively Attorney-General and a judge.

The experiment of Independent Opposition, from this point, passed gently into oblivion. The desertion of Sadlier and Keogh was in no sense decisive; the fact was that the means of organizing public opinion in Ireland were disintegrating. The moral content of the Tenant League was scooped out by the loss of its Ulster supporters. The league of north and south had always been ambiguous anyway. Sharman Crawford had from the start disapproved of one of the League's three policies – the perpetuity principle – and had refused to include it in the parliamentary Bills he framed for the Independent party. In 1853 he left the League. The other northern leaders, in the wake of Dr M'Knight, refused to join in the general execration of Sadlier and Keogh, and they, too, withdrew from the League. In 1858 it was dissolved. By then, anyway, the agricultural recovery which was one of the most extraordinary features of the decade which followed the famine had produced a sufficiently promising period of rural prosperity as to make the tenant agitation appear superfluous.

The collapse of the League was also accompanied – even assisted – by the hardening attitude of the Catholic Church. The earliest sign of this had declared itself when the local bishops supported both Sadlier and Keogh in their re-election campaigns after accepting office. This had drawn the Church into direct confrontation with the League, and had also revealed divisions within the hierarchy. The withdrawal of most of the bishops from the League – by 1855 there were none left on its committee – was an important indication of the enduring strength of their commitment to O'Connellite radicalism and their resulting suspicion of land agitations.

Archbishop Paul Cullen had at first supported both League and Independent party. For nearly thirty years he had resided in Rome, until his return to Ireland in 1850 as Archbishop of Armagh, equipped with legatine powers specifically directed at the reintroduction of strict Roman discipline within the Irish Church. In 1852 he was translated to Dublin. Now Cullen was a Liberal, but there is no sense in which he could be described as politically a nationalist. He has suffered, as a result, at the hands of subsequent nationalist writers. For supporting Sadlier and Keogh he was condemned by the Independent party as a Whig. For his later censure of the Fenians he was vilified by the later republicans. John O'Leary said he had 'apparently no feeling about his country other than that it was a good Catholic machine, fashioned mainly to spread the faith over the world.'

There was logic, however, in the instructions which Cullen brought from Rome. There really were aspects of the Church in Ireland which might not unfairly be represented as 'Gallican', and the lack of coordination among the bishops was serious. The Archbishop of Tuam, John MacHale, seemed to embody this independence in the way most disagreeable to the Vatican: he espoused political principles too closely allied with those which had led to the 1848 revolutions in the States of the Church in Italy. When the Pope had fled to Gaeta, Cullen stayed at his post in the Irish College and had not liked what he had seen of the revolutionary triumvirate. Yet Cullen was not illiberal. He was a supporter of O'Connell. And MacHale was not a revolutionary. But in the easy enthusiasm of the Irish priests for popular politics the Legate saw familiar dangers which he diagnosed as potentially subversive of Catholic order. Above all, of course, he identified the Young Ireland nationalists with the Mazzinians of the *Risorgimento* in Italy.

This equation is not so absurd as it might seem. The shared ideological components of both movements bore some comparison, even though the theological language employed by the Vatican to categorize their philosophical 'errors' might appear somewhat overemphatic. The Vatican and Cullen did not realize, however, that political opinions containing erroneous tendencies, though frightful by the ultramontane standards brought to bear upon them, had quite different associations in Ireland from those they suggested in Italy. The Irish people have a genius for failing to see the ecclesiastical implications of their political logic.

Gavan Duffy had been a Young Irelander. Cullen appears not to have worried unduly about this until 1853. It was then, listening to the uncontrolled language of the 'Young Ireland' priests who defamed Sadlier and Keogh, that he seems to have perceived the writing on the wall. The words of support which he had offered to the Independent party in the general election died upon his lips. MacHale and four other prelates ransacked the reputations of the two 'defectors' with that same abandon which echoed in Cullen's mind like the shouts of the Roman revolutionaries. In Cullen's new clarity of vision, Duffy appeared as 'an Irish Mazzini'. The clergy, he now saw, must at all costs be held back from political passion. Catholic order must be maintained. The result was a series of provincial statutes defining the proper role of the clergy in political agitations. These varied according to the inclinations of the local bishop. Thus in Tuam the new rules were slight; in Dublin the priests were altogether forbidden to attend political meetings. In 1854 national Decrees were promulgated to prohibit the clergy from discussing politics inside their churches.

These new rules were in fact quite moderate. They were a sensible attempt to eliminate the scandal of clergymen tearing each other apart in public, but they were entered by the Independent Oppositionists, and later by the Fenians, in the book of black marks against Cullen. The electoral influence of the Independent party was largely dependent upon the organization undertaken by the priests through local survivals of O'Connell's machine. This organization did not stop, however, even though some of the excesses had been syphoned off. The 1854 Decrees actually encouraged the clergy to take part in the selection of suitable parliamentary candidates. The Independent party, already in radical decline, mistook the opposition of Cullen as the chief cause. When in 1854 one of the Callan curates, Father Keeffe, was suspended by the Bishop of Ossory for allegedly infringing the new rules, the Independent leaders unwisely decided to appeal to Rome on his behalf. Frederick Lucas, the English Catholic convert who had carved a shallow niche for himself in Irish politics, went off to the Vatican full of indignant sympathy for Keeffe and the Independent party. But in Rome, Cullen's influence was supreme, and the rejection of Lucas was coupled with the delivery of a straight papal snub to Archbishop MacHale, who had also turned up at the Vatican to argue for the politics of the politicized clergy.

The disintegration of the Tenant League and the withdrawal of the bishops weathered away the foundations of Independent Opposition. The party was sinking in parliament too, as its members quietly reverted to the easy habit of voting with the Liberals. By 1857 there were only twelve who maintained distinct independence, and even these were in most things supporters of Palmerston. The ambiguity of the pledge made the survival of the party impossible in a parliament characterized, during these years, by well-defined but shifting allegiances. The leaders who might have used their authority to shore up the erosion of the party had themselves slipped away. In 1855 Gavan Duffy took himself off to Australia in a mood of disillusionment. Gray reverted to straight Liberal politics in order to avoid offending Cullen. Shee left the party after quarrelling with the Tenant League. Lucas died. G.H.

Moore survived until 1857, when he lost his parliamentary seat as a result of a successful petition proving intimidation by a group of priests who had pronounced the curse of God on all who refused to vote for him. He retired to private life. In 1859 the rump of the party divided evenly over the question of parliamentary reform, and after the general election of that year the theory as well as the practice of Independent Opposition was allowed to lapse. The discredited principle of independence gave place, in the next decade, to the systematic integration of Irish politics with those of emergent British Liberalism as a whole. A small section of the Young Irelanders in exile, meanwhile, were attempting once more to promote the cause of revolution.

Fenianism was described by Mitchel as an 'enormous sack of gas'. The movement did have important side effects. It forced the liberal politicians and the Catholic hierarchy to consolidate once more around a new version of O'Connellism in the 1860s; it moved Gladstone towards the adoption of those high principles of Irish policy which chanced to bring him to office in 1868. But in itself the Fenianism of the 1860s was, as Mitchel suggested, empty of content and forlorn of success. Nationalist historians overemphasized its importance in a later age for a reason which is certainly not unimportant. After the 1860s the ideal of national independence won by physical force remained alive within the breasts of the Fenian exiles in America and as a continuing tradition among small groups of Irishmen at home: it formed an enduring thread within all national movements up to 1916 and beyond. It was also the first real sign that a greater Ireland had appeared across the seas. Fenianism linked the troubles of the homeland with the Irish-born of America and of England and Scotland.

The movement had its origins in America, in New York and Chicago. Consciousness of Irish nationality had been heightened in the 1850s by the attacks of the nativist political groups upon Irish Catholic immigrants. In 1855 the Know-Nothing party had managed to win control of the New York State legislature; attacks on Catholic property and anti-Irish rioting were then at their most frequent. The realization that the promised land was evidently as incapable of recognizing the virtues of the Irish race as England had shown itself to be soon turned the eyes of a small number of self-conscious exiles back again to Ireland. Fenianism occurred in response to this nostalgic assertion of Irish individuality. In 1859 John O'Mahoney and Michael Doheny, both former Young Irelanders living in New York, dispatched a note to James Stephens in Ireland inviting him to start a new revolutionary movement. Stephens agreed, with the proviso that they would have to give financial support. They did. Between 1858 and 1867 the Fenians received £32,000 from American sources.

The pattern of Fenianism in Ireland followed the American model. When fifty members had taken an oath of allegiance 'to the Irish Republic now virtually established', they constituted a local 'circle', placed under the command of an officer called a 'centre'. The movement was centralized under Stephens, who was self-designated 'Central Organizer of the Irish Republic'. The men received military training and instruction about the historical criminality of the English race. Fenianism had one policy and one method: the achievement of an independent, democratic Irish Republic, by armed-force revolution. It consistently eschewed constitutionalism, and when, in the 1870s, a few Fenians alighted upon the alternative course of infiltrating the existing political structures they were summarily expelled from the movement as deviationists. In 1861 a front organization was established, but the 'Brotherhood of St Patrick' also declined to compromise by adopting constitutional expedients.

Sometime after 1865 the Fenians adopted the title of Irish

Republican Brotherhood – the I.R.B. – a name by which they were subsequently identified. The purity of their aims was on the whole well preserved. They denounced agrarian outrage and condemned the rural secret-societies, though the distinction between Ribbonism and Fenianism was frequently unapparent to Irish constitutionalists and to the government. The ordinary rural crime which continued during the 1860s was often wrongly attributed to the Fenians as a result. There was no evidence, despite the sensational disclosures made at the time of the Fenian trials in 1865, that the movement plotted the massacre of leading sections of society opposed to them. But Fenianism was a secret organization, and this encouraged the public and the government in numerous bizarre fears.

The Fenians also declined to involve themselves with the land question. Revolution against England was the supervening priority, and it was only on the eve of the attempted *coup* in 1867, presumably in the hope of adding the favour of the tenants to their otherwise small assets, that they issued a proclamation supporting agrarian reform and universal suffrage. Fenianism was intended as the most undiluted draught of physical-force revolution. 'Theobald Wolfe Tone and Thomas Davis,' as O'Leary wrote, 'had much more to do with Fenianism than any famine or failure.' It was also purely Irish-American in its social and political vision. Stephens claimed to have adopted the socialism of Louis Blanc, and both he and O'Donovan Rossa became members of the International Workingmen's Association. But these ideas found no expression in Fenianism, and the social thinking of the other leaders, in fact, was extremely conservative.

The Fenians were more successful than the Young Irelanders had been in extending their membership to the lower portions of the social pyramid. Numbers of urban working men were attracted in Dublin, Waterford, and Cork, and some tenant farmers. Exactly how successful the Fenians were over recruitment is uncertain. The secrecy of the movement tended to sensationalize estimates, and the figure of 80,000 members in 1865, given by Stephens, is clearly too generous. It was also in the government's interest to inflate the figures. The numbers who actually turned out in the risings of 1867 can scarcely have exceeded 5,000 or so. Fenianism, of course, had a middle-class intellectual leadership at the centre, and there are signs that the local leaders were drawn, not from the lowest orders in society, but from schoolteachers, shopkeepers, and soldiers. Military organization was given professional assistance by the infusions of Irish-American officers who crossed the ocean in the spring of 1865 when the armies were disbanded at the close of the American Civil War. It is important to notice that Fenianism caught on only in those areas where a middle-class leadership was available. It was successful in getting a foothold in the small towns of Munster and Leinster; but it failed almost completely in Connaught and Ulster. Connaught was the poorest part of Ireland, where the problems of the land were most aggravated. All previous revolutionary movements had failed to stir the province, which was, however, the chief remaining depository of native Irish culture. Ulster, in the 1860s, contained no class which was bordering upon disaffection. It is also important to realize that most of the former Young Irelanders still living in the country kept clear of Fenianism. John Blake Dillon declined Stephen's invitation to join; and in America, Mitchel and Meagher were actively hostile.

Fenianism was created by the lesser heroes of 1848. Stephens, O'Leary, Kickham, Luby, O'Mahony, and Doheny had all taken part in the disturbances of that year, but none had occupied a substantial position of authority within the movement. In Ireland itself, the Confederate clubs of 1848 had nearly all disappeared after the elapse of a decade, and the Fenians, in beginning to reconstruct a revolutionary organization, found the local remnants of Young Ireland largely unsympathetic. After a casual start, recruitment into Fenian circles was stimulated in 1861 when the Irishmen who had fought against the Garibaldians in defence of the papal states in Italy returned – to the manifest relief of the Pope – to Ireland. There is evidence that many perpetuated their military accomplishments by joining the Fenians. In 1861, also, there occurred what the *Guardian* described as 'the ridiculous affair of MacManus' bones'. Terrence Bellew MacManus had died, a Young Ireland exile, in California. Various nationalist groups cooperated to repatriate his remains for burial. On arrival in Ireland, however, the Fenians took control of the arrangements and used the public funeral as an occasion to publicize the cause of revolution. The Young Irelanders dropped out. Cullen prohibited the use of the Dublin churches. Yet 50,000 men followed the coffin through the streets of Dublin to Glasnevin, where a panegyric was delivered by Father Patrick Lavelle, a priest from Co. Mayo already notorious for his support of the Brotherhood of St Patrick. Lavelle was moved, on this occasion, to scarcely veiled advocacy of Fenianism. 'The day for which our fathers yearned, struggled, fought and suffered,' he ended his oration, 'cannot now be very far off.' The MacManus funeral seemed to hasten it. Fenianism received a foothold in Dublin and recruitment elsewhere proceeded briskly – as always in Ireland after a national demonstration over the dead.

But for all its apparent strength and seriousness of purpose, the Fenian movement in the 1860s was essentially futile. It was as resonant of intrigue and hopeless conspiracy as the European revolutionary underground with which Stephens claimed to have cooperated during his years of exile in Paris. There was, within the Fenian leadership, so much excitement about the very commission of intrigue as to leave the strong impression that it was revolutionary agitation *per se* which they enjoyed. The character of James Stephens, and his overwhelming inadequacies of leadership, lend much colour to this conclusion. He was, as Dr Mark Ryan remarked, in his *Fenian Memories*, 'a born conspirator'.

Stephens came from Kilkenny, where he had been a civil engineer working for a railway company. After peripheral participation in the 1848 affray at Ballingarry, he cleared off to Paris, where he and O'Mahony derived an income from giving English lessons. Stephens also translated the novels of Dickens into French. O'Mahony left for America in the mid-1850s, and Stephens returned to Ireland, where he became tutor to Dillon's children. It was from this station that he was called to higher things when the invitation to found a new revolutionary movement reached him from New York in 1858. Stephens was capable of stirring the hearts of men by his oratory – what Irishman in the nineteenth century was not? – but he was inflexibly attached to what he took to be his own infallibility. 'I have no hesitation in saying that I think very highly of myself,' he once told Luby.

He remained the undisputed leader of Fenianism within Ireland until the spring of 1866, when he left for America; but even by that time his stature had begun to diminish. In 1863 he had disappointed the movement by marrying below himself: to a draper's daughter called Miss Hopper. O'Leary noticed the shocked surprise of his associates, who, for all their democratic theory, regarded the union as a social solecism. In the same year a rift had opened between himself and O'Mahony, when the latter, as head of American Fenianism, had laid claim to ultimate command of the Irish movement. There were also those who conceived the impression that Stephens was not manly enough to be the leader of a revolution. John Devoy, for example, has recorded how he lost faith in Stephens when he noticed him trembling with fright as he climbed to freedom during his escape from gaol in

1865. Men who cast themselves as successors of the ancient warriors of Ireland ought not to betray such lapses.

Like the European revolutionaries of this period, the Fenians suffered from lack of effective secrecy. Everyone knew who the local 'centres' were. The organization was also packed with government spies. The Fenian newspaper, the *Irish People*, had Pierce Nagle, an employee of Dublin Castle, on its staff. O'Mahony's secretary in New York was a government agent called 'Red' Jim McDermott: a man who had fought in the papal army and had actually been decorated by the Pope. In 1865 he told the Fenians' secrets to the British consul in New York, and continued his disclosures into the 1880s. In 1867, the proposed Fenian attack on Chester Castle was given away by an agent called John Corydon. During the rising of the same year Godfrey Massey, a Fenian commander in the field, turned informer and became the chief witness for the Crown in the subsequent trials of the insurgents. Irish tradition, of course, has suspected the worst of such men. Massey was said to have fainted in an unmanly fashion when arrested – Devoy even believed that he was illegitimate. Corydon was said to have been the son of a prostitute.

The establishment of the *Irish People* in November 1863 also brought Fenianism into the open. It is a curious tribute to the freedom of the press in Ireland that this paper continued its publication of revolutionary incitement for two years before the government closed it down. It had an able staff directed by Charles Kickham, Thomas Clarke Luby, and John O'Leary. All three had originally intended a medical career. Kickham came from a prosperous Catholic business family in Mullinahone, Co. Tipperary. As a result of a boyhood accident, while playing with gunpowder, he was deaf and almost blind. Luby was the son of a Protestant parson, and was educated at Trinity College. O'Leary was a Tipperary landowning Catholic, who had pursued an education both at

Trinity and at the Queen's Colleges of Cork and Galway. The financial security of the *Irish People* was presided over by Jeremiah O'Donovan Rossa, the organizer of a local 'Phoenix Society' at Skibbereen in Co. Cork which had become incorporated into Fenianism.

The *Irish People* had the importance of bringing to the surface the hitherto partially submerged anti-clericalism of Fenianism. There had been, as Cullen's attitude to the MacManus funeral indicated, early differences between the Church and the Fenians. There had also been a good deal of local resistance to Fenian recruitment organized by parish priests. The Church disapproved of the movement because it was secret and oath-bound. The Vatican had formulated numerous censures of secret societies, and Fenianism fell under this blanket condemnation. Leo XII's Encyclical, *Quo graviora*, of 1826, was therefore paraded by the Church as the chief justification for the opposition to Fenianism. Cullen also knew that the main principles of revolutionism were in direct opposition to Catholic social order. There was also, no doubt, a good deal of resentment from the priests that their control of local affairs was threatened by rival political bosses in the shape of Fenian 'centres'. Cullen, who had not scrupled in depicting the Young Irelanders as Mazzinians, now branded the Fenians with the same mark. 'It is certain,' he wrote in a report to the Propaganda in 1865, 'that they belonged to the school of Mazzini or of Garibaldi.' Since a number of Fenians were also schoolmasters in the National System of education – which Cullen had expended so much effort in attacking – he also had a providential opportunity to associate the two evils. In 1867 the Chief Secretary for Ireland, Lord Naas, revealed that twenty-nine National schoolteachers had taken part in the Fenian rising. Cullen wrote a paper entitled 'The Fenian movement: its connexion with the mixed system of education'. He also feared that Fenianism might establish an organization from which socialists could later benefit – a fear which took on some slight semblance of substance when, in 1869, Marx began to concern himself with the release of the Fenian convicts.

From 1861, the bishops began to issue pastoral letters warning their flocks that excommunication was the automatic penalty incurred by those subscribing the Fenian oath. In 1870 the Pope, after receiving Lord Clarendon's opinion that the Fenians 'would no more scruple in cutting the Holy Father's throat than they would the Lord Lieutenant's if they got the chance', issued a Decree condemning the movement by name.

There were, however, embarrassing exceptions to the Church's solidarity. Archbishop MacHale was clearly less enthusiastic about the censure of the revolutionaries than his colleagues. He publicly accepted a cash present from O'Mahony, and in 1864 went so far as to send three pictures of himself to be auctioned at a Fenian fair in Chicago. Cullen's soul must have trembled within him. But he was, at least, able to turn this additional evidence of MacHale's irregularities to account by denouncing the Archbishop once more to the Vatican.

Such further proofs of the evil of Fenianism as might still be required were furnished by Kickham's abrasive contributions to the *Irish People*. Week after week he flayed the clergy for duping the peasantry into constitutional politics. He maintained that the collapse of the Tenant League in the 1850s, and the clerical support given to Sadlier and Keogh, were lucid enough indications of the need to restrain the priests from political activity. 'Their electioneering blunderings and divisions have shocked all persons possessed of unprejudiced minds,' he wrote. The Fenians also declared that in the future Irish Republic the clergy would be kept out of politics by law: in the 1867 proclamation a separation of church and state was provided for. The rank-and-file membership of the movement, of course, was overwhelmingly Catholic, and in many places young Fenians gave up going to confession. But much more commonly, the mutual hostility of the Church and the revolutionaries had a more inhibiting effect upon the latter than upon the former. Some of the anti-revolutionary propaganda of the hierarchy appears to have enjoyed a length of existence which would have impressed its authors. As Desmond Ryan remarked in 1937, 'the legend that the Fenians lived in luxury on the savings of servant-girls was popular, and dies hard.'

The position of Stephens in 1865 was not unlike that of O'Connell in 1843. Both managed to proclaim a particular year as one of salvation, and both were then stuck with the anticlimatic aftermath of their false predictions. Stephens, who had declared 1865 'the year of action', also ended up in prison. Many of the Fenian leaders urged him to commence the revolution as soon as the close of the Civil War in America had released military trained men. He hesitated, and his leadership waned. The year, indeed, was a disastrous one. In America, the opposition to O'Mahony's leadership split the movement, and the secessionists, under William Roberts, later embarrassed everybody by engaging in a series of futile forays across the Canadian border: in 1866, 1870, and 1871. In Ireland, the police raided the *Irish People* office during September. It is difficult to see why this particular moment was chosen; perhaps an official at the Castle had taken especial exception to the quality of the last edition of the paper, which contained, among others, an article entitled 'The Fenians and the Fairies'. Luby had expected the raid and had with foresight sorted his letters into two packets, one containing the Fenian secrets, the other love letters which had passed between himself and his wife. With uncharacteristic clumsiness, he managed to confuse the labels, leaving the incriminating letters in his desk, where they were found by the police, and carrying off his love letters to safety. From the evidence so fortuitously made available the police had arrested Luby, O'Leary, and O'Donovan Rossa, and then Kickham and Stephens.

Their escape from Richmond Gaol was prepared by John Devoy. Devoy had served in the French Foreign Legion, and it was therefore not so unlikely that it was in a tent in the African desert that he had read about the MacManus funeral in Dublin and had decided to return to Ireland to enlist in the revolutionary cause. He thereafter devoted himself to the conversion of soldiers serving in Dublin. In Devoy's plan Stephens was to escape over the wall of the gaol with the inside assistance of two warders; the Fenians outside were to begin operations with a signal – the simulated call of a duck. The heroic event was all but ruined when, on the night, a real duck appeared on the scene and quacked an authentic but untimely signal. Happily for Stephens this proved to be the only hitch. His successful escape was described by one of those who brought it about as 'the greatest event in history'. It was only an opinion. Early in 1866 Stephens slipped away to America. In Dublin the other Fenian leaders, despite the pleas of Isaac Butt on their behalf, were convicted of treason-felony and imprisoned. The trials were presided over by Chief Justice Keogh, the 'defector' from Independent Opposition. Kickham heard his sentence, of fifteen years' penal servitude, through an immense ear-trumpet. In February 1866, Devoy was arrested. The government secured the suspension of *habeas corpus* as an emergency measure.

In the absence of Stephens, the leadership of the Irish branch of Fenianism fell to Colonel Thomas J. Kelly, an Irish-American officer. During the following year he made copious preparations for the rising which Stephens had been so reluctant to initiate. Arms and officers were promised from the American organization, and Colonel Richard Burke, another veteran of the American Civil War, visited Birmingham occasionally to purchase arms. In February 1867 a contingent of Kerry Fenians began the rising prematurely – unaware that the Dublin leaders had ordered a month's delay. They seized a coastguard station. It was enough to send the local gentry tumbling into Killarney with their families and their valuables, where they occupied the Railway Hotel until it became obvious that nothing further was going to happen. In Killarney Cathedral the Catholic Bishop, Dr Moriarty, lashed the Fenians (with his tongue), denounced their conspiracy as 'an American swindle', and declared that 'hell was not hot enough nor eternity long enough' for their punishment.

On 5 March the main rebellion began. Inevitably, a provisional government was announced, and the Fenians duly trooped out of the cities to convert their virtual republic into a real one on the mountain sides. They were met by the worst snow-storm for fifty years, and within twenty-four hours it was all over. Only in Dublin, Cork, Tipperary, Clare, Waterford, and Louth had there been any response anyway. The rebels were easily dispersed by troops, and the total number of deaths amounted to only twelve. In April, a month too late, an American vessel loaded with forty officers and 8,000 rifles sailed into the western approaches. The officers were landed at Dungarvan and set out on foot to look for the revolution. They were arrested. Their ship, the *Erin's Hope*, sailed back to America. There was another round of state trials and prison sentences, but the government showed considerable restraint: there were no executions, just as there had been none after the 1848 rising. In 1868 a popular agitation began for the release of the Fenian convicts, and in 1871 this prompted the government's concession of a general amnesty. The Fenian leaders departed for America, where most of them resumed the pleasures of conspiracy.

Fenianism had been successfully met by the measures of the government, but this was not the real reason for its failure in the 1860s. It was, in fact, almost totally ineffective and ripped by internal dissensions. It was quite capable of exploiting the antipathy to England germane to Irish society, but it failed to do this during the only period when it might have derived a real benefit from doing so – before the end of 1865. Events in the second half of 1867 were to provide the Fenians with a wider measure of popular sympathy in Ireland, yet it is evident that this sympathy did not extend to the revolutionary programme of the movement, only to the individual Irishmen within it who suffered for their beliefs. The Irish people were not revolutionary, either actually or potentially. Since Fenianism declined to take up reform issues, like the land question, and stuck with puritanical single-mindedness to the attainment of a republic, this wider sympathy of the Irish people was, in practical terms, useless.

In the autumn of 1867 the sympathy of the Irish people received an emphatic confirmation. Colonel Kelly and an American officer called Deasy were arrested in Manchester by a policeman who supposed they were burglars. A group of Fenians, bent upon their rescue, ambushed the police wagon, in which they were driven off on remand, as it passed beneath a railway arch at Bellevue. Kelly and Deasy duly escaped, but in the uproar one of the rescuers, in the words of the popular ballad, 'chanced to kill a man'. This was Sergeant Brett, of the police guard. Three Fenians were executed for his murder in November – William Allen, Michael O'Brien, and Michael Larkin. Ireland was at once swept with emotion; the phenomenon was not dissimilar to that produced on a more generous scale by the executions of 1916. The 'Manchester Martyrs' were also popular with the Church. Masses and memorial services were held in many places; MacHale assisted at a mass for their souls.

Cullen was as usual disquieted, and wrote off in alarm to Rome that the Manchester men were 'not honoured or prayed for because they were good men or died penitent, but because they were Fenians'. In Rome itself, however, the martyrs were not without their sponsors. Fenians in the papal army tried to arrange a requiem for them at Sant' Andrea della Fratte. With Kickham in prison, the *Irish People* suppressed, and the Irish-American officers (who were more agreeably disposed to the participation of priests in politics than the Irish leaders) in key positions, Fenianism and the clergy had suffered fewer occasions of direct confrontation since 1865. The police, indeed, had harboured suspicions of real fraternization: in 1866 they had raided the crypt of the Catholic cathedral in Armagh looking for Fenian arms. There were, of course, none to be found. Now, in 1867, the commemoration of the Manchester men once again allowed the priests a central role in the political emotionalism of the Irish people. J. F. Maguire, the Irish Liberal, in a Commons' speech of March 1868, suggested with pleasing insight the changed balance of opinion: 'As a mere conspiracy Fenianism is not very formidable; but as a principle pervading the Irish nation, and actively influencing the minds of many who have never thought of becoming avowed Fenians, I look upon it as more serious than I can easily find words to express.'

Essentially, however, the Manchester episode had changed nothing: it had merely exposed the ever-popular antipathy to England in a way which characteristically lacked substance. The excitement subsided within a month. Fenian violence was paraded in a less heroic guise. Colonel Burke had been sentenced to death for his part in the 1867 rebellion, but, in some measure due to the personal intervention of Cardinal Cullen, he had been reprieved. In December the Fenians tried to spring him from Clerkenwell gaol in London by dynamiting a hole in the prison wall. A degree of miscalculation resulted in an explosion much in excess of that required. Burke was not rescued, but many houses in the Clerkenwell area were demolished, 120 people were wounded, and twelve died. A number of expectant women living in the district gave premature births induced by the shock. It was impressed upon Gladstone that something would have to be done about Ireland.

7. The Failure of the Liberal Alliance

Fenianism impressed Gladstone that the time had arrived for a new departure in government policy. 'We have reached a crisis,' he told the Conservative administration in March 1868, 'in the affairs and in the state of Ireland.' But the measures he contemplated in 1867 and 1868 were not derived from the proposals of the Fenians, as he was always careful to point out. They were drawn from the programme of reforms agitated during the 1860s by Catholic Liberal politicians in Ireland. For Fenianism had also impressed the Catholic hierarchy with the need to get something done in the country, and an organized movement of constitutional agitation was the result. Fenianism was important in the 1860s because it allowed a few men to rekindle the lamp of nationalism; because it provided a continuing organization capable of transmitting the minority tradition of republican militancy to the twentieth century. But too great an emphasis on the revolutionaries of this decade has led many historians into a disproportionate neglect of the other political movements which then ran their course. In fact, the most substantial political feature of the 1860s was not the Fenians, but the emergence of a coherent Liberal party in Ireland under the direct patronage of the Catholic Church. This Irish movement allied itself with sections of English Liberalism which were just then coalescing – an alliance which was, therefore, already in existence when Gladstone conceived his mission 'to pacify Ireland'. This fusion of Irish Liberalism with other sectional interests within what was to become the Gladstonian party gave Irishmen the opportunity for which they had hoped since the formation of the Independent party of the early 1850s: an administration took office in 1868 which made Irish grievances cabinet questions. During the 1860s, and especially after 1864, the bishops and Liberal politicians in Ireland had reduced their spectrum of grievances to three main items: the Protestant Established Church, the education question, and the land laws. Gladstone's Irish policy received its threefold content from this source.

The Catholic hierarchy were the political descendants of O'Connell, and it was to his brand of radicalism that they looked for a Liberal regeneration in the 1860s. When O'Connell had lived, however, the bishops had been brought in as supporters of his various agitations – they were not the initiators of political opinion. In the 1860s, they assumed that role for the first time. None of the lay Catholic politicians had attained sufficient stature to lead a new political agitation, and anyway Archbishop Cullen was anxious to retain the control of events in order to prevent unreliable men from projecting reforms of too advanced potential. Cullen emerges as a familiar paradox: a devoted ultramontanist yet a Liberal politician. It was, indeed, his soundness on the first count which allowed him to persuade the Vatican to swallow the second. Throughout the decade he was working to bring about in Ireland the very change which the Pope was resisting with such fortitude in Italy – the separation of church and state. Many of his political beliefs sustained affinities with those condemned so squarely in the *Syllabus of Errors* of 1864, and in the end he led the scramble to throw the support of Ireland behind Gladstone's new political vision. It was part of the same paradox that when Gladstone, the well-known antagonist of papal temporal sovereignty, started doing something for Ireland in 1868, it was Pius IX and Cardinal Antonelli, as much as Cullen and the Irish bishops, who applauded the effort. The strange internal contradictions of nineteenth-century Liberal Catholicism find no clearer expression than in Ireland during the 1860s.

The Protestant Establishment, education, the land: these three subjects of complaint had all enjoyed a currency with previous agitations in Ireland. The novelty of the 1860s lay in their espousal by the Catholic hierarchy as the basis of a distinct political platform. The Protestant Church was, as contemporaries in their more restrained moments described it, a 'sentimental' grievance. Its worst characteristics – as far as Catholics were concerned – had already been mitigated by parliament. The tithe settlement of 1838 had considerably diminished much of the popular animus against the Church, and in 1857 Ministers' Money had been discontinued. But the superior legal status of Protestantism still suggested a 'badge of conquest' to suggestible Catholics. 'The social repulsion between Protestants and Roman Catholics is a root of real bitterness in Ireland,' wrote Johnstone Stoney in a memorandum for the government in 1859.

For the Catholic bishops, the question of education was perhaps more urgent. Cullen, certainly, gave it priority. Bishop MacEvilly of Galway wrote in 1866 that he knew of 'no other question which is so peculiarly *our question*, as nothing else so directly affects the souls of men and the salvation of generations yet unborn'. Simply stated, the bishops demanded the adoption of the English structure of primary education: denominational schools with state financial aid – a scheme which could be had only at the cost of dismantling the Irish National System set up in 1831. The separation of secular and religious instruction, and the non-sectarianism of the latter, were now receiving frequent and grave episcopal censure for being not only wrong in principle but hazardously open to the designs of Protestant proselytism. The bishops' university proposals were similar. The Queen's Colleges had been condemned in 1850; Trinity College was under disfavour as a Protestant foundation. In 1859 Cullen described the whole Irish educational structure, at all levels, as one 'which slowly puts in the power of a Protestant government all the education of a Catholic population'. To prevent the continuing resort of Catholic students to the suspect institutions, the Catholic bishops had set up their own university in Dublin and appointed Newman as its first rector. During the 1860s they consistently demanded a Charter, and sometimes a state endowment too, for this venture.

The third grievance, the land question, involved the bishops in disagreement, and their requirements were accordingly formulated with less coherence. Legal recognition of the principle of compensation for improvements got wide enough support – the reform was long overdue anyway – but MacHale and two or three other bishops would have liked to commit Irish politicians to more radical objectives, and especially to fixity of tenure. All these differences, which had complicated the existence of the Tenant League in the early 1850s, were liable to divide and weaken the new Liberal movement. That is essentially why Cullen sought to give the land question a low priority.

By 1864 the need for some sort of renewed organization of Liberal opinion in Ireland was evident both to the Catholic hierarchy and to the Liberal politicians. The bishops had initially sought to manipulate the considerable public outrage elicited by the unofficial sympathy of the Palmerston government for the Piedmontese designs on the papal states during 1859 and 1860. They had tied the question to a joint-Pastoral in favour of general Irish reforms, and had got up *ad hoc* meetings throughout the country to acclaim them. But this had all lacked a sustained basis. The clouds appeared to be gathering in 1864: the Fenians were attacking the political role of the clergy, the Orange order was once again increasing its membership, Garibaldi visited England and was gathered into the arms of working men. It was, therefore, in 1864 that Cullen dared once more to join the Liberal politicians in a new political organization. The National Association of Ireland was founded. The moment was a favourable one: the mid-sixties were characterized by local Liberal groupings throughout Britain. The eventual integration of the new Irish movement with this resurgent Liberalism had paradoxical qualities which were clear from the beginning, however. It was the visit of Garibaldi which inspired the foundation of the English Reform League in 1864 – by men who looked to the sack of the papal states as an iridescent example of Liberalism in the field. The National Association of Ireland was founded by Catholic politicians, who regarded the hero of the *Risorgimento* as the personification of the anti-Christ. But a large deposit of Liberalism was held in common, and the National Association was intended to provide the structure for a radical revival in Ireland.

The National Association, in fact, was shot through with O'Connellism. It originated at meetings of Liberal politicians and Catholic clergy called to provide a national monument to the Liberator in Dublin. Its aim – and here the part of the clergy became clear – was to provide a constitutional vehicle for the agitation of reform as an alternative to Fenian revolutionism. It adopted the threefold programme: disestablishment of the Church, state-supported denominational education, and land legislation to secure compensation for improvements. Seven Catholic prelates headed by Cullen attended the inauguration of the new venture and gave it their literal blessing. Liberal members of the Dublin Corporation were also there, led by Peter Paul MacSwiney, the draper and alderman. And so were some prominent Liberal politicians: John Blake Dillon, O'Neill Daunt, Sir John Gray, J.F.Maguire, and Myles O'Reilly. The new departure, therefore, expressed a union of three groups – the Catholic hierarchy, the city corporation, and the Liberal politicians. The early integration of the Irish movement with the emergent Liberalism of England was suggested by John Bright in a message sent to the new Association.

If the popular party in Ireland would adopt as its policy free land and free church, and would unite with the popular party in England and Scotland for the advance of liberal measures, and especially for the promotion of an honest amendment of the representation, I am confident that good and beneficial changes might be made within a few years. We have on our side numbers and opinion, but we want a more distinct policy and a better organization, and these, I hope, to some extent, your meeting may supply.

This spelt out the real nature of the new Irish movement. It was an experiment in Unionism. The Union was to be made to work by presenting the government with a programme of Irish legislation which was to seem irresistible because it was promoted by the united radicalism of England and Ireland. It was rather like a resurrection of the political mood which had led to the Lichfield House Compact in the 1830s. The leaders, of course, were not unaware of the comparison. 'It is our duty,' Cullen told the new Association, 'to walk in the footsteps of the great Liberator, Daniel O'Connell.' He had secured reforms 'by peaceful means and by force of reason, without violating any law'. Much of the local organization of opinion behind the National Association fell to episcopal control, and it was this which guaranteed the 'force of reason' a circumscribed expression.

The movement, in fact, was dominated by the hierarchy. It aimed, as a result, more at the creation of a public opinion for reform than at direct representation in parliament. The Association was responsible for presenting hundreds of petitions to parliament, which described an entire reform platform: on the Protestant Church, oaths, education, tithe rent-charge, and parliamentary reform. The weaknesses of the Association were familiar ones. Its finances were tenuous; local organization was very imperfect. The episcopal members undermined its authority by deciding matters of policy at their own meetings – their negotiations with the government over the education question, between 1865 and 1868, for example, were conducted without reference to it. The Association was also attacked from outside. The Fenians denounced it at once as a crafty contrivance manufactured by the priests to prevent the people from recognizing the real need for an Irish republic. Orangemen dressed it up as a papist confederacy against the Constitution. There were also those who had blamed Cullen for the demise of the Independent Opposition party of the 1850s, and who regarded the Association, with its professed aim of a Liberal alliance, as a sell-out to English political interest.

MacHale, as was only natural, nursed this opinion, and declined to join the Association. In May 1865 those who tended to sympathize with him sought to reconstruct the rules of the Association in order to redirect the new movement towards Independent politics. These men, led by Bishop Nulty of Meath, also held advanced views on the land question. They were defeated. Their withdrawal from the Association added to its difficulties.

The 1865 general election was not a great success either. When the Association had been founded, Bishop Keane of Cloyne had declared that twenty good men 'by their silent looks and determined countenances' would be sufficiently formidable to reduce parliament to contrition. The Association did manage to get the essentials of such a corps into the

Commons, where they were supported by the agents of English radical nonconformity. But this parliamentary foothold was shallow, and it is important to realize that the considerable influence of the Association resided mainly in its successful propagandist activities and in the direct negotiations between its leaders and individual ministers.

The greatest of the Association's weaknesses, however, lay in the structure of its programme. Three points were too many; they tended to result in a diffusion of interest, and they opened the way to disputation about which of the three was to have priority. The Liberals in the Association were aware of the success of the single-pointed Anti-Corn Law League, whose effectiveness in the 1840s had largely resulted from its partiality of interest, from its bending and relating of all questions to the single one of its selection. The lesson was ignored by the Association, though it was one which had been taught by O'Connell too.

Perspicacious though the founders of the National Association no doubt were, they could not have foreseen, as early as 1864, that Liberalism in England, which still at that time lacked coherence, would emerge in the way it did – garnered by Gladstone, the great political harvester. The Liberal alliance was projected at a time when future developments were unclear. It was especially remarkable that the axis of the new alignment between the popular parties of England and Ireland should have depended upon a union of creeds for political purposes. For this was not the union of north and south inside Ireland, the essential panacea of the nationalist tradition. It was the even more unlikely union of Irish Catholics with English and Scottish dissenters; a union with men most noted for their searing attacks upon Popery.

The Liberation Society was founded by Edward Miall in 1853 in order to promote the disestablishment of the Church of England and the discontinuance of all state support for religion. The Voluntary system ('free-trade in religion') was increasingly propagated by English nonconformity in opposition to Established religion, until it was raised by them, indeed, to the level of dogma. The extraordinary alliance between the Liberation Society and the National Association of Ireland was brought about by W. J. O'Neill Daunt, the former secretary to O'Connell. In 1862 he had managed to persuade the Society to give up their attacks upon Maynooth, and he had already suggested the common policy of Voluntaryism which was to cement the alliance with the National Association at its foundation in 1864. The Voluntary System of endowments was largely foreign to Catholicism, but the peculiar circumstances of Ireland, where the Catholics had relied upon it with incredible success since the penal days, made it a natural enough basis for agreement. Cullen had spoken in support of Voluntaryism at the National Association, and the hierarchy, with the exception of the Bishop of Kerry (Moriarty) were in agreement that the Protestant Church in Ireland should be disendowed as well as disestablished. The Association did not formally adopt the principle of 'uncompromising Voluntaryism' until 1867, but it had always been implicit in its policy. Daunt had drawn in the threads. 'It was no easy task,' he later wrote, 'to get Irish ecclesiastics to place confidence in the Liberation people whose anti-Catholic bigotry in theological matters was notorious.' But he managed it, with the support of Dr Patrick Leahy, the Archbishop of Cashel. The implications were considerable. Since the only point of agreement between the Irish Catholics and the English dissenters was that the Church should be disestablished, it lifted the Church question to immediate priority in the National Association's programme. Gladstone adopted the policy of disestablishment as a result.

The Liberation Society acted as the publicity agent of the Association in England, promoting the causes of the Irish

Catholics through the nonconformist press and through its own generous machinery for political pressure. It prepared agitation to support motions against the Irish Establishment placed before the Commons, on behalf of the National Association, by Sir John Gray in 1866 and 1867. In 1867, Carvell Williams was deputed by the Society to visit Ireland and learn the opinions of the Catholic leadership at first hand. In March 1867, Gray felt well enough prepared to make tentative approaches to Gladstone on the Church question. In July the two men met in London to explore the ground they might hold in common. Gladstone's principles, it transpired, were flexible. He was, he intimated, personally favourable to any settlement of the Church question which Catholic opinion in Ireland might declare their 'approved plan'. This left it to the Catholics to articulate their 'approval' of disendowment, and of the redeployment of the resources of the disestablished Church to secular uses like poor relief. In October 1867, the hierarchy duly responded by resolving in favour of the secularization plan. The union of Irish Catholicism and English nonconformity was now, as a result, presided over by Gladstone. One of the most important of the sectional alliances which raised the Liberals to office in the 1868 election was ready for testing.

While these extraordinary agreements were being made, the bishops had been negotiating with the Conservative administration of Lord Derby about the Irish university question. The government, no less than the bishops, were anxious for a settlement. During the summer of 1867 they had appointed a Royal Commission under Lord Powis to inquire into the condition of Irish primary schools; another commission was examining the need for reforms in the Irish Protestant Establishment. In February Lord Naas, as Chief Secretary, had introduced legislation for tenant improvements, but this had been dropped when the Irish members began to insist on nothing less than fixity of tenure. With two of the three main points of Irish agitation under commission, there was, therefore, a real sense in which the Conservatives' Irish policy was, by the start of 1868, pinned to a satisfactory solution of the university question. In March, a motion on the 'state of Ireland' was introduced to parliament by J.F. Maguire, representing the National Association, and the government selected the occasion to announce their university scheme.

This, as outlined by Mayo (Lord Naas), conceded a Crown Charter for a new Catholic university. Cullen accepted this as the basis of a settlement in the belief, which was probably correct (and which he shared with Gladstone), that the administration intended to give an endowment to the new university once it was established. The endowment of a denominational institution was too much for Gladstone's new Liberalism, however, and he at once swept the entire question to one side by proposing, instead, three motions calling for the disestablishment of the Irish Church. Gladstone's new Liberalism was also good tactically: he had, after all, to keep his new supporters in alliance, and this meant that the education question – the one in which the Irish Catholics and the English nonconformists had no common ground – was the one to be taken up last. His superior bid for Irish power was successful. The government withdrew its university proposals; the Irish hierarchy acclaimed Gladstone. In the general elections of November 1868, the National Association and the bishops urged the electorate to support candidates pledged explicitly to Gladstone. The sixty-five who were returned on this understanding signalled the effectiveness of the Liberal alliance. Irish politics had become integrated with those of the United Kingdom as a whole. The Union had been made to work. A prime minister took office in 1868 with an Irish policy agreeable to the leaders of Irish opinion. Gladstone declared that he had taken up the Irish question in the name of 'the God of Truth and Justice'. Cullen could scarcely have hoped for a more suitable announcement. 'We should turn our eyes and hearts to the Supreme Lord and Ruler of the earth,' he informed his clergy, 'humbly imploring Him to fill our lawgivers with wisdom and a desire of doing what is just.' But, as it turned out, the God of Abraham and of Isaac and of Gladstone had prepared a more ambiguous response to their intercessions.

During the election campaign, Gladstone had alighted recurringly upon the need for Irish measures conformable to Irish opinion. Yet the legislation introduced by his ministry after 1869, although suggested to him by the programme of the Irish Liberals, was his own. With neither the Church nor the Land Bills did he seriously undertake amendments pressed by the Irish Catholics. Gladstone explained his position clearly enough to an Irish delegation in March 1870. 'What I meant to say,' he told them, 'was not that legislation for Ireland should proceed according to the behests of Irish opinion taken by itself, but in conformity with that opinion, as modified and qualified by public opinion in England and by public opinion in Scotland.' The nineteenth century offers no more explicit definition of Unionism.

Legislation to disestablish and disendow the Irish Protestant Church was introduced in March 1869. 'The working of our constitutional government itself is upon its trial,' Gladstone told the Commons. The revenues of the Irish Church were to be secularized, after due attention to vested life-interests, and state support for Presbyterianism (the *Regium Donum*) and for Roman Catholicism (the Maynooth grant) were also to be discontinued on the first day of January 1871. On that day the Establishment would cease to exist. The Bill created a new incorporated body to govern the disestablished Church, and conveyed around £10 millions of the £15 millions estimated value of ecclesiastical property to that body. The balance was to be appropriated, as the preamble read, 'not for the maintenance of any Church or clergy, nor for the teaching of religion, but mainly for the relief of unavoidable calamity and suffering not touched by the poor law.' There was also a provision for state loans to assist tenants on Church estates to purchase their holdings. This Act was therefore the first to advance land purchase with the important precedent of state aid; 6,000 peasant proprietors were in fact created as a result. The general principles of the Church Bill were exactly according to the plan approved by the Irish hierarchy and the National Association. The generous reinvestment of capital and property in the disestablished Church were not. But the Catholic bishops accepted the measure with gratitude. Opposition came from parliamentary Conservatives, who still hoped that a radical reform of the Irish Church might prevent its spoliation, and from the House of Lords, who attempted to introduce the principle of concurrent endowment by inserting amendments intended to redistribute ecclesiastical property among the leading Irish denominations. Gladstone saw these amendments as contrary to the chief object of the Bill: the creation of a complete state neutrality in the religious affairs of Ireland. After a short and acute constitutional crisis, the Lords were prevailed upon to withdraw their amendments, in return for which the government dropped the secularization clause. But Gladstone had the substance of a victory.

The Irish agitation for disestablishment had enjoyed almost universal Catholic support, but when Gladstone came next, in 1870, to the redemption of his second pledge, he faced the reopening of divisions among his Irish supporters which had remained as a legacy from the preceding decade. Land legislation was certain to divide the National Association, especially since Cullen had already committed himself to accepting Gladstone's proposals before they were even drafted. The bishops, indeed, were fully aware that they were about to be caught with their cassocks down. 'They urged,' as Archbishop Manning reported from Rome, where the prelates had all gathered for the Vatican Council, 'that they had so openly staked their influence over the people in the confidence of a satisfactory Land Bill, that if in this they seem to have failed, their power for good will be gone.' The Bill was before parliament in February 1870. Its chief intention was to extend and recognize, in moderation, the principle of tenant-right: compensation for improvements according to a scale based on rent. Despite Gladstone's own reservations, the Bill also contained a small measure of land purchase – the 'Bright clauses' – enabling state loans for privately contracted land sales to tenants. The bishops almost fell off their thrones in acclaiming the Bill. But the National Association, and opinion in Ireland generally, was divided. Gray used his *Freeman's Journal* to express the views of those who would accept nothing less than fixity of tenure; a principle to which Gladstone, who introduced it in 1881, was at this time implacably opposed. MacSwiney sided with the episcopacy. The Bill passed through parliament, despite the clamours of Gray and his followers; in Ireland the National Association fell apart.

The bishops and some of the laity maintained their adhesion to Gladstone. But the foundations of the Liberal alliance began to slip away with the defection of many of the most influential of the Catholic politicians to the new movement for Home Rule launched by Isaac Butt in 1870. To these men, Gladstone's Irish policies had turned out to be something less than volcanic: a little ash had scattered across the fields of grievance, but no more. The alliance of Irish Catholicism and English nonconformity was in reality brought to an end with the disestablishment of the Church, for this disposed of their only common sympathy.

Education was now the problem, and the bishops remained

desperately loyal to Gladstone in the belief that he might be persuaded to implement some of the denominational recommendations made in the Powis Report, and to concede a solution of the university question agreeable to their consciences. Yet the education question was the one which most divided them from the English nonconformists – who looked for the extension of the existing Irish system of non-sectarian state schools to England as the only way of defeating the Church of England's practical supremacy in education. In higher education, they also looked for the elimination of denominationalism. Gladstone hoped to patch something up which would elicit the support of both his Irish Catholic and his English dissenting followers. The Irish University Bill of 1873 was the result. It proposed a non-sectarian 'national university' with affiliated denominational colleges.

The collision was immediate. The Irish bishops rejected the scheme, in the words of Cullen, since it 'perpetuated the mixed system of education', and since it failed to envisage a Charter or an endowment for a distinct Catholic university. The English dissenters attacked it as too great a concession to the denominational principle – they had just, after all, tasted blood with the passing of the English Test Act in 1871, which had removed many of the surviving traces of religious confessionalism at Oxford and Cambridge. Gladstone's third great Irish measure was therefore the immediate cause of his undoing. The same forces which had united in agreed policy to lift him to office now united in their disagreement to push him out. In February 1873 the Irish Catholics joined with the 'advanced' Liberals and English dissenters to defeat the University Bill. Gladstone resigned. A general election was postponed until the following year by Disraeli's refusal to accept office at the head of a minority administration; but the election, when it came, revealed the disintegration of Gladstonianism in Ireland.

MacHale and three other prelates had already subscribed to the new policy of Home Rule, but in the 1874 election most of the bishops continued to stick forlornly to the Liberals rather than see Home Rule candidates carry the seats. But of the Irish members returned to Westminster, fifty-nine were Home Rulers, and only twelve were Liberals. The intervention of the Catholic hierarchy in Irish politics during the 1860s had, therefore, failed to sustain the incorporation of Irish sectional interests within a British reform party. The bishops themselves finally abandoned their loyalty to Gladstone over an issue of considerable gravity. In 1874 Gladstone went into print to attack the Decrees of the Vatican Council. They had, he alleged – and in language of quite advanced 'No-Popery' – declared a war upon civil obedience; they had refurbished the 'rusty tools' of theological medievalism. This served to confirm Cullen's creeping belief that Irish Catholicism and Gladstonian Liberalism were, after all, incompatible. When the Land Bill had been introduced in 1870, Cullen had told Gladstone that 'Ireland will be eternally grateful to you for the glorious effort you have made'. But the Vatican controversy, coming on top of the university proposals, had changed all that. Eternity reduced itself to seven years. When Gladstone arrived for his only visit to Ireland, in 1877, Cullen refused to dine with him. 'No other statesman, however hostile,' he then said, 'ever ventured to treat Pius IX as he has thought fit to do.'

Contemporary Irish Liberals rather overstated both the novelty and the radicalism of the Home Rule movement which superseded their influence. In Butt's vision, in fact, Home Rule implied a constitutional revisionism which tended to reinforce the imperial bonds within the United Kingdom. Where the disgruntled Liberals were correct, and where the ambiguity in the national following which Butt managed to accumulate lay, was in the strange diffusion of that diluted Fenian sympathy which had begun with the Manchester executions in 1867 and which had gathered strength during the 1870s. This is not to be misinterpreted as a growth of revolutionary republicanism. It was the manifestation of a renewed momentum of the rural radicalism which the Liberal politicians and the Catholic hierarchy had largely managed to ignore. It was, through the contrivance of Parnell, to infiltrate and to destroy Butt's interpretation of Home Rule as well.

Isaac Butt was not obviously qualified to be the inheritor of Irish political leadership in the difficult conditions which the sharp rejection of Gladstonianism had brought into existence. He was the son of a Protestant parson. At Trinity College, and as a member of the bar, he had established himself as a Tory polemicist, and had survived the honour of clashing with O'Connell over Repeal in the 1840s. He had entered parliament as a Protectionist in 1852, and left it after losing at the polls in 1865. Like O'Connell, his legal career drew him increasingly into national politics: he had defended the Young Irelanders in the state trials of 1848, and after 1865 he accepted briefs for the Fenian leaders too. His promotion within national politics was thenceforth rapid. In 1869 he was a member of the committee of the Amnesty Association, striving to secure the release of the Fenian convicts. He was president of a new Tenant League. By the start of 1870 he had already prepared the main outlines of the Home Rule policy in cooperation with G. H. Moore, but the unhappy death of the latter within a few months left Butt with the sole responsibility of bringing their new programme to fulfilment. He was then a man of fifty-six. Yeats, who was invariably wrong in his judgement of character, once described Butt as 'a man of genius lost in law and politics'. He was, in fact, a likeable man of very ordinary perception, much given to the cultivation of personal comfort. In this pursuit, as in his political career, he was largely unsuccessful. Like so many public men in the nineteenth century, Butt was permanently short of cash. Even in this he enjoyed excess – in 1868 he endured eighteen months in Kilmainham gaol for debt. By 1871 he owed £10,000 again. The perpetual search for funds considerably interfered with the amount of time he was able to devote to politics. He also enjoyed the diversions of female society beyond the restrictions of his marriage with the sort of abandon which, though just tolerable in the age of Palmerston, was to bring Parnell, in the age of Gladstone, to the termination of his public life. Butt had at least two illegitimate children, which circumstance has led to his being described by more than one Irish historian as 'sensuous'. Butt was not especially sensuous: he was in some measure uninhibited by the middle-class prudery which spread in his day but which is now no longer general.

Such political genius as Butt was able to muster went into the Home Rule movement of 1870. He was then able to float the vessel of imperial federalism upon a lake fed by the diverse streams of Fenianism, Conservatism, and the remnants of Young Irelandism and of disenchanted Liberalism. The curious popularity of the Fenians had been demonstrated by O'Donovan Rossa's invalidated election as member of parliament for Tipperary at the end of 1869 – which was, as Lord Kimberly remarked, 'just what might be expected from the ruffians who inhabit that county'. Just before his death, G. H. Moore is supposed to have taken the Fenian oath, and both Joseph Biggar and O'Conor Power were members of the Supreme Council of the I.R.B. until 1877, when they were expelled after failing to surrender to a majority decision condemning the use of parliamentary methods of national agitation. The Conservative element was most obvious in Butt himself – a lifelong Tory. It also comprised those who looked with (temporary) despair upon an imperial relationship which had enabled the spoliation of the Church of Ireland. As King Harman said, 'by the disestablishment of the Protestant

Church, the Act of Union had been broken by English statesmen with as little concern as if it had been a Turnpike Bill or a Railway Bill.' The Tory element in the Home Rule movement particularly alarmed the Catholic bishops and the Liberals. It was also distrusted by the electorate, which accounted for the early failures of Conservative Home Rule candidates in the by-elections of 1870. But they did not stay the course: in 1871 the *Irish Times*, which had at first supported Butt, relapsed into orthodox Conservatism, and in the 1874 general election Tory influence was exchanged for that of converted Liberals hungry for another slice of the cake. It was in the same year that John Cashel Hoey suggested that the new party 'though Home Rule in the carnal part' were 'still good liberals at heart'. The Liberals had at first been held back by the Catholic hierarchy. Cardinal Cullen's hostility remained consistent until his death in 1878. Many of the lower clergy predictably went over to Home Rule with their flocks, however, and the defeat of Chichester Fortescue, Gladstone's Chief Secretary for Ireland, in the 1874 contest at Louth, symbolized the readiness of the priests to sterilize the influence of the hierarchy when it was still deployed on the Liberal side. Gladstone's own attacks on the Vatican Decrees, which began after the elections, pushed many more Catholic clergy into the Home Rule movement. The Young Ireland tradition was represented by the early adhesion of the venerable John Martin, whose election at Meath in January 1871 was the first of the Home Rulers' parliamentary successes.

The meeting in May 1870 at Bilton's Hotel in Dublin revealed the exact proportions of the Home Rule components. Of the committee of sixty-one, twenty-eight were Conservatives, ten Liberals, seventeen radical constitutionalists in the Young Ireland tradition, and six Fenians. The programme of the Home Government Association, which they founded, was drawn in Butt's own image. Simple Repeal in the O'Connellite sense was laid to rest; the scheme outlined in Butt's 1870 pamphlet on federation was adopted instead. England, Scotland, and Ireland were each to have domestic parliaments for internal affairs, and each was to continue to send representatives to the Imperial parliament. There was also to be a common executive and a single sovereign. These proposals, of course, amounted to the creation of a federal state, but they were also a frank testimonial to the value of the British Constitution and to the need for Ireland to take an integral part in its future operation. Home Rule, in the Butt scheme of things, was a proposal for making British constitutionalism more efficient as well as more equitably operated. The revived Irish parliament was to consist of a House of Lords as well as a lower chamber. It was extremely remarkable that so conservative a plan should have received the support of such diverse political interests as were represented by O'Neill Daunt, Father Lavelle, Joseph Biggar, Mitchell Henry, and Charles Stewart Parnell.

The growing popularity of Home Rule in Ireland after 1870, however, owed little to the constitutional niceties which were propounded in Dublin. Local political interests attached themselves to Home Rule without any direction from the centre, and their interpretation of it revealed wide variations of opinion. In November 1873, the Association was superseded by the Home Rule League, which incorporated both the personnel and the programme of its predecessor, and which also failed to exert any sort of control over local political groups in the country. That it did not do so was not a blemish in its efficiency: it was a conscious decision of policy arrived at by Butt himself. He disliked the principle of pledging public men; and he was opposed to the idea, implicit in the doctrine of Independent Opposition, that every act of government ought to be opposed until Irish interests were attended to. The Home Rule League, as a result, had no local branches and no executive authority. There had been, at the 1873 conference which set up the League, some opposition to this *laissez-faire*. A motion to create a strong, centralized executive had been proposed by Joseph Biggar, but was withdrawn because of its potential to divide the Conservatives from the other Home Rulers. Biggar himself was a deformed hunchback who had risen from employment as a pork merchant in Belfast to considerable wealth. Butt died penniless; Biggar managed to leave £100,000. In many things loyal to Butt, he achieved prominence in the party as the leading practitioner of parliamentary obstructionism. He was also noted for causing an uproar in the Commons in 1876 when he spattered Disraeli with abusive epithets which were identifiably anti-Semitic.

Perhaps the most striking feature of the Home Rule movement was the support it received from the Irish overseas. Not only did remittances from America increase, but in England and Scotland the Home Rule Confederation gathered in support. This was founded in 1873 on what Butt, who was its president, supposed was the model of the Anti-Corn Law League. It was soon strong in sixty British cities, a success largely owing to F. H. O'Donnell, a former army officer who was elected for Galway in 1874 but unseated for intimidation. The vice-presidency of the Confederation fell to him as a compensation, and he was good at it. In 1877 he got the parliamentary representation of Dungarvan after an election campaign of notable, even ostentatious, propriety.

It was the general election of 1874, the first since secret balloting was introduced, which gave the Home Rule party a real existence. The fifty-nine members returned to Westminster met under Butt and agreed to 'take counsel' together in future. Compared with the pledges and undertakings which had been commonplaces for Irish radicals in the mid century, this was clearly a very slight thing. In practice, the party quietly evaporated. In 1876, only thirty-one attended a conference of

Home Rule members which Butt called at the opening of the parliamentary session; in the next year the number was down to twenty-seven. The huge periods during which members absented themselves from the House – and Butt was himself culpable in this – were the subject of constant and unfavourable remark in the Irish press. Without any party discipline, those who did attend parliament voted according to their own judgement, which is no thing for a parliamentarian to do.

Nor did the Home Rulers have much financial backing. This meant that they could scarcely have done anything to organize local political effort in Ireland even had they elected to do so. The League membership paid a small annual subscription, and cash arrived from America. But the party was always rather dependent upon Mitchell Henry, a Manchester magnate who had deployed his riches in good works among the Connemara peasantry, with whom he had chosen to dwell, in the anonymity of a fake Gothic castle. The movement had graver weaknesses than finance. Despite the early adhesion of the Protestant Conservatives, Ulstermen consistently remained outside it. Many of the rivets fell out, too, over the Eastern question in 1878. Butt, Biggar, and O'Donnell were pro-Turk, and therefore supported Disraeli's policy. This got them into trouble at home, where all forms of support for the government were thought to be incompatible with Irish representation. Parnell, on the other hand, in a dress-rehearsal for his later alliance with Gladstone, was an 'atrocitarian', a supporter of Russia and of the Liberals. This split within the party tended to widen another which existed – over obstructionism.

Despite the informal nature of its composition, the Home Rule party did prosecute a parliamentary policy. Each year they trundled on about fifteen Bills of their own – on the franchise, taxation, an amnesty for the remaining detained Fenians, coercion, grand-jury reform, economic development, education, and tenant-right legislation. And, of course, there were motions praying the House to inquire into the possibility of Home Rule for Ireland. These were all, as everybody expected, defeated. On the first occasion, in June 1874, only ten non-Irish members supported Butt. Disraeli had delivered a sizzling and slightly unfair dismissal of Irish grievances, and a not too favourable impression had been established by the Irish speaker who closed for the Home Rule side, Major O'Brien, who was rather badly drunk. But in Ireland the Home Rulers were landing the catch. The hopelessness of a Liberal revival was superabundantly indicated in August 1875, when MacSwiney, one of the authors of the National Association and now Lord Mayor of Dublin, attempted to convert the celebrations of the O'Connell centenary into a new Liberal Catholic political movement. A procession through Dublin – whose centrepiece was O'Connell's own coach, with a bust of the Liberator inside – was broken up by supporters of the Fenian Amnesty movement and by Home Rulers. The Confederation had sent 6,000 members from England explicitly for the purpose, even though local talent for such things was well known. The official banquet was no more decorous. Gavan Duffy, who had returned on a visit from Australia, was howled down, until the gas lights were extinguished and the guests groped their way from the scene of the shambles. MacSwiney's new political venture, which he had called 'Faith and Fatherland', was buried with the debris of the centenary.

The essential conservatism of the kindly Isaac Butt was most obviously revealed in his dislike of party discipline. But it was this quality which caused most impatience among his critics within the party – men who could point to the increasing restiveness of the Irish press, and to the need both for bolder tactics in parliament and for the creation of a party machine. The obstruction crisis was only superficially about tactics: Biggar and Parnell were really out to reconstruct the whole basis of the Home Rule movement. Parnell was elected for Meath on the death of Martin in 1875. After remaining unmoved during his first two parliamentary sessions, he leapt to prominence through obstructionism. Delaying parliamentary business by talking out debates was not an unfamiliar device employed by pressure groups. Butt himself had done it in 1875 over the passage of the Irish Coercion Bill. He had drawn a careful distinction between interfering with Irish legislation, which was fair enough, and with imperial legislation, which was not. Parnell and Biggar, however, began a systematic campaign of obstructing general imperial legislation, which reached a climax in July 1877 with a twenty-six hours' sitting on the South Africa Bill. This was popular in Ireland; at Westminster it brought disunity. Butt's attack on Parnell divided the party into moderates and militants, with the latter clearly enjoying most support at home in Ireland. Parnell, from this point, emerged as a contender for the party leadership, and he worked carefully to cultivate a national following. His public speeches began to suggest that ambiguous reference to physical force which was the authentic mark of successful Irish leadership. In July, at Manchester, he ridiculed the idea of reform: 'What did we ever get in the past by trying to conciliate?' It was, he explained, the example offered by the Fenians which had forced the government to propose legislation. In August 1877, the Home Rule Confederation elected him as president in place of Butt. Disagreements within the party were now difficult to conceal. Intermediaries poured oil on troubled waters; the result was merely a gigantic slick.

Butt was drawn increasingly towards the Conservative administration. By the end of 1878 he was advising Sir Michael Hicks Beach about Irish measures. The government, in fact, had taken advantage of the Liberals' unpopularity in Ireland, and was engaged in an attempt to displace their influence with the Catholic hierarchy through a programme of reforms. In the process some impressive additions were made to the accumulating machinery of state education in Ireland. An Intermediate Education Board was created in 1878 to provide grants for denominational secondary schools. The money came from the Temporalities fund of the disestablished Church. This acceptance by the state of the principle of denominationalism in the field of secondary education was welcomed by the bishops, who had, of course, been demanding it for two decades. In 1879 the government passed a University Act. The ground here was unsure: the question had brought down the Gladstone administration; Butt had himself introduced legislation in 1876 which had been dropped after failing to satisfy the Catholic hierarchy. In 1877 and 1878 O'Conor Don had tried to secure parliamentary approval for the creation of a 'St Patrick's University', also in vain. Now, in 1879, the government suppressed the Queen's University and replaced it with the Royal University of Ireland. This was an examining body only – on the model of London University – to which affiliated denominational colleges could present candidates for degrees. As such, it was agreeable enough to the bishops, since it allowed Catholics to acquire legal degrees without the hazards of attendance at Protestant or secular institutions. Disraeli also made a gesture of goodwill when, in 1879, he accepted a motion to repeal the 1793 Convention Act of the old Irish parliament brought forward by the Home Rule party. The Act had placed troublesome obstacles in the way of political organization in Ireland, and although it could always be avoided by the device of 'aggregate meetings', as O'Connell had discovered, its repeal made mass political association much simpler to organize. The Land League was the immediate beneficiary.

Butt's declining health brought him to the grave in May 1879. The party elected William Shaw as his successor: a

Congregationalist minister from Co. Cork who was intended to ensure the continuation of moderate leadership. Moderation, however, was no longer possible. Agrarian radicalism, American influence, Fenian contrivance, and Charles Stewart Parnell were seeing to that.

8. Parnellism

There is really nothing very enigmatic about Parnell, although it is quite easy to see why so many have found him difficult to understand. Parnell did not enter politics because of any burning passion to see justice done to Ireland; nor was he a mere political tactician, weaving himself the clothes of power for the casual pleasure of wearing them. He was an Anglo-Irish landowner whose prejudices were almost exactly those of his class – a class which adhered to a belief in the earnestness of public service, and which, having a certain detachment from the central avenues of British political interest, had shown itself adept at furnishing the world with men of objective judgement and almost eccentric originality. Rationalist bishops and nationalist politicians were the speciality.

Charles Stewart Parnell belonged to the second category. He was born in 1846. His education had shown some peculiar features: he was, for a couple of years, the only boy at a girls' boarding school in Somerset. At Cambridge he could not bring himself to read books – which was then an unfashionable failing, but one which did not matter anyway, since he was sent down in 1869 for assaulting a tradesman in Station Road. He afterwards retired to the life of the landed gentry in Co. Wicklow, established a reputation as a cricketer, became a member of the Synod of the newly disestablished Church, and began what was to become the diversion of his existence: fruitless mining operations for gold on his estate. When, in 1875, he was elected to parliament for the Meath constituency, he was devoid of political ideas and appears to have taken up a political career rather in the manner of his class – because it was a suitable employment for the Protestant gentry. He was a Home Ruler, but this was less a matter of conviction than of inclination.

A great deal has been made of the anti-English vituperations of his American mother, and some of these no doubt dusted off on to the young Parnell. His loathing of England was well known. Yet he was, as A.M. Sullivan said, 'a regular Englishman' in manners and in speech. Of native Irish culture he knew little; nor was he disposed to interest himself in it. His knowledge of any form of culture was not extensive. His conversation was of sport. Nationalists like to suppose that his searing references to the wrongs inflicted on Ireland came flopping from a brain brimful of political learning. In fact he had no knowledge of Irish history and did not bother to read any. He wrote almost nothing himself, and of the two slight articles which appeared as the sole testimony to his poverty of literary skill, one is known to have been written by his sister Fanny. He was a superstitious man, perpetually afraid of contracting contagious diseases, and with a compulsive aversion to the colour green, which for an Irish national leader can only be considered a disadvantage, especially as he had to speak from public platforms draped with green flags and decorations. He was, perhaps as a result, a notably poor public speaker.

Parnell's social conservatism may, perhaps, explain his political energy. He was an arrogant man, and it is difficult to avoid the conclusion that he used the Home Rule movement as a prop to injured pride. He thought Englishmen arrogant.

He felt slighted by his own class in Ireland, too. 'He betrayed acute family pride amounting to conceit,' as F. H. O'Donnell remarked in one of his more reliable moments; 'and this family pride seemed to have been bitterly affronted by a number of persons and families of his class, local aristocrats of English descent.' The strange translation from sacked undergraduate to 'Uncrowned King of Ireland' adjusted the score. Labouchère once recorded how, in 1882, Tim Healy had said that 'Parnell in his heart cared little for the Irish', and had been 'obliged to admit that personal feeling actuated his leader's policy at times'. Parnell had no especial love of his new political supporters, either. He called the Home Rulers both 'sweeps' and 'gutter sparrows'. It was, in the circumstances, perhaps a good thing that he had no profound ideas about the policy of Irish legislative autonomy which he came to adopt. 'He was not,' as R. B. O'Brien, his supporter and biographer put it, 'in the habit of forecasting the future to an extent which would interfere with the operations of the present.' A good thing as well: it was the greatness of Parnell to have held the conflicting requirements of Fenians, land radicals, constitutionalists, and Liberals in a temporary suspension – not for long enough to lessen the focus of their differences, but long enough to allow the construction of a tight party discipline controlled by himself.

Of all Irish political leaders he knew the least, perhaps even cared the least, about Ireland. Once, in the ripest years of his political career, he read some speeches of O'Connell for the first time, and was astonished to discover that the Liberator had said the sort of things that he was inclined to say. How could such innocence of a political tradition have occurred, in Ireland of all places? The truth is that Parnell's political ideas were of the simplest; it was his deployment of political organization and his tactical accomplishments which were complicated.

He was an opponent of landlordism early in the 1880s, and saw its destruction as necessarily related to his definition of Irish nationality. 'I feel confident that we shall kill the Irish landlord system,' he said in Cincinnati in 1880, 'and when we have given Ireland to the people of Ireland we shall have laid the foundation upon which to build up our Irish nation.' But by 1882 he was working to subordinate land radicalism to the question of Home Rule. It was not a progression in his ideas. It was the arrival at a point of political supremacy at which he could reveal what he had always sought. Of the mass-meetings of the Land League, of which he was president, he then wrote 'I cannot describe to you the disgust I always felt with those meetings, knowing as I did how hollow and wanting in solidarity everything connected with the movement was.' But if simple legislative autonomy for Ireland was the unalloyed expectation of his career, it was plainly unconnected with any clear vision of what sort of policies an Irish parliament would actually pursue. In 1886 he told Davitt that it would end the land question, yet there would be 'no attack upon the land system as a whole'.

Parnell's early speeches, during the Land League days from 1879 to 1882, were in fact declaring the same principle. His supporters had responded to the tangy hints at militancy; when examined for actual policies, however, his views on landholding were even then moderate. His conversion to protectionism as a necessary safeguard for Irish industry was similar: he was quite prepared to drop it in order to ease a Home Rule Bill out of Gladstone in 1886. He also accepted that Bill as a final settlement of Irish national claims, although it fell some way short of even O'Connell's Repeal demands.

Parnell, in fact, appears to have avoided defining Irish nationalism. 'No man has the right to set a boundary to the onward march of a nation,' he declared in a memorable speech of 1886. But what was the nation? It was certainly not the misty Celtic culture which was beginning to grab most exponents of Irish autonomy. Nor was it Catholic Ireland. Parnell's Protestantism was latitudinarian, but it did not go so far as to suggest any liking for the Church of Rome, whose clergy, indeed, he used bluntly to refer to as 'those fellows'. The hierarchy were first upset with him for championing Bradlaugh's right to atheism, and although they did, at last, formally declare in favour of Home Rule in 1886, their enthusiasm for Parnell's leadership was always something less than ecstatic, and their exhalations of relief when they were able to condemn him on moral grounds in 1890 were actually audible. Parnell was perhaps the last representative of those Protestant gentlemen who had appealed to an autonomous Ireland in the age of Grattan. He sought no social revolution, no political upheaval. Ireland was to be run by the men of influence who lived in it. Parliamentary institutions, which he found so disagreeable in England, were to operate with complete felicity when under Irish control. He was only a nationalist in the sense that he looked to a self-governing Ireland: nationalism, for him, had no suggestion of cultural virtue or racial distinction. He was, in reality, a constitutional radical with a limited programme.

There is, then, in Parnell, a curious hollowness. In all that he said, and in all that has been written about him, there is extraordinarily little about his political beliefs. So attention has turned instead to his supreme abilities as a political manager. In that he was impressive, although it is still difficult to escape the impression that many of his successes happened by accident. Parnell's following in 1880 was still comparatively slight. After the general election he defeated Shaw in the contest for chairmanship of the party by only five votes. The Parnellites were only twenty-four of the 103 Irish members of parliament. Shaw's supporters sat on the government side of the House. The smallness of the Parnellite wing was to some extent a reflection of Irish conditions. Parnell was not universally popular, despite the inflation of his reputation during the obstructionist campaign. At Enniscorthy during the election excitements, he had been pelted with eggs and had his trousers torn away by a mob. Yet in the 1885 elections a Home Rule party of eighty-five was returned to Westminster under Parnell's personal banner, a result assisted by the extension of the franchise to the Irish agricultural labourers by the Reform Act of 1884. Parnell had created a centralized political machine which, while in part inspired by the example of the National Liberal Federation in England, had some features more advanced than hitherto seen. The Irish National League, founded in 1882, provided a network of political influence. In 1884 a new pledge made it impossible to return a Home Ruler for any Irish constituency who was not bound to Parnell. Candidates were selected by local conventions under centralized direction. An election fund helped defray the costs of a contest, and after 1885 over forty of the Home Rulers in the Commons were receiving a salary from the party. Finance came from America – although this fluctuated according to a scale set by Parnell's apparent militancy – and from the assets of the Land League, which, after 1882, came within Parnell's personal control. In England the Irish vote was organized by T. P. O'Connor and the English National League, the successor of the old Home Rule Confederation. For propaganda, Parnell founded a newspaper, the *United Irishman*, with William O'Brien, the ex-Fenian journalist from Co. Cork, as editor. Its rank presentation of the case for Home Rule was not made more agreeable when, in 1884, it chose to disclose the incidence of homosexuality at the viceregal court. The condemnation of a political system on grounds of sexual misconduct was not a good precedent for Parnellism.

It was the 'New Departure' of 1879 which prepared the

transfiguration of Parnell, but his own part in the novel fusion of forces which took place was not great. He was the beneficiary rather than the architect of the new alliances. Agrarian radicalism and political organization were combined; so were Irish-America and the homeland, the constitutional, and the revolutionary movements. None of these groups ever really worked satisfactorily together, but until 1882 their ambiguous support lay roughly behind Parnell. Michael Davitt was responsible for the new departure. Davitt had been brought up in industrial Lancashire, had attended a Methodist school, lost an arm in a factory accident, and became a commercial traveller. In 1870 he had been imprisoned for Fenian conspiracy. At the end of 1877 he was released from Dartmoor, and, in the following summer, sailed to America to visit his mother. He also met John Devoy and sounded out the possibilities of a new alliance of Irish-American forces. Devoy had already begun to consider the chances for a union of revolutionary and constitutional movements – a strategy at complete variance with the doctrine of pure revolutionism embraced by both the Irish Republican Brotherhood and Clan-na-Gael in America. Parnell's obstruction tactics in the House of Commons, however, had suggested that constitutionalism might, after all, prove a useful weapon. Parnell's public appraisals of Fenianism and his informal contacts with leading Irish Fenians added to the impression that he was a suitable leader for a new alliance. In this Devoy and Davitt were mistaken. Parnell was to ditch the revolutionaries as soon as they had lifted him to the head of Irish politics. The 'New Departure' was, anyway, conceived in misunderstanding. Devoy assumed that Parnell was prepared to set up a parliament in Dublin on his own authority should the Imperial parliament refuse Home Rule. Parnell, of course, had no such intention. In reply to the overtures of Devoy and Davitt he had carefully agreed merely to drop the Buttite policy of federalism and to make a simple declaration in favour of Irish self-government. That appeared to be enough, and the 'New Departure', despite its ambiguities, received the support and the cash of Patrick Ford's *Irish World* in New York. The Supreme Council of the I.R.B. in Paris, presided over by Kickham and his ear-trumpet, refused to commit Fenianism, although individual members were allowed to take part in the new policy. A very large number did so.

Davitt saw the 'New Dèparture' as the battle-front of an agrarian war. A new land agitation had already begun quite spontaneously in 1878. The agricultural distress which prompted it was in fact general throughout the British Isles; its effects in the congested areas of the west of Ireland were grave, especially in the winter of 1879–80. Beaconsfield's administration passed a Poor Relief Act to make £1 million available for relief works. A large quantity of maize was also imported by the government to prevent starvation, and, as in 1846, to stabilize food prices. The wife of the Viceroy, the Duchess of Marlborough, formed a committee to collect for the peasantry. The peasantry of the west, meanwhile, formed themselves into Tenants' Defence Associations. It was the first time, in the nineteenth century, that an organized agrarian movement had caught on in the west. Many landlords reduced rents; others evicted their tenants. In 1879 there were 1,238 evictions (of 6,239 persons). Davitt returned to Ireland to exploit the discontent, and to convert the Ribbonism of the distressed into the currency of local Fenianism. Rural outrage was increasing with disagreeable acceleration: in 1879 there were 863 burnings, shootings, cattle-maimings, etc., and by 1880 the number had risen to 2,590.

Davitt revealed a considerable flair for coordinating misery. The centre of the new agrarian movement was in Co. Mayo. At Irishtown in April 1879, he opened his land war with the first of the great mass-meetings to denounce the landlords.

The district had just been disturbed when a new owner had evicted his tenants from the largest local estate. He was a Catholic priest called Canon Burke. In the same month Parnell joined in with one of his militant utterances at Limerick: 'Stand to your guns, and there is no power on earth which can prevail against the hundreds of thousands of tenant farmers of this country.' An unearthly power, indeed, visited the west during the summer. At the height of the agrarian disturbances in Co. Mayo, in August, an apparition of the Virgin appeared beside the Catholic chapel in the small village of Knock. The thousands who gathered for the land agitation now resorted to Knock at the same time, where miraculous cures were being received by those able to bring themselves to swallow mortar from the chapel wall.

While local Protestants were still trying to find the magic-lantern through which the deception, as they imagined it, had been contrived, Davitt was imparting a national organization to the land war. The Land League was established in October 1879 in order to defend tenants evicted 'for refusing to pay unjust rents'. It aimed to achieve peasant proprietorship. Local leadership was in the hands of Fenians and ex-Fenians almost everywhere. But Parnell accepted the presidency; Patrick Egan, a Dublin businessman and a Fenian, became treasurer. Money rattled in from America; by the end of 1880 Egan was receiving £100 a day. Due to a certain amount of local intimidation quite prosperous farmers felt obliged to join the League. Davitt was delighted to find what he called 'a respectable class of men' were giving tone to his movement. Parnell, at Ennis in September, had already given the Land League a practical policy – to treat any man who took over a holding from which the previous tenant had been evicted 'as if he was a leper of old'. As everybody knows, the League applied this moral and physical isolation to the unlucky Captain Boycott with notable success. The League's activities also drew John Dillon, the son of the Liberal politician of the 1860s, into the centre of Irish politics for the first time. His extreme speeches, which landed him in gaol several times, became one of the most purple features of the agitation. 'We shall see that every man in Ireland shall have a rifle if he likes,' he declared at Kildare in August 1880. John Dillon was an austere politician, possessed of the double disadvantage of chronic hypochondria and actual ill-health; a man given over entirely to politics, and, at this period, considerably to the left of Parnell. He later emerged, however, as a tried constitutionalist and became Redmond's chief lieutenant and eventually his successor. In 1880 he accompanied Parnell on a lecture-tour of America whose success was represented by the $300,000 they collected for 'bread and lead'.

The general election of that year returned sixty Home Rulers of various loyalties. Gladstone formed an administration which had no distinct Irish policy. Most public men assumed that when the worst of the distress passed – as it did in the summer of 1880 – the land agitation would fall away. This was a calculation which failed to account for the ulterior motives of both Davitt and Parnell. W. E. Forster, as Chief Secretary for Ireland in the new administration, was an early convert to the need for coercion; which was hardly surprising in view of the frantic reports which were arriving from the Viceroy. 'Something like a general massacre of all landlords,' wrote Lord Cowper in November, was 'a conceivable and possible event.' Bright and Chamberlain, however, were enough to frustrate Forster's enthusiasm for strong measures, and the Chief Secretary, instead, found himself manoeuvred into a piece of conciliatory legislation by the Irish members. The Compensation for Disturbances Bill, introduced in June 1880, would have provided for tenants evicted when non-payment of rent was due to a crop-failure. Its defeat by the House of Lords pushed the Parnellites into open hostility and ruined the government's reputation among the forces of the 'New Departure' in Ireland.

The inflationary spiral of disturbance and outrage continued in the Irish countryside. In January 1881 the leaders of the Land League were brought to trial for conspiracy to prevent the payment of rent. They were acquitted. The government looked a bit foolish. Coercion was now the thing, with Harcourt assuring the Irish people that it was in reality like caviare, 'unpleasant at first to the palate, it becomes agreeable with use'. Forster's Coercion Bill was heavily obstructed by the Parnellites: so heavily, indeed, that they were suspended from the House by the Speaker, Henry Brand – whose procedural difficulties over the Bradlaugh case were anyway reducing business to chaos. Brand also used his authority to close one debate which had been prolonged to forty-one hours by Biggar. The House was obliged to accept new procedural rules, which were anyway required due to the increasing volume of parliamentary business. The Irish obstructionists unwittingly enabled a reform of procedure to pass which, in ordinary circumstances, would probably have divided the English parties. In February Davitt was arrested for violating his ticket-of-leave, from Dartmoor prison, and in March the Coercion Act became law. Gladstone asked Newman to use the influence of the Vatican to quieten Ireland. But the number of outrages continued to increase; in the last three months of 1881 there were eight agrarian murders and thirty-four attempts at murder. Davitt, fearing the effects of coercion, established the Ladies' Land League, to carry on the good work should the men be shuffled off to prison. Parnell was himself opposed to the Ladies' League, but his sister organized it with fierce efficiency. The Catholic Archbishop of Dubin, Dr McCabe, issued a Pastoral Letter condemning the League for interfering with the 'modesty' of Irish womanhood. It is difficult to see what he imagined was about to happen.

The government, meanwhile, had received the report of the Bessborough Commission on Irish Land which, to almost universal surprise, had opted for something not far removed from the demands of the tenants. Gladstone's conscience quivered: he now proposed fixity of tenure, the right of out-going tenants to full compensation for improvements, and judicially agreed rents. The Duke of Argyll resigned from the cabinet. Gladstone introduced his legislation in April 1881. Its leading feature was a Land Commission to adjudicate rents, and therefore to write the principle of dual ownership of land, by both owners and tenants, into the law. It was very radical. The dangers for Parnell were clear: since the tenants were likely to consider the measure a very satisfactory concession its passage would sap the Land League's authority. But Parnell could hardly oppose it. Happily, Dillon was arrested again – for a violent speech in Ireland, against the Bill – and this enabled Parnell to declare an abstention of Irish members on the Second Reading as a protest. The Land Act, when it passed, was a very considerable benefit to the tenants. In the following twenty years over eighty-five per cent of those entitled to use its provisions did so. The three Land Commissioners were overwhelmed with applications for judicially fixed rents, and sixty sub-commissioners had to be appointed. A state machinery was thus created far in excess of anything imagined by the authors of the Act. Landlords experienced reductions in rent which averaged out at around twenty per cent. There was an unpleasant irony in this. 'The landlords who have suffered least have probably been those who simplified their properties by wholesale evictions,' as Lecky observed; 'It is the improving landlord . . . who has suffered most from the legislation . . . and in most cases rendered the sums he had expended an absolute loss.' King Harman, for example, the Buttite Home Ruler, sustained a twenty-per-cent loss in rent-receipts from his tenants, and this sum was exactly the difference between his total income and his debts in mortgages and encumbrances. His annual income from his land, as a result, was nil. The Fry Commission, however, in 1898 reported that the Act had not uniformly injured the landowners.

The Act was rather a trial for the Land League. It was manifestly popular with the tenants, and there were those inside the League who wished frankly to accept it. Others were opposed. Parnell faced the possible disintegration of crucial components in the machinery of the 'New Departure'. In September, at a conference of the League, a compromise was agreed which prevented collapse. The League was to bring test cases to the new land courts to see how adequately the Act improved the lot of the tenants in reality. Parnell probably hoped the Act would stand the test, despite his militant language. But Gladstone thought he could see through the device at once. 'Parnell means to present cases which the Commission must refuse,' he wrote to Forster, 'and then to treat their refusal as showing that they cannot be trusted, and that the Bill has failed.' Early in October 1881, in a famous speech at Leeds, he warned Parnell that those who obstructed the operation of the Act would find that 'the resources of civilization are not yet exhausted'. This exhortation on the civilizing character of coercion was just what Parnell hoped for. He had already decided that the only suitable way of dodging the contradictions within his movement, and a way which would earn him the advantage of suffering for a cause which he did not care to define, was to disappear behind bars. He therefore produced a deliberately provocative reply at Wexford, advising Irishmen not to throw away their arms and ridiculing Gladstone's threats: 'They are very brave words that he uses, but it strikes me that they have a ring about them like the whistle of a schoolboy on his way through a churchyard at night to keep up his courage.'

There is some evidence that Parnell then decided that arrest was not in his best interests. He planned a vacation, instead. But it was too late. He was dispatched to Kilmainham gaol, where he joined Dillon, O'Kelly, and other Leaguers detained under the Coercion Act. From gaol he signed the 'No Rent Manifesto', written by O'Brien, which called for a general rent strike by the tenants. It was ignored by them and condemned by the Catholic hierarchy and by Liberal opinion generally. But it gave the government the opportunity to move in for the kill: the League was suppressed.

Life in Kilmainham was not too disagreeable, and it served Parnell's purpose well. By April of the following year, however, he was all set to ride again. When he was released on parole in order to visit his nephew in Paris, he broke his journey in London to see Captain O'Shea and to begin the discussions which resulted in the Kilmainham 'Treaty'. This was an informal understanding that the Home Rule Party would use their influence to restore the rule of law in Ireland and, as Parnell stated his terms in a letter to O'Shea, 'to cooperate cordially for the future with the Liberal Party in forwarding Liberal principles and measures of general reform'. In return the government would drop coercion and introduce a measure to assist tenants in arrears with rent. Parnell and the League leaders were duly released from Kilmainham. Davitt was also released as a gesture of goodwill. Forster, who had vainly insisted on a public statement from Parnell that he would stop outrage in Ireland, resigned. Cowper retired from the Viceroyalty. The Queen was furious.

Parnell was clearly rearranging the basis of his support by turning away from the more extreme groups. Within a month of the 'Treaty', the murders of Lord Frederick Cavendish, the new Chief Secretary, and his Under Secretary, Thomas Burke, completed the change. The two men, returning through Phoenix Park from the installation of Lord Spencer as the new Viceroy, were set upon by members of an extremist Irish-American conspiracy known as the 'Invincibles'. They were carved to death with long surgical knives which had been taken to Ireland beneath the skirt of Mrs Byrne, the wife of the London Secretary of the Land League – a skirt made ample by the expansion of her person due to pregnancy. The Invincibles had made earlier attempts to assassinate Forster, each one frustrated by their own lack of punctuality. Public opinion was inflamed. Parnell learned of the murders as he was returning from a weekend at Eltham with Mrs O'Shea, and wrote at once to Gladstone offering to retire from public life. The Home Rule party had no knowledge of the Invincibles, and Parnell, Dillon, and Davitt issued a manifesto addressed to the people of Ireland condemning the crime. It was hardly an auspicious start to the Kilmainham arrangement, especially as the government renewed coercion by introducing a new Crimes Bill on 11 May 1882. It was, however, accompanied by a measure providing public money to enable most of the 130,000 tenants in arrears to pay off their debts and receive the benefits of the Land Act.

From this point, the way was clear for Parnell to reveal himself. He had now separated himself from the extremer elements who had made the 'New Departure' possible, and a broad feeling of confidence in parliamentarianism existed in Ireland. He began to quieten the land radicals, quarrelling with Davitt and his schemes for land nationalization; dismantling the Ladies' Land League – which had always been more savage in its demands for violence than the men's one – and providing the machinery for a national agitation aimed at Home Rule rather than agrarian revolution. The National League, of October 1882, was the result: it completed Parnell's personal authority within the Home Rule movement by subordinating the constituencies to his control. The appalling crimes of 1882 were an important incentive to quieter politics.

The Maamtrasna murders in August, in which a whole family had been brutally slain, removed any lingering romanticism which might otherwise have still attached to the exploits of 'Captain Moonlight'. The series of bomb and dynamite outrages in English cities during 1883 and 1884 were not planned in Ireland. They were the work of Irish-Americans, drawing on the vast resources of the 'Skirmishing Fund', by then under the control of Clan-na-Gael, and in themselves an indication of the separation between Parnellism and the extremists and Fenians. During 1883 and 1884, in fact, Parnell was usually absent from parliamentary life, wrapped either in ill-health, or in the arms of the lovely and politicized Mrs O'Shea.

It is important to notice the extent to which Irish policy had become, during Gladstone's administration, increasingly bi-partisan. Both the Conservatives and the Liberals were moving towards peasant propriety as the solution of the land question. W. H. Smith and E. Gibson (Lord Ashbourne) had adopted the policy on behalf of the Conservatives in 1882. In 1883, when it became official policy, Balfour said in parliament that with peasant ownership of land 'the very class which would otherwise be ranged against law and order in Ireland would be amongst its foremost upholders.' The Liberals were rather slower off the mark, principally because Gladstonian retrenchment would not concede the huge expenditure of public money involved in the provision of state loans to assist the tenants to purchase their holdings. But a Bill to accelerate peasant ownership was introduced by Gladstone at the time of his Home Rule measure in 1886, following the Conservative lead in the Ashbourne Act of the previous year. Both parties also acknowledged the need for some sort of reform of local government in Ireland, but here the Liberals stole an advance. In April 1882 Gladstone had produced a plan for provincial councils. Chamberlain, who was at that time more interested in committing the administration to an extensive programme of state-aided public works in Ireland, produced his own scheme, for Irish local councils under the direction of a central board, in 1885. It was rejected in the cabinet. Both parties were opposed to the principle of Irish legislative autonomy, and both were prepared to use coercion to preserve order.

Gladstone's preparedness for coercion, in fact, was his undoing. In May 1885, when he decided to renew the Crimes Act, Parnell determined to punish what he considered a violation of the Kilmainham terms. His party voted with the Conservatives to defeat the government over the liquor duties in the budget proposals, and Gladstone resigned. The Conservative administration under Lord Salisbury, which succeeded without an election, made immediate conciliatory moves to the Parnellites by allowing coercion to lapse. They then succeeded in passing Ashbourne's great Land Act, which advanced £5 millions to the tenants to set the scheme of a peasant proprietorship in motion. Parnell welcomed the measure, which, indeed, established the foundations upon which the modern fabric of small freeholding was built. The Conservatives were not as flexible in their Irish policies as Parnell was led to suppose, however. Lord Carnarvon, the new Viceroy, was persuaded of the virtues of Home Rule on his arrival in Dublin, where he found that most of the Castle administrators were Home Rulers. Carnarvon's secret meeting with Parnell in London in the summer of 1885, when both men agreed upon a Home Rule solution and protectionism for Ireland, was wholly unauthorized by the government and did not represent their views. Salisbury's conciliatory speech at Newport in October, and Lord Randolph Churchill and his 'Fourth Party', also gave a false impression of the extent to which the Conservatives were prepared to compromise over Irish questions. But Parnell had picked up the scent, and in the November general election he committed the Irish voters in England to support Conservative candidates. The election, which was not fought primarily on Irish questions, did not increase the Conservative representation very significantly, but it did, with 335 Liberals and 249 Conservatives, give the Home Rule party of eighty-five (plus T. P. O'Connor, representing Liverpool) a balance in the House of Commons. The Home Rulers were now tightly organized behind Parnell's direct leadership, too. The elections in Ireland had seen the elimination of the Buttite group and the Liberals.

In December the Salisbury administration found itself entirely dependent on Parnell's goodwill. Parnell, as it transpired, was clean out of goodwill. Gladstone, who had offered no clear Irish policy in his election address – but who had certainly rejected Home Rule – at first seems to have supposed that Salisbury would introduce a Home Rule Bill which the Liberals could then support. Salisbury, learning of this, said 'his hypocrisy makes me sick'. On 15 December came Herbert Gladstone's celebrated gaffe/calculated leak, the 'Hawarden Kite', carrying the gospel of his father's conversion to Home Rule. When parliament met in January 1886, the Speech from the Throne made it obvious that Home Rule, as far as the Conservatives were concerned, was off. Coercion was offered instead. The Parnellites, in an Irish paradox, voted with the Liberals over Jessie Colling's motion for agrarian reform in England, and so brought down the government. In February, Gladstone was back again, with Spencer as Viceroy and Morley as Chief Secretary: an Irish administration wholly committed to Home Rule.

Gladstone introduced his Home Rule Bill in April 1886. It projected a quite extensive devolution. An Irish parliament of two houses – the Commons, and a Senate composed of Irish peers – was to be established in Dublin. Irish representation at Westminster was to cease. There was to be a distinct

Irish executive. Certain reserved issues were to continue within the control of the Imperial parliament: the armed forces, defence, war, foreign relations, titles, trade, currency, the post office, and treason. The Irish parliament was explicitly prohibited from passing laws respecting the establishment of religion, tariffs, or educational freedom. Ireland was to contribute one fifteenth of the Imperial exchequer – a sum rather larger than the one twentieth which E. W. Hamilton had judged equitable. The Bill did not, therefore, with its principle of exclusion from Westminster, envisage a federal constitution for the United Kingdom, as Butt had proposed, and as Chamberlain (who later suggested the 'adoption of the Canadian Constitution') would have preferred. Yet it was a very considerable piece of constitutional revision. 'Home Rule,' as Dicey wrote in *England's Case Against Home Rule* (1886), 'is no doubt primarily a scheme for the government of Ireland, but it is also much more than this: it is a plan for revolutionizing the Constitution of the whole United Kingdom.' It was, as a result, 'more dangerous to England than Irish independence'.

This argument became, in effect, the basis of the Conservative and Liberal Unionist opposition to the Bill. This was not an opposition, as is so frequently assumed, which resided in the self-interest of English magnates with Irish landed properties. The Conservatives had themselves just passed the most radical Land Act yet, explicitly aimed at the break-up of large estates. The Unionists were afraid that the whole Constitution would be dissolved. The separate consideration of Ireland within the general structure of constitutional relationships seemed wrong in principle to them. Chamberlain, who led the radical opposition to the Bill, was especially explicit on this point. He also favoured the partition of Ireland, should the Bill pass, to allow the Ulster counties to opt out.

The north, in fact, was already beginning to organize its

opposition to Home Rule. The Ulster Conservatives formed their own party in January; Randolph Churchill made Orange speeches in Belfast in February; and an Anti-Repeal Union was drawing the northern Liberals into alliance with the Tories. At Westminster, Hartington led the Liberal opposition to the Bill, and Bright – who forfeited his reputation of twenty years' standing as a friend of Ireland – was among the ninety-three Liberals who voted against Gladstone. The Parnellites, with the sole exception of Captain O'Shea, voted with the government. The Conservatives, now coalescing around a hard Unionism, all voted against.

The Bill was lost, by 343 to 313, on the Second Reading. A Land Bill, which Gladstone had made an integral part of the Home Rule settlement, lapsed at the same time. Gladstone sought a dissolution, and the ensuing elections returned a Unionist majority of 118: the country was even more opposed to Home Rule than parliament. The Liberal party, which had aspired to gather the fruits of the franchise reform of 1884, found itself excluded from office for most of twenty years. Yet it is important to notice that the Home Rule issue only dispatched a party which was already advanced in sickness: there were longer-term dissensions among the Liberals. The party had torn itself apart at the hustings in 1885 by differences of opinion over Chamberlain's unauthorized programme – a proposal for state expenditure wholly at variance with orthodox Gladstonian economics. Sections of the middle classes and the intelligentsia, increasingly disgusted by Gladstone's apparently democratic appeals to mass opinion, had been slowly defecting from Liberalism for over a decade. The Caucus was being disrupted by local opposition to Birmingham centralization. All the inherent weaknesses of the Liberal party, that is to say, were moving it to destruction by the mid eighties, before Home Rule arrived to administer the dispatching blow.

Salisbury's return to office in August 1886 completed the alliance of the Parnellites with the Home Rule Liberals. For the next four years their mutual cooperation was both edifying and unrestrained. Parnell was once again a frequent absentee from the House, electing to live in a convenient anonymity, under the name of Preston, in Tressilion Road, Brackley. In 1888 he emerged for the sensational hearings of the Special Commission appointed by the government to investigate allegations made by *The Times*, in the previous year, under the title 'Parnellism and Crime', that the Home Rule leaders had been in collusion with extremists and had approved of the Phoenix Park murders. Salisbury went so far as to inform the Primrose League that he considered Parnell tainted with 'conniving at assassination'. Parnell, however, who happened to be innocent, was vindicated when Richard Piggott confessed to having forged the literary evidence, fled to Spain, and committed suicide.

Parnell was also faced with another problem: the reopening of the agrarian movement in Ireland. By the mid eighties agricultural prices had fallen to the point at which many tenants found it impossible to meet rent demands. In December 1886, Timothy Harrington, the Secretary of the National League, had launched the 'Plan of Campaign' with O'Brien and Dillon. The scheme was a simple one. The tenants were to offer 'fair' rents to the landlords, and if they were refused the money was to be entered in a bank account and the tenant to resist eviction. The Plan was adopted on about 120 carefully selected estates. Its ability to disrupt parts of the Irish landed economy was considerable, even though most of the tenants were more interested in trying to take advantage of the Ashbourne Land Act. By 1889 the Plan had cost its organizers £200,000. The government watched the situation with careful reserve, and prevented the earth catching fire by using influence to prevent landlords evicting tenants on the Plan estates.

Parnell was embarrassed by this resurgence of agrarian militancy. A number of his parliamentary colleagues were openly abetting the Campaign, but he remained as detached as possible, anxious to avoid upsetting the Liberal alliance. The Vatican came to his assistance in April 1888 by issuing a Rescript, based upon evidence collected during a mission to Ireland by Mgr Persico, condemning both the Plan of Campaign and the practice of boycotting. Parnell was able to direct the Home Rule Party into the safe diversion of telling the clergy where to get off. He announced that he could leave the question to the resolution of his Catholic supporters. They duly met and declared 'that Irish Catholics can recognize no right in the Holy See to interfere with the Irish people in the management of their political affairs'. So much for the supposition that Home Rule would mean Rome Rule. The authority, both of Parnell and of the parliamentary party, was enhanced by the crisis. The Plan of Campaign continued.

The Conservative administration passed a new Land Act in 1887, which included the leaseholders, of whom there were some 150,000 in Ireland, in the benefits of the 1881 Act. This was welcomed by Parnell and denounced by Dillon. Both men, happily, were able to unite in condemning the government for the renewal of coercion. A Crimes Act was passed. Balfour had replaced Hicks Beach as Chief Secretary for Ireland in 1887 – the latter had retired owing to ill-health – and easily acquired a grim reputation for strong measures which was scarcely justified. Three men were killed at Mitchelstown when the police opened fire upon a riotous crowd, and the Chief Secretary refused an inquiry. Balfour, who had previously been known to his English acquaintances as 'Pretty Fanny', became 'Bloody Balfour' in Ireland. Gladstone was publicly upset by Mitchelstown, as indeed was everybody else, including the unhappy Balfour.

Parnell's almost reclusive life was at length interrupted in

December 1889, when Captain O'Shea filed a petition for divorce citing him as co-respondent. Divorces were not, in those days, exactly a fillip to a political career; Dilke's had been ruined by one in 1886. Parnell's relationship with Kitty O'Shea was both moving and, in its way, honourable. His terrible loneliness found consolation. 'Life is not supportable without the friendship of a woman,' he once told William O'Brien. There are aspects of the O'Shea liaison which will always remain obscure – the extent of Captain O'Shea's awareness of it, for example. Parnell had taken lodgings near Kitty's house at Eltham, where she lived apart from her husband, and the relationship had gone on since 1881. O'Shea had certainly rumbled them by 1886, the year in which Parnell had intruded him to the parliamentary seat of Galway against the wishes of the local Home Rulers. Biggar had then told the electors quite publicly that O'Shea had only been selected because his wife was Parnell's mistress. Everyone in London knew about it, especially since the secret service men who protected Parnell had had to shadow him down to Eltham every weekend for almost ten years. The divorce in 1890 had special features which made it appear particularly scandalous to those who find such things scandalous. O'Shea was a Catholic. Kitty was an Englishwoman. Parnell at first assured his colleagues that he could refute O'Shea's allegations, but then allowed the petition to go uncontested. Irish puritanism and Irish nationality were doubly offended: Parnell could be represented as having jettisoned his love of the Irish cause for the affections of an Englishwoman. Sections of the English press could scarcely bring themselves to mention the dreadful hanky-panky which the uncrowned King of Ireland had got up to down in Eltham. They did just manage it, however. Parnell might have survived the moralists had not Gladstone's susceptibilities got in the way. The Irish Catholic hierarchy were at first restrained, hoping that the Home Rule party would force Parnell's resignation of the leadership. As soon as it became apparent that this was not forthcoming they tore into him. The English nonconformists were their equals in high-minded rectitude. The Reverend Hugh Price Hughes was perhaps the most high-minded of all. 'We do not hesitate to say,' he announced in the *Methodist Times*, 'that if the Irish race deliberately select as their recognized representative an adulterer of Mr Parnell's type they are as incapable of self-government as their bitterest enemies have asserted.'

Most public men accepted the notion that adherence to conventional morality was a necessary qualification for public service, and Parnell's refusal to resign as chairman of the Irish party flew in the distended face of accepted behaviour. Gladstone was worried about the image of the Liberal alliance, especially as his nonconformist followers were racing after Parnell with their consciences hanging out. Cardinal Manning urged him to repudiate Parnell; to the Irish party he hinted subtly at 'the opportunity of your regaining the lead and direction' once Parnell's authoritarianism had been overthrown. But the National League in Dublin, and the parliamentary leaders, declared their continued loyalty to Parnell, with only Davitt, at first, in declared antipathy. Gladstone changed all that. In November 1890 he wrote a letter to Morley, which was published at his own request, threatening to relinquish the leadership of the Liberal party unless Parnell was ditched. Parnell himself published a manifesto defending his position, but the defections had begun.

In December the Irish party debated the issue at length in Committee Room 15 of the House of Commons. By then the cleavage was apparent: a large anti-Parnellite group led by Justin McCarthy, Dillon, O'Brien, O'Connor, and Healy confronted a smaller band of loyalists collected together by Redmond. It was soon clear that the party was split upon principles that went far beyond the question of Parnell's leadership. The Anti-Parnellites were the exponents of party decentralization; they stood for the rights of the constituencies against the discipline of Parnell's machine, they were sceptical of the Liberal alliance. All the issues, in fact, which had decimated the Independent Opposition party of the 1850s were cropping up again. Negotiations between Parnell and O'Brien, held at Boulogne – the latter could not appear in England because a warrant was out for his arrest – produced no signs of a settlement. Parnell, however, showed no inclination to surrender, and at by-elections in Kilkenny, Sligo, and Carlow, he threw all that he had against the Anti-Parnellite candidates pitched against his own nominees. They were bitter campaigns, in which the clergy opposed him with all the vulgarity of moral fervour. He suffered decisive defeats. Exhausted by strife, yet still determined, he caught a chill and died at Brighton, in October 1891. He had married Kitty O'Shea a few months previously.

9. Consolidation and Dissent

It has usually been supposed that the fall of Parnell, and the resulting divisions among his followers, created or symbolized a sort of fluidity within which new forces flourished. 'A new kind of Ireland, as full of energy as a boiling pot,' according to W. B. Yeats, 'was rising up amid the wreck of the old kind.' And 'the national life was finding a new utterance.'

There were, indeed, new departures between 1891 and 1914, but it is important to get the perspective and the scale in proper vision. These years in fact saw the consolidation of parliamentary constitutionalism in Ireland. The Home Rule party – usually rather confusingly called the 'Nationalists' at the time – were, despite their rancorous disagreements, established and secure in the political aspirations of the great majority of the Irish people. Governments of the day, both Conservative and Liberal, consulted them about Irish appointments and generally treated them as a sort of shadow administration in Ireland. In some ways they actually were, too. Having captured most of the popularly elected county councils set up by the Local Government Act in 1898, the Home Rulers were effectively controlling large areas of Irish public life.

There was no sign, not even as late as 1916, that the party might be swept away – as it was – virtually overnight in 1918.

The new forces, the 'boiling pot', which so excited small coteries of litterateurs like Yeats, of discontented constitutionalists like Griffith, or a racist nationalist like Moran, were almost unknown not only to the mass of the Irish people in these years but to most of the professional classes and to the remnants of the landed aristocracy. The spread of respectability, which so upset men like Joyce, was in fact a reliable sign of the very real assimilation of Irish life to the general British type. There was no 'cultural crisis', except for those who said there ought to be one; Ireland did not appear to be upon the point of disintegration, and the renaissance of native literature and custom, though it enjoyed a certain vogue in the drawing-rooms of Lady Gregory's friends, or upon the hurley fields of Tipperary, did not attract either the interest or the sympathy of most people living in Ireland. The litterateurs and the Gaelic revivalists, in fact, like the Parliamentary party, ignored the growing urban society of Ireland. Militancy in labour politics was certainly a new feature in these years, and it was in direct contrast to the rural romanticism of the leaders of public life. But like the parliamentarians, the urban working class was to find itself excluded from the new Ireland to which the small minorities of Gaelic revivalists appealed.

Between 1890 and 1914 the policies of the government considerably assisted the social and economic improvement of Ireland through a series of reforms which Dillon said were intended to 'kill Home Rule with kindness'. The phrase, which received immediate currency and has been uncritically repeated by commentators ever since, suggests a view of the origin and nature of these policies which is in most aspects quite false. State initiative to promote national development was as much a feature of the policy of the government towards England as it was towards Ireland in these years. In England it was expressed through increased expenditure and activity in education, sanitation, land reform, and local government; in Ireland, it was through land reform, technical and agricultural improvements, the replanning of overpopulated areas, education, and local government. The Conservative administration of Lord Salisbury was perhaps in a better position to initiate policies like these, less tied, as it was, to Gladstonian retrenchment. But the Liberals under Asquith continued in the new century where the Conservatives had begun.

Those who suppose that the development of Ireland was a conscious attempt to quieten national aspirations will no doubt also believe that the English counterparts of these years were inspired by a hope of buying off socialism. Development, in fact, was according to Wagner's Law, which applied no less in Ireland, by the end of the nineteenth century, than in other progressive countries. 'The ever-growing complications of civilization,' as Winston Churchill said at Glasgow in 1906, 'create for us new services which have to be undertaken by the state.' Or, as Dillon came to realize in 1910, 'Irish politics is, and has been for a considerable time, a much more complex problem than it used to be.' State activity had always been rather advanced in Ireland due to its relatively underdeveloped condition. The country caught up in the scale of development at just the right moment to benefit from a frank acceptance by the government of obligations which it had previously undertaken only under the heading of 'exceptional legislation'. In 1896 the Childers Committee on the Financial Relations of England and Ireland reported with evidence suggesting that, since the Union, Ireland had been annually overtaxed by about £2¾ millions. The country, on the other hand, had also received greater benefits from state expenditure than England during the same period; but whatever injustices might have existed were certainly eliminated by the start of the twentieth century. By 1912, the year in which Asquith declared that Ireland was in receipt of a 'copious flow of imperial doles', the government was spending £2 millions more than it received from taxation in Ireland each year. British tax-payers had also advanced £108 millions to assist the Irish tenants to buy their land.

The policies of social improvement were, therefore, the result of far more general growths in the responsibility of government than 'killing Home Rule with kindness' suggests. That the policies reduced still more the social dislocation, the emigration, the poverty of Irish society, no doubt also blunted the edge of the Home Rulers' appeal – which is why some of them opposed the works of improvement, and why the Gaelic Leaguers, fearing the contentment of a people increasingly assimilating to the securities of modern British society, went hammer and tongs for cultural separatism. The improvements were, indeed, impressive.

In 1891 the government set up the Congested Districts Board, with an annual budget of £86,000. It resettled estates in the overpopulated areas of the west, established sea-fishing industries, improved livestock and sent out itinerant agricultural instructors.

The Local Government Act of 1898 abolished the old grand-jury control of the counties and replaced them with county, urban, and rural district councils. State funds met half the costs of county and poor rates. The new councils were popularly elected, with a female suffrage. Redmond said of the Act: 'It worked a social revolution: it completely disestablished the old ascendancy class from its position of power and made the mass of the Irish people masters of all the finance and the local affairs of Ireland.'

By an Act of 1899, a Department of Agriculture and Technical Instruction was established. Its annual expenditure, of £166,000, on educative schemes carried out in cooperation with the new county councils, accelerated the transformation of the peasantry into independent small farmers.

Their legal transformation, through state-aided land purchase, was also assisted by Wyndham's Act of 1903 and an amending statute of 1909. The Act was prepared by a national meeting of representatives of landowners and tenants, called in 1902 by Captain John Shawe-Taylor (the nephew of Lady Gregory), which met in Dublin with the blessing of the government. Their unanimous recommendation that the land purchase initiated by Ashbourne in 1885 should be extended was embodied in the government legislation brought forward by Wyndham. Three Estates Commissioners were established within the old Land Commission to negotiate the sales of whole estates; landlords were encouraged to sell up by being given a financial bonus. Despite a rise in land prices caused by the tenants' immediate rush to use the Act, it was a huge success. 'The Act undid the confiscations of James I, Cromwell, and William III,' as Healy remarked with Irish historical reckoning. By the time of the Treaty in 1922, 200,000 peasants had purchased their holdings with state loans. The land question had been solved.

Another long-standing grievance disappeared in 1908, when the government passed the Irish University Act. Queen's College in Belfast became a separate university, and the colleges in Dublin, Galway, and Cork were incorporated into a national university. This fell at once beneath the influence of nationalists, and became, in effect, a lay Catholic university. Trinity remained untouched as the sole college of the University of Dublin, which it still remains.

Another benefit, the extension of old-age pensions and the other social advantages of the Insurance Act of 1911 to Ireland, was the occasion of curious disagreements. Some of the Home Rule party, led by O'Brien and Healy, objected on the ground that the Irish Medical Charities Act of 1851 already provided for the poor. They voted against the Bill. The Catholic hierarchy condemned state old-age pensions as undue state interference. By 1914, the government had also introduced reforms in rural and urban housing, and had increased the education grant. Parliament was attentive to the urban problems of Ireland even if the Irish nationalist politicians were not.

The work of social improvement was also initiated by private agencies with government encouragement. Sir Horace Plunkett's cooperatives greatly helped the revolution in the rural economy. Plunkett was born in 1854 in Gloucestershire, the son of an Irish Protestant peer. After Eton and Oxford he went off to Wyoming in 1879 as a rancher, returning ten years later, on his father's death, to manage the Dunsany estates in Co. Meath. From 1892 he was Unionist member of parliament for South County Dublin, though he later, after 1908, became a Home Ruler. Plunkett first began experimenting with rural cooperatives in 1889, interested in both the economic and the educative benefits of cooperation for the small-farmers. In 1893 he founded the Irish Agricultural Organization Society, to promote cooperative dairies and banks and generally to stimulate self-help among the farmers. The movement, which was at first resisted in many places by the farmers themselves, and which was always disliked by those nationalists opposed to any economic improvements which might diminish the appeal of their own solution to the Irish question, was highly successful. By the start of the twentieth century there were around 800 cooperatives in existence, with an annual turnover of £3 millions. The movement was supported by both local and central government, and also by Plunkett's close collaborator George Russell ('AE'). Russell – who was unkindly described by D.P. Moran in his nationalist paper as 'the Hairy Fairy' – was an Ulsterman who came to Dublin as a draper's assistant. He was also a leading practitioner of the current literary revival. It was Plunkett who, in 1895, secured the parliamentary inquiry, known as the 'Recess Committee', which reported in favour of increased state aid to promote Irish agriculture and industry. The Report became the basis of the Act of 1899 which created the Department of Agriculture and Technical Instruction. Plunkett became its most influential member.

While all these good things were being wrought, the Home Rule party had disintegrated into factions. It is important to notice, however, that in the resulting decade of division, and until the 1918 general election, the actual size of the Home Rule element returned from Irish constituencies never fell below the eighty or so which Parnell had established. There was no drifting back, as on previous occasions of Irish party disagreement, to the English parties. The minority group of Home Rulers loyal to Parnell's memory had met in Dublin in October 1891 – on the day after the Chief's funeral – and repudiated the Liberal alliance. In the 1892 general election the Parnellites were cut down to a party of only nine, led by John Redmond. Redmond came from the Catholic gentry of Co. Wexford. His father, who had been a Buttite member of parliament for Wexford, also had brewing interests. Redmond was sent off to be educated by the Jesuits at Clongowes Wood, and it was there, while still a schoolboy, that he decided to enter parliament. After an interlude at Trinity College, Dublin, and in helping his father with official duties in London, his desires were consummated in 1881 when he entered the Commons as Parnellite member for New Ross. His loyalty to Parnell never faltered. Like the great man he was essentially conservative in his final political analysis. 'Our demand for Home Rule does not mean that we want to break with the British Empire,' he once said. 'We are entirely loyal to the Empire as such, and we desire to strengthen the Imperial bonds through a liberal system of government.'

The majority Anti-Parnellite party, led rather nominally by Justin McCarthy after 1891, was in a state of constant mutation. They got seventy-one seats in the 1892 elections, but the frequent resort to internal disputation allowed no great solidarity to appear among them. In the early days, in fact, it was only the common hostility to the Parnellites which sustained any degree of coherence at all. They had the Catholic hierarchy to thank for that. Bishop Nulty of Meath, the most outspoken of Parnell's detractors, went to especially extravagant lengths to provide an ideological basis for the majority. 'Parnellism, like many great rebellious movements which heresy had from time to time raised against the Church, springs from the root of sensualism and sin,' wrote the Bishop in one of his Pastoral Letters. 'The dying Parnellite himself will hardly dare to face the justice of His Maker.' The Anti-Parnellites had less grave problems to contend with. Rivalry between Dillon and Healy occupied a lot of their time. Tim Healy was blunt and insensitive. Within three weeks of Parnell's funeral he had denounced Mrs Parnell as 'the British Prostitute' in a public speech at Longford. Two days later he was horse-whipped in Dublin by a relative of Parnell's called Tudor McDermott – who was, as a result, presented with an inscribed gold-mounted whip by his friends in recognition of his services to justice. Healy was a Catholic from Bantry in Co. Cork. His father was both postmaster, and clerk in the local workhouse. He had left school at thirteen, and in 1871 had emigrated to Newcastle-upon-Tyne to become a railway clerk. In England he had thrown most of himself into the Home Rule Confederation, and in 1880 he had been elected as member of parliament for Wexford as Parnell's personal nominee – much to the disgust of Redmond, who had wanted his father's old seat. Healy was a difficult man.

Dillon was concerned with reconstructing the Anti-Parnellites into a centralized and disciplined machine on the Parnell model. Healy stood for the sovereignty of the constituencies and for the local principle in Irish politics. After the general election in 1895 the Anti-Parnellites fell to pieces over the difference. There were also, of course, frequent altercations with the Parnellites during these years, as well as splintering disagreements over the attitude to be adopted towards government policy. Redmond, for the minority, accepted the virtues of social development. Dillon broadly opposed the policies. Healy tended to support them. It was all very confusing. Dillon, who enjoyed a slight majority within the Anti-Parnellites, became chairman on McCarthy's retirement in 1896. While he expended his energies upon the reimposition of centralized authority, yet another agrarian movement was generated – this time by William O'Brien and his United Irish League. The League was founded in the west in 1898 as a non-political agency for resettling the populations of congested districts; a sort of rival to Plunkett. Its political potential was obvious from the start, and nearly all the Home Rule politicians therefore had an interest in keeping the League under control. Dillon kept clear of the new movement, and began negotiations with the Redmondites to explore the possibility of a reunion of the party.

There was also some disillusionment in Ireland with the parliamentary party. The significance of this can easily be exaggerated; there was disillusionment with parties in England during the same decade. Ireland was really enjoying a period of repose: the pressures had relaxed. But the sensation of political relaxation did not commend itself to Dillon, and there is no doubt that his alarm at the growing political lethargy of the Irish people increased his determination to seek some accommodation with the Parnellites. A reunion was achieved in 1900. Redmond, with the support of both Dillon and Healy, was unanimously elected chairman. He also became president of the United Irish League, so bringing it within the safe anchorage of parliamentarianism. Healy's continued independence of action – he sponsored his own candidates at selection conventions – led to his expulsion from the party in December 1900. O'Brien resigned in 1903 after Dillon had attacked Wyndham's Land Act. The ground having been cleared, it was possible for Redmond and Dillon to reconstruct the Liberal alliance when it became apparent, as it did in 1905, that the Liberals would win the next election and could be committed once more to Home Rule legislation.

There were no real threats to the supremacy of the Home Rule party in Ireland between 1891 and 1914. The Unionists' claim to a decisive voice in the future destinies of the country resulted, by 1914, only in their acceptance of the principle of Ulster separatism. Extreme nationalist groups were so far on the fringe of national life as almost to escape the political calculation altogether. Dillon, for example, remarked in 1906 that the new Sinn Féin party 'will not become very formidable because it has no one with any brains to lead it'. Like most public men, he confused Sinn Féin with the Irish Republican Brotherhood, so little was known of either. Only the organization of labour politics was latently threatening to the Home Rulers, for this could provide the urban working classes of Belfast, Dublin, Waterford, and Cork with an alternative to the middle-class politics of nationalism. As it turned out, the alternative was an empty one. The Labour candidates who were elected in a few places to the new local councils created by the 1898 Act all looked to the Home Rule party for guidance. So did most Irish trade unionists, despite the efforts of Larkin and Connolly to convert them to socialism – just as the working classes in England remained loyal to Gladstonian Liberalism. In 1916 Labour was drawn into an alliance of convenience by the middle-class nationalists, and they were betrayed. Labour was allowed no voice in the creation of the new Ireland of 1922. The urban workers of Belfast had opted for Tory Unionism; the workers of Dublin were largely ignored by the new governors of the small-farmers' Free State.

Labour politics in Ireland almost exactly paralleled those in the rest of the British Isles for most of the nineteenth century, though there were minor chronological disparities. The opportunities were also comparable. The predominantly agricultural economy of Ireland should not be allowed – as it has sometimes been allowed – to screen the fact that there had been an industrial revolution in Ireland too. As in England, it had occurred regionally. Belfast's cotton, linen, and shipbuilding, Dublin's trades and small manufacturing industries, had fostered the growth of a working-class population whose concern with wages, security, apprenticeship, and housing were precisely those of their English and Scottish counterparts.

Trade unions had established themselves, especially after the repeal of the Combination Acts in 1824-5, for the same reasons as in England: they were primarily charitable societies of skilled artisans out to protect themselves from the competition of the unskilled, and to provide themselves with social and educative benefits. Their political interests were radical, which in Irish terms translated rather awkwardly because O'Connell, the leader of Irish radicalism, kept trade unionists out of his political movements. He disapproved of all combinations in restraint of trade. Finding no outlet in O'Connellite radicalism, therefore, Irish trade unionists were more politically retarded than some of their English equivalents. O'Connell's extirpation of Chartism had a similarly arresting effect. From the mid century, therefore, Irish trade unionists formed a middle group of urban men unable to ally effectively with the O'Connellite Catholic commercial interests – who were both the employing class and the opponents of trade combination – or to ally with the Young Ireland nationalists, who, like Thomas Davis, had a romantic antipathy to industrial society and sought a return to the domestic system. By the second half of the century, as a result, some Irish trade unionists had lent their support to the Tory interest, but most had found allies overseas – in the English unions. During the 1860s Irish unions began to integrate with the general movement of British trades unionism by becoming branches of the new English amalgamated unions. The British unions were not disinterested: by acquiring this influence over Irish unions they hoped to prevent the haphazard emigration of unskilled labour to English and Scottish cities, where, as Engels noticed in 1844, by their threat to wage and living standards through competition with native workers, 'the Irish immigrants in England have added an explosive force to English society.'

In 1880, when the British Trades Union Congress met in Dublin, half the Irish unions represented were branches of British amalgamations. By the end of the century there were only ninety-six independent Irish unions left. By then, however, the movement for integration was in reverse. Irish trade unionists had become Gladstonians during the later 1860s. They passed, with most of the other components of Liberalism in Ireland, into the ranks of Home Rule during the 1870s, and by the end of the century were stressing the devolution principle. They also tended to resent the financial control exercised by the English executives of the amalgamated unions. In 1894, as a reflection of these feelings, the Irish Trades Union Congress was founded, and this inevitably drew Irish unions into sectional political questions. From 1904 the annual Congresses suffered divisive discussions about the rival merits of supporting the Home Rulers or a distinct Labour party. The question remained unresolved, though most union members were solid Home Rulers. A few drifted into Sinn Féin; and a few more were co-opted into socialism by Larkin and Connolly.

Socialism in Ireland was in direct opposition both to the Catholic Church, whose bishops quoted prolix papal censures of the creed, and to the nationalists, who stressed the sinking of material class interests beneath the pure waters of national self-consciousness. Its development in Ireland also paralleled the experience of England. There were early Utopians. William Thompson of Roscarbery, Co. Cork, whom Connolly rashly described as 'a forerunner of Marx', threw his all into workers' cooperative communes. He supposed that the wealth of the ruling class derived from the plunder of labour. He eschewed the state as the basis of the new order, and during the 1820s published several tracts to suggest why. Reserving the utopia until after his own demise, he left the whole of his estate to establish a workers' community. His relatives postponed the new dawn by successfully contesting his will on the ground that 'immoral objects were included'.

Owenism was also transplanted to Ireland, and by the master himself. Robert Owen visited Dublin in 1823 and in 1832. His ideas were diluted by becoming fashionable. The platform of his great Dublin meeting on the latter occasion was groaning with such dignitaries as the Duke of Leinster, the Archbishop of Dublin, and the Lords Meath and Cloncurry. The Hibernian Philanthropic Society, which was the fruit of the visitation, was heavily subscribed in the salons of Dublin and did some good works for a number of years. But one interesting Owenite community was set up – by Arthur Vandeleur, a landowner from Co. Clare. At Ralahine, in that county, he established a community in 1831 with the help of a Manchester Owenite called Craig. During its brief existence the workers went in for agricultural improvements, social security, and education. They also issued a special currency, the 'Labour note'. It was soon devalued. Vandeleur lost his fortune on the gambling tables of Dublin and did a flit. His creditors dissolved the Ralahine utopia. The appeal of rural socialistic communities has never quite disappeared in a country so given over to agriculture – as late as 1911 the Countess

Markievicz was running one at Reheny, Co. Dublin. It lasted two months and lost her £250.

Socialist groups in Dublin and Belfast at the end of the nineteenth century were, like the English and Scottish ones, the diversion of a few middle-class intellectuals. In 1894 Keir Hardie managed to establish branches of the Independent Labour Party in Dublin, Belfast, and Waterford. But it was James Connolly who made the first systematic attempt to apply socialism in Ireland. Connolly was the son of an Irish lamplighter who had emigrated to Scotland. At the age of fourteen he joined the King's Liverpool Regiment and in 1882, when the regiment was posted to Cork, he saw Ireland for the first time. It was there that he was converted to socialism. He returned to Edinburgh, became a carter for the Edinburgh Corporation, and worked for the Social Democratic Federation. He was preparing to emigrate to Chile when he received the call to return to Ireland in 1895 as organizer of the Dublin Socialist Club. In the following year he launched the Irish Socialist Republican Party, whose principles were obvious, and between 1898 and 1903 published the *Workers' Republic* to popularize them. Their popularity, however, was never quite apparent, and in 1903 Connolly emigrated to the United States. Only in Belfast did socialism acquire a genuine working-class following, and even that was slight. But in his book, *Labour in Irish History* (1910), Connolly explained the Marxist analysis of Irish history with that simple lucidity which always manages to captivate. The book was a direct assault upon Irish nationalism – 'a movement which would lay aside class contentions to gain national ends, so enabling the bourgeoisie to prevent working-class expression'. That, at any rate, was certainly true.

'Larkinism' succeeded Connolly's propagandist work. As a movement for the infiltration of trades unionism with socialist doctrines it was no more successful than its contemporary

English equivalents, but as a stimulus to the growing self-consciousness of labour in Ireland it had a considerable importance. James Larkin came from a Liverpool working-class family of Irish Catholic descent. As an adolescent youth he had been profoundly shocked by the widespread incidence of prostitution in the city. He also supposed that the wealth of the upper classes in some part derived from the profits of the houses of ill-fame, and this managed to convert him, other considerations notwithstanding, to socialism. Larkin's puritanism was well suited to Irish conditions. Its linear qualities were evident throughout his life: he always denounced his working-class opponents, who were multitudinous, as '*pimps*'. He was a teetotaller. In 1907 he went to Belfast to organize the dockers and there he converted a minority élite of the workers to industrial militancy. His first success was the Belfast dock strike of 1907, which lasted six weeks. Then, in Dublin, he organized the Transport and General Workers' Union at the end of 1908. As in the north, the militants who rallied to his brand of syndicalism were unrepresentative of trade unionists. Larkin's new union was formed only by breaking with Sexton's National Union, and by quarrelling with the majority of orthodox union men. But his success at industrial disruption was impressive. He was adept at exploiting the unrest which was general in Britain after 1911. Connolly had returned from America in 1910 and in the following year became the secretary of Larkin's union; so there emerged the influential alliance of socialism and unionism for the attainment of Connolly's 'Workers' Republic'.

In 1913 came Larkin's celebrated confrontation with the employers. William Martin Murphy was a Catholic Home Ruler, a millionaire newspaper baron, a hotel and store owner, and also chairman of the Dublin Tramway Company. In 1913 the Tramway Company refused recognition of Larkin's union and dismissed some of his members. The six months'

strike and lock-out which resulted was not without violence:
a mass-meeting of the strikers broken up by police charges
ended with two deaths and many injuries. There was,
however, some success for both sides. The government
court of inquiry which arbitrated in the contest pleased
Murphy and the Dublin Employers' Federation by condemning sympathetic strike action; it pleased Larkin by censuring
employers who refused to allow their men to join unions.
But the workers really lost; they had to return to work on the
employers' terms. Larkin had by then quarrelled with almost
everyone. He had attacked the British trade union leaders.
He had been rapped by the Catholic hierarchy as a result of a
clumsy mishandling of public relations in October 1913. It
chanced that Mrs Dora Montefiori, a lady of philanthropic
largesse, had proposed a scheme to export the children of the
Dublin strikers to temporary fosterage in England. Larkin
supported the plan. Archbishop Walsh and the Catholic
hierarchy, on the other hand, had scented a threat to the faith
and morals of the children, and a posse of priests had actually
seized the chosen band of children from the corporation
baths just as they were being scrubbed down in preparation
for shipment to England. Mrs Montefiori was arrested on a
kidnapping charge, and the Catholic public of Ireland rounded
sharply on Larkin. It was an unfortunate turning-point.
Larkin shortly resigned as General Secretary of the Transport
Union. In 1914 he denounced the outbreak of the First World
War as a capitalist plot, and emigrated to America, where he
became a German agent. In the Land of the Free he also had
to serve three years in prison for trying to overthrow the
government. Larkin's work for the neglected slum-dwellers of
Dublin should earn him tribute, however. He even went so
far as to purchase a cow which he trundled through the back
streets to familiarize the working classes with Ireland's
rural economy.

It was, in fact, the exponents of rural Ireland who were laying the intellectual foundations of a new nationalism in these years. Theirs was the movement of a minority – or rather, of groups of minorities – cut off from the widely accepted developments which were converting Ireland into a modern state. The Gaelic revival projected an Irish-Ireland. It was a right-wing movement at first scarcely conscious of its own political implications. The Gaelic League and the Athletic Association described a society based squarely upon the principles of racial discrimination. The literary revival was studded with suggestions of authoritarianism. Gaelic nationalism, which in some measure came to be represented by D. P. Moran's paper *The Leader*, founded in 1900, distinguished between genuine Irishmen, of original Milesian blood, and 'West Britons' – unfortunates of Saxon or Scots descent who had, or ought to have, no community with the purity of the race. Most of the leaders of this sort of thinking were themselves of Saxon descent, but they were so divided among themselves as to render such blemishes unimportant. The old doctrine of the United Irishmen that a union of races was the essential pre-requisite for national independence was now thrown to the wide windy acres. The idea of subordinating class and religious differences to the solidarity of the nation state was not. The language of the new nationalism truly revealed its nascent fascism. 'A nation is sacred as it holds few or many of those to whom spiritual ideals are alone worth having,' declared George Russell. 'International misunderstanding is one of the marks of nationhood,' said D. P. Moran. 'We may make mistakes in the beginning and shoot the wrong people,' suggested Patrick Pearse, 'but bloodshed is a cleansing and a sanctifying thing, and the nation which regards it as the final horror has lost its manhood.'

The first real expression of the new culture came with the founding of the Gaelic League in 1893. The League hoped to revive the Irish language. By 1900 it had 120 local branches, and by 1904 nearly 1,000. There were also branches in England, America, and the colonies. Yet it was largely an affair of middle-class townsmen, another example of the buoyancy of rural romanticism in Ireland – for the language which was to be revived was one conceived and useful only in a rural society. The peasantry were extremely suspicious of the language revivalists: they frequently mistook the curious townsmen who came among them to learn their tongue as Protestant proselytizers. The League was non-political and non-sectarian. Its president until 1915, in fact, was a Protestant. Douglas Hyde came to be known as An Craoibhin Aoibhinn ('The Delightful Little Branch'). He was a gentle man, the son of a Protestant parson from Frenchpark, Co. Roscommon. He was fascinated by the Irish language from an early age, and claimed to dream in Irish. His position in the League was something of a guarantee of its moderation. The League's main function, after all, was educative. It organized such distinctively Irish diversions as *ceilidhthe* (dances) and *turas* (outings), as well as opening reading-rooms and holding classes in the language. But its political potential was always obvious. Pearse later declared that it was 'the most revolutionary influence that ever came into Ireland', and Michael Collins once said that the birth of the League would be recognized as the most important event in Ireland's history during the nineteenth century.

After 1900, indeed, I.R.B. members began to infiltrate the local organization, and it was the League's eventual commitment to work for a 'free Ireland' which in 1915 prompted the resignation of 'The Delightful Little Branch' from the presidency. The League had enjoyed some notable successes. The 1900 Commission on Intermediate Education had provided for the teaching of Irish in schools as a result of League pressure. This was a victory over the combination of

Doctors Mahaffy and Atkinson of Trinity College. The former believed that Irish was, at best, 'useful to a man fishing for salmon or shooting grouse in the west'; the latter, himself an Irish scholar, had, with exquisite taste, declared that 'all folk-lore is at bottom abominable'. The League had also managed to get compulsory Irish as a requirement for matriculation at the new National University, created in 1908. Hyde got the chair of modern Irish.

Interest in early Irish culture and society rippled out beyond the confines of the language movement. Celtic La Tène art-forms became indiscriminately fashionable: the Ardagh chalice, for example, was reproduced as a racing-cup, complete with the incised names of the Apostles. Members of the League took to dressing in what they imagined was the dress of the pure Celts – 'trews fastened to the legs with thongs,' as the astonished French commentator, L. Paul Dubois, noticed; 'a tunic caught in with a leather belt, and a brath or coloured sash thrown across the shoulder.' Sean O'Faolain, though less surprised, has also recorded 'a kind of tradition among these people, too, that to be formal, or to be polite – even with some to shave or to wear clean linen – was to ape the manners of the sophisticated and decadent Saxon': a phenomenon recognizable in many generations. The revival of Irish sport was slightly less rarified, though its appeal was exclusively to rural areas. The Gaelic Athletic Association had grown out of several local movements, and had been consolidated at Thurles during 1884 by Michael Cusack, the head of an academy for preparing students to take the civil service examinations, and by Archbishop Croke of Cashel, the former sympathizer of Young Ireland. Croke became the patron of the G.A.A. Not all his pleasures were Gaelic: he was a rich man, generously addicted to claret and snuff. He looked to the revival of such ancient Irish games as 'leaping in various ways' and 'foot-ball' – as he wrote in his letter accepting the office of patron: 'We have got such foreign and fantastic field sports as lawn tennis, polo, croquet, cricket and the like – very excellent, I believe, and health-giving exercises in their way, but still not racy of the soil but rather alien, on the contrary, to it, as are, indeed, for the most part, the men and women who first imported and still continue to patronize them.' The G.A.A., accordingly, organized the boycott of 'foreign' games, but, as Dr Cruise O'Brien has pointed out, this in practice meant excluding all Protestants, the Catholic middle classes, and the whole urban population of Ireland from the new 'national' pastimes. Archbishop Croke and his Tipperary hurley-players were the only ones to pass the racial athletic test.

The literary revival was the work of a quite easily definable group of Irish men and women who mostly belonged to the rump of the Protestant Ascendancy: W.B. Yeats, J.M. Synge, Lady Gregory, Maud Gonne, Oliver St John Gogarty, Standish O'Grady; and, in a second gasp, Joyce, Shaw, and O'Casey. Yeats and his circle were addicted to romantic nationalism. Few of them could actually speak or read Irish, but they were, in their way, true enough representatives of the strange attempt to exploit the supposed literary and artistic merits of folk culture. This was a movement with English counterparts too. William Morris, the lesser Pre-Raphaelites, and all those Anglican clergymen who began wearing 'sarum' cassocks girded about with rustic leather belts, were excited by the same fascination for popular rural culture. Daniel Corkery and others have sought to depict the Irish literary revival as non-national, as a 'colonial' literature, the work of the 'Anglo-Irish': an analysis which shares with Yeats the unwarranted assumption that truly national literature (whatever that is) has to be multi-class in its appeal. The Irish literary crowd, at any rate, fell headlong into nationalism. Like the Gaelic revivalists, they ignored urban society and wrote about the simple people of the Irish countryside. Yeats, especially, represented the reactionary qualities of the new nationalism, with his forthright admiration for charismatic leadership and authority. His most politically suggestive play, *Cathleen ni Houlihan*, actually concerned the rebels of 1798. They were represented romantically. Other nationalists were usually unmoved by the litterateurs. Moran said that Yeats was 'one of the most glaring frauds that the credulous Irish people have ever swallowed'.

The first translation of the new national consciousness of these minority groups into political currency came in 1905, when Arthur Griffith founded Sinn Féin. Griffith was the son of a Dublin printer; a Catholic. He was also an unusually agile man – he took almost daily swims in Dublin Bay – despite the fact that he had deformed feet. Apprenticed in the printing trade at fifteen, he became a compositor, emigrated to South Africa, and returned to found his newspaper at the age of twenty-seven. He existed on the fringes of literary society, actually cooperating occasionally with Maud Gonne. In 1900 he founded an educative society, Cuman na nGaedhal, to disseminate the ideals of national self-help. Also in 1900 he was imprisoned for a month after horse-whipping a journalist who had ventured to suggest that Maud Gonne was in receipt of a pension from the British Government.

Sinn Féin was, characteristically, a conservative constitutional movement. The start of the Boer War in 1899, and the possibility that Irishmen in the Crown forces might have to fight against the South African Republics, did something to stimulate political organization, just as pro-Boer feeling in England did. An Irish Transvaal Committee sent off a volunteer force under John MacBride, armed with copies of the Irish Coercion Acts for Kruger, to fight against British troops in the field. Arthur Griffith used his paper, the *United Irishman*, which he founded in 1899, to campaign against the war. As

R.M. Henry wrote of Irish resistance to recruitment, 'the excesses of the British army in Burmah, and the charges made against the soldiers for offences against Burmese women, were insisted upon to prove that no decent Irishman could join the army.' In fact, thousands flocked to the colours. Griffith was moved to try other tactics.

It was in 1902, at the annual convention of the Cuman na nGaedhal, that Griffith revealed 'the Hungarian policy'. After slight but excited readings of Austro-Hungarian history he had fallen upon what he imagined to be a close parallel to Ireland's relationship with England. In 1861 Deak and his band of men had declined to attend the Imperial parliament in Vienna and had stayed at home in Hungary to safeguard their national rights. This had led to the Dual Monarchy: a constitutional expedient which Griffith now advocated for England and Ireland. His reflections appeared as a book in 1904, *The Resurrection of Hungary*. It was crammed with inaccuracies and conveniently overlooked the subsequent misgovernment of Hungary by the Magyar landowning class. The book also revealed all the reverence for history which characterizes those who have never quite understood historical scholarship. But the main outlines of the Hungarian policy became the basis of his new political party.

In 1905 Sinn Féin ('Ourselves Alone') proposed a legal return to the Irish Constitution of 1782, with a personal union of the Crowns of England and Ireland, but separate governments. A Council of 300 was to meet in Dublin – this was an idea borrowed from O'Connell – after the Irish members of parliament had abstained from attendance at Westminster. Native industry would be encouraged by protection, and a population of 20 millions would soon cover the land. Griffith's economic doctrines were inspired by Frederick List, whom he called 'the man who saved Germany from falling a prey to English economics'. Ireland was to be de-anglicized. The structure of society, however, was to remain unaltered. Griffith was a solid opponent of socialism, he feared the idea of class conflict, and he attacked Larkinism. '"The solidarity of labour" is a phrase used by the British working man to get Irishmen to help him in his disputes,' he wrote. 'It does not work the other way.' As Sinn Féin was clearly non-Republican, it was coolly received by the I.R.B. Its inaugural meeting, which was very poorly attended, was chaired by Edward Martyn, a Catholic landowner from Co. Galway who had been expelled from the Kildare Street Club for opposing the visit of Queen Victoria to Ireland in 1900. He was educated at Christ Church, Oxford.

Sinn Féin had no popular appeal. It remained a fringe company of Dublin sages; its national paper circulated no more than two thousand copies a week during most of its existence. In 1908, when the party contested the North Leitrim parliamentary seat, it was convincingly defeated. In the 1910 general election the party declined to put any candidates into the field, which was wise. Sinn Féin was by then all but dead. A number of Republicans, working through the Wolfe Tone clubs, tried to infiltrate the party after 1910, and small groups of Dublin working men were sympathetic. But the popularity of the Home Rulers had in reality left no room for even a small-scale rival. The Fenian tradition was no better represented in these years. It had never recovered from being ditched by Parnell. By the end of the 1890s, according to P. S. O'Hegarty, who was then a member of the Supreme Council of the I.R.B., the 'whole membership could have been comprised in a concert hall'. In 1910, to keep the tradition alive, Bulmer Hobson, the Quaker from Belfast, edited a new I.R.B. paper, the *Irish Freedom*, which presented the familiar thesis of physical force republicanism.

In an age which was beginning to worry itself about the question of women's rights, it is interesting to notice the large part taken by women in the Irish movements of these years. The grant of a local franchise to qualified women in the Irish Local Government Act of 1898 had offered many a taste of blood. In 1900 Maud Gonne had founded the Inghinidhe na h-Éireann (Daughters of Ireland) to spread the lucid ideals of Irish culture throughout the linen-rooms of the land. In 1911 an Irish Women Workers' Union had been set up by Delia Larkin, the sister of the labour leader. During the Home Rule crisis after 1911 both sides organized the ladies: the Ulster girls had their own Covenant to sign in 1912, and in 1913 the southern sirens recruited themselves into an auxiliary army known under the revived name of Cuman na mBan. But of all the prominent women of Ireland, none was more prominent or more political than the Countess Markievicz.

Born in London of Anglo-Irish stock in 1865, Constance Gore-Booth matured into an unusually emancipated girl. She smoked heavily, chewed gum, carried a revolver, and kept a pet snake which she wore in her hair. Her marriage to Count Markievicz was not happy. Constance was not the most feminine woman in the world (how many leading feminists were?), and she was soon straining after the outside diversions of politics. She joined the Gaelic League but had to give up trying to learn the language after a few barren months. She sought out Arthur Griffith – who was actually opposed to female suffrage – but was not encouraged. 'She was,' as Sean O'Faolain has written, 'possibly not the first society woman who had come to him in search of a new thrill.' So she turned instead, in 1909, to the organization of a corps of nationalist boy scouts in Dublin. The inspiration for this venture came both from Bulmer Hobson's Belfast scouts of 1902, and from Baden-Powell's English movement of 1908. Constance's scouts were known as the Fianna Éireann, after the force of super-youths described in early Celtic literature.

She trained them personally in the use of firearms, dressed them in green shirts, and drilled them into manly discipline. They remained a useful aid to the Volunteers in 1914 and a source for the recruitment of rebel soldiers during the next couple of decades. Roger Casement, then in Africa, sent a £10 cheque to purchase 'kilts for the boys'. The movement was not large until after 1911, when Liam Mellowes got regional branches established.

The amount of space allowed to the Gaelic revivalists and the new nationalism is wholly out of proportion to the real influence they were able to exert in Ireland at the end of the nineteenth century. But their ideas formed the political culture which was to sweep through the country after the fortuitous demise of the Home Rule parliamentary party between 1916 and 1918. Into the vacuum then created, the extreme nationalist minorities poured the heady atmosphere of Irish-Ireland. But between 1891 and 1914 the general consolidation of Ireland continued.

Beneath it, however, the question of the government of Ireland lay in a dangerous slumber. In April 1893, Gladstone had introduced a second Home Rule Bill. The exclusion principle had been dropped; there were now to be eighty Irish members at Westminster eligible to vote on all questions. Certain issues were still to be reserved to the control of the Imperial parliament, as in 1886. The Bill had been defeated in the Lords, and Rosebery, succeeding to the premiership upon Gladstone's retirement, had shelved the whole question in 1894.

There the matter had remained virtually undisturbed until 1904, when Lord Dunraven and his Irish Reform Association – a body of progressive landowners – had proposed a generous measure of devolution with the blessing of Sir Antony MacDonnell, then Under Secretary. Orthodox Unionists denounced the scheme. Carson called it 'a gross betrayal'. Wyndham was obliged to resign as Chief Secretary. The Liberals, returned to office in 1906 with an overall majority of more than a hundred, and therefore untrammelled by the support of the Irish party, were reluctant to take up the Home Rule question.

In 1907 an Irish Councils Bill was brought forward. It envisaged better local government rather than Home Rule, was rejected by the Irish members, and withdrawn. The patience of the Home Rule members during these empty years was impressive. With the extended constitutional crisis resulting from the Lords' rejection of Lloyd George's 'Peoples' Budget', however, and with the passing of the Parliament Act in 1911, which removed the Lords' veto over legislation, the day of the Home Rulers had at last arrived.

As a result of the crisis elections, the Irish party also had a balance in the Commons once more. Asquith felt called upon to introduce a new Home Rule Bill in 1912. It was a measure of noticeable moderation: there was to be an Irish House of Commons of 164 members – a disproportionately large number of whom were to sit for rural seats, a point which made the proposals especially agreeable to the Redmondites, and especially distasteful to Larkin – a Senate of forty members, and a separate Irish Executive. Forty-two Irish members were to continue to resort to Westminster. The usual list of reserved issues was appended, with some additions. The police were to remain under Imperial control for the first six years. Redmond accepted the Bill on behalf of his party and it passed the Commons, after ruthless applications of the guillotine, by a hundred votes, in May 1912. For the next year the Bill shuttled between the Commons and the Lords, growing heavy with the accretion of amendments and sour with the putrefaction of its good intentions.

The initial passage of the Bill through the Commons set Ulster alight, and the deep shadows cast over the next two years brought the country to the edge of civil war and the British Constitution to its most critical test in modern history. In Ulster, the Orangemen faced the Ancient Order of Hibernians – a Catholic association led by Joseph Devlin, a bar-tender – across a religious divide which had not diminished, in either beliefs or manners, since the seventeenth century. In June 1912, a group of Hibernians attacked a procession of Protestant Sunday-school children from Belfast who were on a day's outing in Castledawson, Co. Londonderry. Several children were wounded. Reprisals followed in the Belfast shipyards. In the same month a Liberal member of parliament, Agar-Robartes, moved an amendment to the Home Rule Bill proposing the exclusion of the Ulster counties of Antrim, Armagh, Down, and Londonderry from its terms. The Ulster Unionists at first opposed this: they were reluctant to desert the Southern Unionists, and they also believed they could procure the defeat of the whole Bill. Redmond was also, at this point, unwilling to accept the partition of Ireland. 'The idea of two nations in Ireland is revolting and hateful,' he said; 'the idea of our agreeing to the partition of our nation is unthinkable.' Ulster, meanwhile, under the leadership of Carson, was preparing for its own defence.

Edward Carson was born in Dublin, the son of a prominent architect and devoted Presbyterian, in 1854. He had aspired to the ministry of the church, but his father had insisted upon a legal career. Despite his unreliable health – he had a weak heart – he managed to play the Irish game of hurley when up at Trinity College, Dublin, in 1871. Thereafter he became a member of both the English and the Irish bars, establishing himself in a number of celebrated cases. It was Carson who conducted the cross-examination of Oscar Wilde while defending Lord Queensberry in the libel action of 1895. In 1892 he had become Irish Solicitor-General, and in the same year was elected to parliament as one of the representatives of Dublin

University. His Unionism was inflexible; his Toryism often surprisingly liberal. He supported both female suffrage and the abolition of capital punishment. He was also a man with many friendships. Tim Healy, a legal though scarcely a political colleague, once lavishly remarked that he would trust his soul to Carson. In 1910 Carson became the leader of the Irish Unionist party, and in September 1911 he made his famous appearance at the Belfast meeting which introduced him to the Province whose champion he was so shortly to become. 'We will yet defeat the most nefarious conspiracy that has ever been hatched against a free people,' he said of Asquith's Bill. The vast gathering of the northern working class roared their approval. From this point Carson coordinated the opposition to Home Rule upon the basis of a popular movement in Ulster. His principal manager was Captain James Craig (Lord Craigavon), a self-made man who had transformed himself from a clerk in a whiskey distillery to a millionaire Unionist member of parliament. English support came especially from Bonar Law, now the leader of the Conservative party, and from F. E. Smith (Lord Birkenhead).

The support of Bonar Law, indeed, was given with very few reservations. In July 1912, with the full knowledge that the Ulster Unionists threatened unilateral action should Home Rule reach the statute book, he committed the English Conservatives to their cause. 'I can imagine no length of resistance to which Ulster will go,' he said in Belfast, 'in which I shall not be ready to support them, and in which they will not be supported by the overwhelming majority of the British people.' Winston Churchill, in the same month, was down in Co. Cork kissing the Blarney Stone and assuring the Home Rulers that the Liberals would enforce the law. Further confrontations seemed unavoidable. In September 1912, the Solemn League and Covenant was drawn up in Belfast, pledging loyalty to the king and committing its signatories to refuse recognition to any parliament which might be set up in Ireland under the terms of the Liberals' Home Rule Bill. It was immediately signed by 219,000 men. Five hundred religious services were arranged to celebrate the occasion. In December an armed Volunteer force was raised to defend Ulster. Carson kept it within the law by applying to the Belfast magistrates for authorization to train men in arms. By the end of the following year there were 100,000 men in the force.

Events then moved swiftly upon a collision course. In January 1913 the Lords threw out the amended Home Rule Bill. Under the terms of the Parliament Act their delaying powers could prevent it becoming law only until 1914. In September 1913 a provisional government was set up in Belfast with Carson at its head. All actions were taken in the king's name. A situation was contrived, that is to say, which is legally comparable to the Rhodesian declaration of independence in 1966. The executive of the Ulster government was a 'Central Authority'. There were subordinate councils and committees for military defence, local government, volunteer forces, education, customs, and postal services – many of the functions, in fact, which in the Liberals' Home Rule Bill were reserved to Westminster. On each committee there was a representative of the Ulster Women's Unionist Council. An indemnity fund soon raised over £1 million. The provisional government had the support of the Protestant clergy, the Orange democracy, large sections of the English press, and the Conservative party. In a Bradford speech, Churchill described it as 'a self-elected body, composed of persons who, to put it plainly, are engaged in a treasonable conspiracy'. It was certainly unusual to find half the nation, and the most conservative half at that, tendering aid and comfort to a combination openly preparing to defeat the legal government by force of arms.

The example also proved irresistible in the south. In October 1913, an article entitled 'The North Began' appeared in *An Claidheamh Soluis*, the paper of the Gaelic League. Its author was Eóin MacNéill (John MacNeill), Professor of Early Irish History in the National University, and Secretary of the League. His suggestion that a Volunteer force should be formed to defend the south in the event of unilateral action by Ulster fell upon receptive ears. The I.R.B. had anyway been hoping to create something of the sort, and the appearance of an independent corps which they could convert into a front movement was beyond their expectations. At a Dublin meeting in November the Volunteers were established, with MacNeill as president. Four thousand enrolled at once, many of them Redmondites; but Sinn Féin and the Republicans entered the movement from the beginning as well. Some labour militants were rather less than enthusiastic, and a party of Larkinites tried to break up the first meeting of the Volunteers. The Gaelic League also remained formally outside the movement, although its more activist elements, those seeking to nudge the League into politics, were early recruits. By 1914 the Volunteers numbered 200,000. The Home Rule party were anxious to exercise some sort of authority over this new force in national life, and in June 1914 Redmond succeeded in intruding twenty-five of his own nominees to the Committee of the Volunteers. Dublin labour received military organization in October when Larkin set up a 'Citizen Army', in order, as he said, 'that Labour might no longer be defenceless'. Most of its small membership, however, defected to the Volunteers, and the remnants, gathered once again into military ranks by Captain White, an Ulster Protestant, were not very formidable. But they survived long enough to take part in the rising of 1916.

The government responded to the new militancy in December 1913 by posting two Royal Proclamations prohibiting the importation of arms to Ireland. In March 1914, Asquith compromised his Home Rule Bill still further by introducing the principle of temporary partition: individual counties could vote to opt out of Home Rule for the first six years. Redmond agreed to this. Worse difficulties declared themselves in the same month. Sir Arthur Paget, the Commander-in-Chief of the Imperial forces in Ireland, reported that officers domiciled in Ulster were prepared to resign their commissions rather than undertake any military coercion of the north. The Secretary of State for War, Colonel Seely, gave General Sir Hubert Gough at the Curragh an unofficial assurance that Crown forces would not be used against Ulster. Asquith had this assurance negatived and sacked Seely. The 'Curragh mutiny', however, made the British forces in Ireland look vulnerable, not only to Irishmen, but to Germans, too.

The Larne gun-running in April 1914 did not improve the prospects for a peaceful conclusion to the crisis, either. It was Frederick Crawford who planned the arming of the Ulster Volunteers. He was an Ulsterman of unusual, not to say eccentric talent. He had once formulated a plot to end Home Rule by abducting Gladstone on Brighton promenade and marooning him upon a Pacific island with a Bible and an axe. But he was a solid enough businessman. Twenty thousand Mauser rifles and ammunition were purchased in Hamburg, through an agent called Spiro, and shipped to Ulster through a marine adviser called Agnew. The only casualty of the enterprise was a coastguard at Donaghadee, whose zealous exertions in bicycling to warn the police that illegal shipments of arms were being landed resulted in his unfortunate death from a heart attack.

The atmosphere of crisis was unrelieved in the following month, when Asquith gave notice of his intention to introduce legislation to exclude Ulster temporarily from Home Rule. The Lords promptly added an amendment to make the exclusion permanent. In July 1914, King George V summoned the disparate parties to a conference. Redmond and Dillon represented the Home Rule party, Carson and Craig the Ulster Unionists, Bonar Law and Lansdowne the Conservatives, and Asquith and Lloyd George the government. After four days they were unable to agree either on the areas of Ulster to be excluded or for how long, and the Buckingham Palace Conference broke up. During the same month the situation in Ireland deteriorated still more when the southern Volunteers landed guns at Howth from Erskine Childers' yacht. The police attempted to intercept the Volunteers and the boys of the Fianna as they marched into Dublin with their 900 rifles. But they got safely away, and the only bloodshed of the day occurred in Bachelor's Walk, on the quays of the Liffey, when three persons were killed in an incident between a hostile crowd and a party of Scottish Borderers.

It was at this point of frightening tension that the war in Europe began. Irish enthusiasm for the entry of the British Empire was immense: altogether 200,000 Irishmen volunteered to join the Crown forces. 'No English city,' as Larkin's paper, the *Irish Worker*, despairingly remarked in September, 'is displaying more enthusiasm than Dublin in sending its bravest and best to murder men with whom they have no quarrel.' Redmond pledged the support of Ireland in a famous and moving speech in the Commons, whose theme he extended at a public meeting in Woodenbridge, Co. Wicklow. This was too much, however, for the republican and Sinn Féin components of the southern Volunteers. Twelve thousand of them seceded under the leadership of MacNeill and Pearse to form the 'Irish Volunteers'. The majority, of some 160,000 men, calling themselves the 'National Volunteers', stayed with Redmond and were in due course mostly recruited into the British army. The Ulster Volunteers were absorbed, virtually unaltered, into the Crown forces by special arrangement with the War Office. The differential treatment of the two Irish forces was ill received in the south. But the European war imposed urgent national priorities which were accepted even in the supercharged crisis atmosphere of Ireland. The lights were going out for the extreme nationalist minorities. They were despised by the public for denouncing the 'English' war, and three months after the declaration of hostilities the government suppressed the Sinn Féin, Republican, and Larkinist newspapers.

In September 1914, the Home Rule Act had finally received the royal assent. Its operation was postponed until the end of the war by the simultaneous passage of a Suspensory Act. Rather surprisingly, the entire political basis of the Home Rule movement had by then been destroyed.

10. The Revolution

Those custodians of the thesis that England's difficulty is Ireland's opportunity – the Supreme Council of the I.R.B. – decided that an armed rising at some point during the general European hostilities had definite advantages. There were, among them, those like Pearse who looked merely to a staggering blood sacrifice which would arouse the soul of nationality in preparation for a greater struggle to come; there were some who imagined that a rebellion would establish the international status of the Irish question and so bring it eventually before the peace settlement at the end of the war; others even conceived a successful conflict, the countryside rising with eager idealism while the forces of the Crown were away in Flanders surrendering their lives in a cause for which they could find no sympathy. The I.R.B., of course, only numbered a few hundred. But those who had joined Pearse and MacNeill in the minority secession from the Volunteers, the 'Irish Volunteer' force of some 12,000 men and women, were extremely susceptible to I.R.B. manipulation, and it was they who were to form the 'Army of the Republic'. Since the I.R.B. was a secret society, few in Ireland beyond its own officers had any intimation of the stirring demonstration which was in preparation. In January 1916, the military council of the I.R.B. decided upon the date of the Rising: it was to be an Easter Sunday, 23 April – an especially suitable day since it was followed by a Bank Holiday, and this meant that people would not have to break into their working week in order to join the revolution. These early plans were guided by Tom Clarke, a Fenian who had survived sixteen years of penal servitude for blowing up public buildings. He was, by this time, running a small tobacconist's shop in Dublin, and it was from the back-room of that establishment that the New Ireland was conceived.

Patrick Pearse was both the Director of Organization in the Irish Volunteers and a member of the military council of the I.R.B. He was the theorist of the Rising. Pearse had been born in Dublin during 1879, the son of an Englishman who had moved to Ireland to practise his trade, which was the decoration of gravestones. The young Pearse was educated by the Christian Brothers and entered the legal profession. As a boy he was romantically inclined towards the ancient world of the Celtic heroes, and discharged his enthusiasm by reading up the stories of their military valour. At other times, it seems, he used to dress up as a girl and wander around the streets in the centre of Dublin. The fantasies of his boyhood never left him. His later poetry, written in both English and Irish, carried the legendary brutalities of the ancient warriors into the parlours of the Edwardian Dublin.

He was especially attracted to the Celtic custom of child fosterage; as a bachelor he no doubt overlooked the family objections which were likely to be raised against a revival of the practice of sending boys away to be brought up by others. Yet in part he attempted a revival. Abandoning the legal profession in 1908, he set up St Enda's, a boys' boarding and day school, with a staff headed by his brother Willie, by Thomas MacDonagh, a poet, and by Desmond Ryan, a litterateur. Con Colbert, a former acrobat, took charge of physical education and promptly recruited most of the boys into Countess Markievicz's Fianna. There were other teachers too, all of whom left at the end of the first year. St Edna's was frankly dedicated to a revival of Celtic society, and Pearse poured out all his *penchant* for blood sacrifice to the boys. They appear to have perceived the tone of the establishment quite rapidly. 'One of the boys said there was no fun in telling lies to Mr Pearse,' as James Stephens, the poet, reported, 'for however outrageous the lie, he always believed it.' A curious man, therefore, to find in charge of the military operations of 1916. He was visually an odd figure; his features, as John Horgan wrote, 'somewhat marred by a cast in one eye which his popular portraits, usually taken in profile, mercifully hide'. But the heroism and loyalty which he inspired among the young men who followed him to death was real enough.

The preparations for the Rising were not helped by conflicts between the I.R.B. and the Irish Volunteers. Neither MacNeill, as Volunteer Chief-of-Staff, nor Hobson, the Secretary, was let in on the plan. Arthur Griffith and the Sinn Féin party were left in the dark, too. This resulted in a great deal of confusion in Holy Week. James Connolly, the head of the Citizen Army, had to be kidnapped to prevent his small body of workers from starting a rebellion of their own. When told of the I.R.B. scheme he decided, after a couple of days of secret persuading – of which no details are known – to throw in his lot and join the military council. In the middle of the week MacNeill rumbled what was going on, and after frenzied interviews with Pearse sent out, on Easter Saturday, a countermanding order instructing the Volunteers not to turn out for 'manoeuvres' on the following day. Griffith supported him. The military council of the I.R.B., however, decided to go ahead anyway, and rearranged the Rising for Easter Monday.

As a result of the confusion only 1,500 Volunteers actually turned out for the Rising, together with 219 members of Connolly's army. The help expected from Germany was also unforthcoming. Some of the expectations were anyway false ones inspired by Sir Roger Casement. On retirement from the British Consular service in 1913, Casement had returned to his native Ireland and supported the Volunteers. The start of the First World War saw him in New York proclaiming the friendship of Germany for the Irish people. In October 1914, in pursuit of the logic of this conclusion, he travelled to Germany in the company of a young Norwegian sailor whom he had chanced to meet on Broadway on his first night in America. In Berlin he found the German government willing to help him raise and arm an 'Irish Brigade' from among the prisoners-of-war interned at Limburg. To these troops he revealed his vision of an independent Ireland. They hissed him into inaudibility and one of them grabbed his umbrella. Casement was desolated, and retired to a Munich hospital with a nervous breakdown. Only fifty soldiers joined his brigade during the course of the war. He was also, unhappily, distrusted both by the German government and by the I.R.B., who had sent their own agent, Joseph Plunkett, to Berlin in 1915.

While Casement languished in Bavaria, the German government heard of the projected Rising in Ireland from John Devoy in America, and agreed to send a shipload of arms – but no officers, as had been requested – to support it. The British government, as it happened, had intercepted the messages conveying these arrangements, and the vessel bringing arms to Ireland was stopped on Good Friday by a patrol boat. The German captain scuttled his ship and the arms for the Rising went to the bottom of Queenstown harbour. Casement, aware at the last minute that German aid was anyway completely inadequate, tried to return to Ireland in time to warn the I.R.B. leaders to call off the Rising. He was landed in Tralee Bay from a submarine on Good Friday and had the ill-fortune to be spotted by a farmer who was apparently looking for a holy well to say his rosary. Casement was arrested, sent to London, and executed for treason later in the year. His actual contribution to Irish nationalism was, to say the least, slight. But his death became a symbol of the forlorn idealism of the struggle for independence. He was also a noted diarist.

Easter Monday was a Bank Holiday. Dubliners had departed in large companies to the near-by coastal resorts or to the races at Fairyhouse; government offices were almost empty. When the small contingents of Volunteers marched out to begin the rebellion the streets were quiet and the city taken by surprise. For the previous couple of years the police had avoided interfering with the Volunteers. There had been numerous rumours of revolution and everyone was used to the spectacle of the Volunteers marching through the capital in the green uniforms from which, no doubt, they derived sensations which went in some measure beyond their nationalism. The government had even remained unmoved in October 1915 when Countess Markievicz had conducted a simulated attack on Dublin Castle. MacNeill's public cancellation of the Easter manoeuvres had satisfied the officials that the latest shadow *coup* was now off. The population as a whole, of course, was equally surprised when they returned to Dublin from their various outings to discover the rebels in occupation of public buildings. 'Neither in England nor in Ireland had the public an inkling of what was brewing,' as Tim Healy later remarked. Since the rebel orders had been issued only to key officers most of the Volunteers were themselves surprised.

The strategy of the rebellion was the work of Joseph Plunkett, a consumptive who actually rose from his hospital bed to take part. The centre of the city was to be sealed off and held until the brigades of Volunteers arrived from the country. The plan was only partially in operation on Easter Monday because not enough men turned out. Apart from a couple of local skirmishes, the Volunteers failed to rise in the provinces. The Dublin brigades, cut off and besieged in the buildings they had occupied, merely waited to be attacked. Nowhere did any members of the civilian population join the insurgents. The overwhelming majority, indeed, were unmistakably horrified by the action which the Volunteers had taken.

The first violence occurred on Monday morning, when twenty Volunteers turned up at the gate of Dublin Castle and demanded to be let in. The unarmed policeman on duty refused admission – the Castle was closed for the holiday – and was shot dead. The Volunteers ran off without further engagement. The General Post Office in Sackville Street (now O'Connell Street) became the headquarters of the military council led by Pearse and Connolly. It was from here that Pearse read out the Proclamation of the Republic to an astonished gathering of Dublin citizens, some of whom made derisory noises. It all seemed a bit unreal. Printed copies of the Proclamation were to be posted up throughout the city, but Pearse discovered that the military council had forgotten to buy any glue. The first looting therefore occurred when a packet of flour was seized from a grocer's shop to make into adhesive paste. Seán T. Ó Ceallaigh (O'Kelly), later a President of the Republic, then trundled a little cart around the streets with the notices, and the new state was in existence. The Provisional Government of the Republic, with Pearse as its first President, had been named by a secret meeting of the I.R.B. The seven members of the military council signed the Proclamation.

At St Stephen's Green the Citizen Army dug trenches across the superb lawns and built barricades. Countess

Markievicz, wearing a green uniform which she had made for herself, with a leather belt, gun-holster, and kinky boots, was second-in-command of the forces in occupation. There were twenty more armed ladies in the Square and a number of armed boys. A man who tried to get his lorry out of the barricades was shot to death by the rebels. The crowd which had gathered exchanged their curiosity of the insurgents for heated anger. The Dublin Veterans' Corps, a group of unarmed old men, many of whom were Fellows of Trinity College, were returning that evening from a day's marching in the country when they were shot down by rebel soldiers from de Valera's garrison at Boland's Bakery. Five veterans were killed and forty-six wounded. A party of Lancers, carrying swords but not firearms, were escorting some wagons to Phoenix Park when they entered Sackville Street unaware of the rebels in the G.P.O. The rebels, however, opened fire and killed four Lancers and one of their horses. The spectators supported the British soldiers, the women, especially, infuriated with the rebels for shooting at the horses. These unprovoked killings earned Pearse and his followers the bitter hatred of the population.

Nobody knew exactly who the rebels were. Pearse was a mysterious figure to most Irishmen. Mistakenly, the public referred to his followers as 'Sinn Féiners', and it was this misidentification which accounted for much of the popular acclaim which Sinn Féin in fact acquired in the reaction which later succeeded the executions of the leaders of the Rising.

During Easter week, the public had nothing but scorn for the rebels. Redmond later spoke of the general feeling of 'detestation and horror' which was then prevalent. British troops entering the city to put down the Rising were surprised to find themselves being cheered by the people of Dublin. Women brought food to the soldiers in action against the rebels. Discomfort is always a stimulus to irritation, and the public had to put up with a lot of it. Dublin was cut off for the whole week; little news came in or out, and there were wild rumours of German landings which added to the universal disquiet. Food ran out, pets were killed and eaten. The police disappeared from the streets: several had already been shot by snipers, and as the Dublin metropolitan police were an unarmed force the government could hardly leave them to be picked off. And then there was the looting. Hundreds of people emerged from the slums to ransack the fashionable stores in Sackville Street and surrounding areas. Drunkenness followed the looting of public houses. The Easter Rebellion was all idealism for the amateur politicians who conceived it: for the public it meant squalor and hardship. Nearly a third of Dublin's population needed public relief by the end of the week. Property to the value of £2½ millions was destroyed.

On Tuesday the first troop reinforcements arrived from England, and on Wednesday a gunboat nosed up the Liffey and opened fire on Sackville Street, setting fire to the G.P.O. and other buildings. Connolly had assured the military council that a capitalist government would never destroy capitalist property. He was wrong. One of the most beautiful streets in Europe was devastasted; 103 British soldiers, and 450 rebels and civilians were killed. As not all the Volunteers wore uniforms a number of civilians who got in the line of fire were shot down by guns from both sides. One of the most lamentable losses of the week was Sheehy-Skeffington, an eccentric Dublin savant who, with two journalists, was shot by a British officer later found to be insane.

On Saturday Pearse signed an unconditional surrender, and the rebellion came to an end. Conditions in the G.P.O. were by then frightful. Pearse mused dreamily among the debris. Connolly had been wounded. Now from their strongholds the rebels came out to surrender their arms. De Valera spoke ruefully to the people who stood at the doors of their houses to see the prisoners go by: 'If only you would have come out with knives and forks.' They came out, instead, with abuse.

General Sir John Maxwell had been ordered to bring the rebels to justice, a task which he performed with expeditious efficiency. Fourteen leaders of the Rising were shot, including the seven signatories of the Proclamation of the Republic. Pearse had achieved his ambition of sacrificing himself for his country. De Valera's ambitions were less extreme: his capital sentence was commuted to life imprisonment, in part because of his American citizenship. Seventy-five others sentenced to death were also given prison terms instead. The execution of the leaders, which elicited such a revulsion of opinion in Ireland, has often been taken as an indication of the ferocity of the government. In fact it is difficult to see what else could have happened. The country was at war and appeared to have been literally stabbed in the back. The rebels had clearly appealed to Germany, as Redmond pointed out in his press statement of 3 May condemning the Rising. Casement did not deny his activities in Germany. Pearse's Proclamation had referred to the 'gallant Allies in Europe'. In the prevailing conditions, indeed, Maxwell might even be represented as having shown considerable restraint. The government, anxious to bring the U.S.A. into the war, was trying not to offend the Irish-American political groups. In the event the rebels got off rather lightly: the 2,000 detained at Frongoch in Wales were released before the end of the year, and de Valera in the following June. But terrible damage had been done by the executions. The reputations of the dead revolutionaries were transformed overnight – because they were Irishmen who had self-confessedly died for Ireland, an appeal which never failed. Masses were offered for them in almost every Catholic church. Processions held in their honour turned easily into political rallies which the more extreme converted to their own ends. 'You are letting loose a river of blood,' Dillon wrote to Asquith when the executions were taking place in May, 'and make no mistake about it, between two races who, after three hundred years of hatred and strife, we had nearly succeeded in bringing together.' Pearse's blood sacrifice had turned out to be a fair calculation after all.

In June Lloyd George attempted to conciliate Ireland by offering immediate Home Rule, but the situation had not changed since the start of the war, and the internal degree of compromise required proved too much for the Irish politicians. Ulster was to be excluded from the settlement until the end of the war. As no undertaking could be given by the government that the exclusion would be only a temporary one, however, Redmond withdrew from the arrangement. Southern politicians were anyway suspicious of the wartime cabinet because it contained Carson as Attorney-General. In a last hope of settlement the government arranged a Convention of all Irish parties to deliberate upon a constitutional device agreeable to everyone. The Home Rule party, representatives of local government, Ulster and Southern Unionists, Catholic and Protestant bishops, labour representatives and businessmen, met together from July 1917 to April 1918. Their efforts were in vain.

Sinn Féin, who refused to attend the Convention, were by this time reaping a harvest which they had not sown. Their intervention at by-elections was not uniformly successful – they won several seats from the Redmondites in 1917, failed to win some in the first half of 1918, and then began to pick up again as the general election drew closer. But they were clearly a formidable challenge. The political situation, in fact, was extremely fluid, and the later transcendence of Sinn Féin in the south of the country owed a great deal to the secret activities of the I.R.B. Since the urban middle classes tended to rally to Sinn Féin as the best alternative to the old Home Rule party – it was, at least as promoted by Griffith, a constitutional party – the labour tradition, drawn into nationalism by Connolly, found itself increasingly isolated. Sinn Féin was gradually losing its economic policy as bourgeois shopkeepers and clerks filled its local organization. Nor were the I.R.B. men who pulled the strings of the Sinn Féin revival interested in social conditions.

In October 1917, Sinn Féin adopted a more militant constitution. The party now aimed at 'an independent Irish Republic', and when this was in existence the public would be given the opportunity of choosing the form of government. This prejudicial mechanism incorporated both the Republicans and the Sinn Féin Dual Monarchists. Griffith himself stood down in the election for the presidency of the party, and de Valera, who was also the head of the Volunteers, took over. The party was being manoeuvred towards the frontiers of more extreme nationalism. By 1919 the conversion was complete. The Sinn Féin convention of May in that year was packed with I.R.B. members and Volunteer officers; the elections of the representatives were so rigged that a large number of them did not know the areas they represented until they were told on arrival in Dublin. The Volunteers were also, by this time, controlled by the I.R.B.

The two men principally responsible for the capture of the political movement in Ireland by the small minority of Republican extremists were de Valera and Collins. Eamon de Valera was an austere theoretician; 'tall, spectacled, schoolmasterly, of Jewish cast', as Healy described him. St John Gogarty said he was like 'something uncoiled from the Book of Kells'. As the only military commandant to survive the Easter Rising he enjoyed immense prestige. De Valera was born in New York City in 1882, the son of a Spanish father and an Irish immigrant mother. In 1885, after the death of his father, he was moved to Ireland and brought up by relatives among the Catholic peasantry of Co. Limerick. Until the age of fourteen he went to the local national school at Bruree, and then, for a brief period, he was educated by the Christian Brothers. At sixteen he passed on to Blackrock College near Dublin with a government scholarship, and subsequently became an instructor in a Ladies' College for training teachers. Attracted to the current vogue for Irish literature, he joined the Gaelic League and married his Irish teacher. Family life at Donnybrook in the Dublin suburbs was thereafter interrupted only by his activities in the Volunteers. He joined the I.R.B. in 1914. In 1916 he secretly believed that the Rising ought to have been called off, but also believed, with puritanical conviction, that his first duty was to obey orders. De Valera was at this time a typical intellectual revolutionary. He insisted on correct attitudes, correct tactics.

Michael Collins, on the contrary, was certainly not an intellectual. He was born in 1890 at Clonakilty, Co. Cork, and after a national school education emigrated to England to become a postal clerk. In 1916 he returned to Dublin and was in the G.P.O. during the Rising. He was imprisoned for six months at Frongoch and then returned once more to Ireland where his revolutionary interests left no time for any sort of work. He was a member of the Supreme Council of the I.R.B. Collins was a man of violent impulse who liked nothing so much as to tumble his colleagues on the floor and to bite their ears in playful affection. He had no political ideas, seeking only the independence of Ireland. When asked about the future of his country he once replied that he looked to 'the sort of life I was brought up in'. He was a simple man of common sense, ruthless in the achievement of his ends. His emotional instability did not deter the loyalty of others, and from 1918 he was accompanied everywhere by Joe

O'Reilly, a lad whom Frank O'Connor described as 'slim, delicate, sensitive, had the stuff of the medieval page in him'. He was also 'courier, clerk, messenger-boy, nurse, slave' to Collins.

The government did not interfere with Sinn Féin, despite its new Republican constitution, until April 1918. The Volunteers continued to drill openly: Sinn Féin clubs, under the careful control of local I.R.B. men, were established throughout the country. It was the anti-conscription crisis of April 1918 which revealed the full extent of national political unrest. Ireland had been excluded from the general introduction of conscription in 1916, but within two years voluntary recruitment proved insufficient to meet the demands of the war effort, and the government therefore proposed legislation, early in 1918, to extend compulsory military service to Ireland. In Ireland, this prompted national indignation so intense as to give temporary unity to the various parties and factions. The Parliamentary party, led since Redmond's death in March by John Dillon, came out decisively against conscription – so did the trade unions, who called a one-day national strike; Sinn Féin, who called the government by disagreeable names; and local government bodies, who sent deputations to Dublin. A national conference at the Mansion House condemned the new legislation. The Catholic hierarchy, meeting at Maynooth under Cardinal Logue, declared against 'an oppressive and inhuman law which the Irish have a right to resist by every means that are consonant with the laws of God'. De Valera, in fact, had gone up to Maynooth to present the case in a correct perspective. His arrival, as one bishop said, was 'like the descent of the Holy Ghost upon them'. The government passed its law but decided to leave it unenforced.

Sinn Féin, however, was suppressed. The occasion was provided by the 'German Plot'. In April the commander of what was still remaining of Casement's mini-brigade in Germany, a man called Joseph Dowling, was landed in Galway and captured. The government rushed to the conclusion that Sinn Féin was plotting a second Rising, and crammed Griffith, de Valera, Joseph Plunkett, Countess Markievicz, Maud Gonne, Darrell Figgis – seventy persons in all—into goal. There was no real evidence of a conspiracy, and the detention of the Sinn Féin leadership was not especially good publicity in the months preceding the general election of 1918. Those who escaped arrest were not inactive either. Michael Collins, Cathal Brugha (Charles Burgess) – a maker of ecclesiastical candles – and Harry Boland occupied themselves by going through the list of Sinn Féin candidates and eliminating all the moderates. National self-consciousness had been heightened in the previous September when Thomas Ashe, who had been imprisoned for sedition, died while on a hunger-strike in Mountjoy gaol. Two hundred Roman Catholic priests walked in his funeral procession. The Roman Catholic Archbishop of Dublin followed in a carriage.

In December 1918 the general election confirmed the trend. The anti-conscription movement had revived the fortunes of Sinn Féin at a time when they would otherwise have wilted into extinction. There was, during the polling, a generous measure of intimidation; dead men voted for Sinn Féin candidates, moderates were hustled from meetings. The Home Rule party, as a result, was almost wiped from the psephological map: only six were returned. There were also twenty-six Unionists. Of the seventy-three Sinn Féiners elected, all but three were Catholics. Thirty-four of them were in gaol. Dillon's reward for his long service to Ireland was to be ousted from the representation of East Mayo by de Valera. Sinn Féin had almost entirely superseded the Home Rulers as the national political party. But their victory was not quite so overwhelming as it looked at first sight. Only forty-seven per cent of the popular vote had gone to Sinn Féin, and since a lot even of that represented an explosion of protest-voting, and since few of those who actually voted Sinn Féin intended to alter the main lines of the old Home Rule policy, the result cannot be taken as a national mandate for republicanism. Father Flanagan, a member of the Sinn Féin executive who had been suspended by his bishop for electioneering, was quite frank about it. 'The people have voted Sinn Féin,' he said. 'What we have to do now is to explain to them what Sinn Féin is.'

The successful Sinn Féin candidates declined to take their seats at Westminster and assembled instead on 21 January 1919 at the Mansion House in Dublin as the first Dáil. It was an unusual gathering. As a result of the detentions, only twenty-seven members turned up. Cathal Brugha became acting Priomh-Aire (first minister) or 'president'. The Dáil endorsed the Republic declared in 1916, and adopted a 'democratic programme' intended to signify their prepared-ness to formulate a social policy. In fact the document, which vaguely refrained from mentioning any actual reforms, was passed unanimously after a brief debate in a house denuded of all the party talent. Social revolution was shelved in half an hour.

Collins and Boland, meanwhile, were planning to spring de Valera from Lincoln gaol. An impression of his cell key was made in the wax of an altar candle. Two copies enclosed within two cakes sent into the gaol turned out to be the wrong shape, and a third broke in the lock; but in February 1919 de Valera just managed his escape. The rest of the detainees were anyway released within four weeks.

Back in Dublin, during April, de Valera assumed the presidency of the Dáil at the head of a cabinet which included Griffith as Minister for Home Affairs, Collins for Finance, Brugha for Defence, Cosgrave for Local Government,

MacNeill for Industry, and Countess Markievicz, the first woman M.P. in Britain, as Minister of Labour. Most of these departments of government were without real existence; they were a propagandist front to suggest to the world, as well as to the Irish people, that the new national leaders were seriously in business as a government. The Dáil Loan organized by Collins, and the military departments, were real departments, however. The Volunteers, now notionally under Dáil direction, became the Army of the Republic.

In September 1919 the Viceroy, Lord French – himself a convinced Home Ruler of the traditional sort – declared the Dáil an illegal assembly. By then attacks on the police and the outbreak of politically inspired outrages were already obliging the government to recognize the disruptive potential of the Sinn Féin parliament. The Dáil went underground, and the cabinet, seeking to avoid total elimination by a chance arrest, never met together. It was, indeed, the selective consultation with individual ministers which enabled the president to exercise a direction over the government which most administrations would have found intolerable. The ministers took to wearing disguises, some of which were detectable at a glance: Harry Boland, for example, forgot to have glass fitted into his false spectacles.

The seizure of political initiative by the I.R.B., working through front organizations, had finally cut labour and trade union interests out of the proposed new Ireland. The extremist leaders espoused – where they espoused social concepts at all – a vision of a lower-middle-class society. Labour took no part in the first Dáil, and failed to contest the elections of 1921 to avoid splitting the Sinn Féin vote. In throwing in his lot with the Republicans in 1916, Connolly had bequeathed a divided legacy of nationalism and socialism, of which the former proved itself the stronger partner. Union membership began to decline; between 1920 and 1921 membership of the Transport and General Workers' Union was reduced by half. Many Irish workers continued to belong to British amalgamated unions. In 1923 Larkin returned from America, but he was quite unable to reassert his old leadership: socialism was being drained off from the labour movement. In the 1922 elections, seventeen Labour members were returned to the Dáil representing pro-Treaty trade unions, but they sided with the middle-class objectives of the nationalists.

The socialists had, however, staged an interesting finale. Extremism of many tinctures found a place in post-war Ireland, and it was there that the only soviets set up in the British Isles had their brief existence. In April 1919, British troops were called in to close off the centre of Limerick during a state of emergency proclaimed after the shooting of a policeman by the Irish Volunteers. The Limerick Labour Council, representing thirty-five local trade unions, took over the city, declared a strike, and announced itself as a soviet. A small company of Bolshevist sympathizers was attempting to reproduce the example of Russia on the banks of the Shannon. The strike committee appointed sub-committees of propaganda, finance, food, and police. A daily workers' paper was turned out on requisitioned presses, currency notes were uttered, private cars abolished, and shops allowed to trade only at prices fixed by the Food Committee. No one was allowed into the city without a permit from the soviet authorities. The experiment had some publicity because Limerick happened to be full of journalists awaiting the arrival of Major Woods, who was attempting an Atlantic flight. Sir Stephen Quinn had to obtain the permission of the soviet to get fuel for the aircraft. After two weeks, however, the bourgeois shopkeepers had had enough, and at their request the troops moved in and occupied the city. In May of the following year workers at Bruree and Knocklong, Co. Limerick, and at Arigna, Co. Leitrim, set up their own soviets in factories, mills, and mines. These were autonomous local spasms of enthusiasm, without direction from trade unionists either in Dublin or abroad. Their ephemeral existence was a bizarre symptom of the disorganization of Irish life caused by the collapse of the Home Rule constitutionalists.

The Republicans were no less disorganized. Despite frantic efforts to present a united front there were frequent conflicts and personal animosities. The location of sovereignty in the new government was unclear, for a start. The I.R.B. pledged loyalty to its own Supreme Council as the republican government of Ireland: by its own constitution the I.R.B. head was also President of the Republic. Yet the Dáil had its own president, and the relationship between the two offices was never defined.

The Volunteers, similarly, never quite found out their real status as the Army of the Republic. Were they, indeed, controlled by the I.R.B. or by the Dáil Ministry of Defence? Even after August 1920, when the Volunteers took an oath of loyalty to the Dáil, they still appear to have remained an autonomous body. Sometimes these practical difficulties were bridged by personalities, for quite a number of the new political leaders were members of the I.R.B. or the Volunteers as well as of the Dáil. But these personal links proved disastrously useless when the politicians at the top fell out, as happened so often before the Treaty, and with monumentally frightful effects in 1922 when the country was sliced open by civil war.

The ambiguity of leadership also allowed a larger measure of local direction than was judicious in the guerrilla warfare against the police and the troops between 1919 and 1921. The politicians were unrestrained in their rivalries. Collins sought to undermine the influence of the moderates by attacking Griffith. Griffith refused to allow Erskine Childers the right to be heard in the Dáil, denounced him as a British agent, and accused him of mental derangement. Childers, in fact, had been an intelligence officer with the Royal Flying Corps during the war. Brugha and Austin Stack scarcely contained their loathing for Collins, in which sensation they received the distant sympathy of de Valera. It was, therefore, hardly surprising that the rancorous cabinet meetings should finally have led to the ambiguities which encompassed the disruption over the Treaty in 1921.

These disagreeable political realities, however, formed a mere superstructural shell beneath which, in the streets of the cities and in the fields of the countryside, the extremists were bringing the ordinary conduct of society and government to a halt. Between 1919 and 1921 small bands of Volunteers engaged the police and the forces of the Crown in a lamentable series of bloody incidents known as the 'Anglo-Irish War'. The expression is not particularly appropriate. The conflict approximated much more accurately to a civil war, for the antagonists on both sides were usually Irishmen. It was essentially a confrontation between a majority of men who were traditionally Home Rulers or southern Unionists, and a minority of Republicans. The officials of central and local government were nearly all Irishmen; so were most of the army officers and most policemen – until reinforced in 1920. The Republicans were nearly all Irish; the men who fought in the guerrilla bands were typically drawn from the artisan classes of the towns and from the rural small-farmers. A rather high proportion were very young men, a surplus of whom had accumulated in Ireland during the war years, when emigration to America had abruptly ceased. Many of these men were unemployed; some used employment merely as cover for the more serious undertaking of revolution. Few were encumbered with family responsibilities. They were ruthless in the prosecution of a cause which must, in many cases, have received no political definition beyond the single pursuit of national independence. Their idealism was no less uncompromising than that of the men of 1916, but they were more professional and less sentimental than their predecessors in the business of killing people for political purposes. There were atrocities in the war as a result. Appalling brutalities occurred on both sides; but who is able, as George Orwell remarked of the Spanish Civil War in *Homage to Catalonia*, to apportion the blame or to assess the accuracy of atrocity stories which seep through the propaganda of any conflict?

The Volunteers first disturbed the fragile peace by attacking the Royal Irish Constabulary in the hope of capturing arms and ammunition. In the process they built up, during 1919, a machinery of terror whose effectiveness was easily assessed by the reluctance of the public to come forward and testify against them. It is a later gloss to suppose the public to have been naturally friendly to the rebels because they were Irishmen. In the first year of the terror campaign the public were immeasurably hostile; in the second, apathetic and reluctant to stand between the opposing guns. The Republicans certainly entertained some drastic tactics. Liam Lynch and Cathal Brugha proposed the bombing and machine-gunning of civilian crowds in theatres and cinemas as a way of assisting the polarization of opinion. The Dáil cabinet rejected the scheme as impractical; but Brugha's campaign for wrecking signal boxes in England in order to derail trains was carried out, with horrible results. Collins, whose original proposal to steal the Stone of Destiny from Westminster Abbey had somehow seemed inadequate, instead produced a plan to assassinate the British cabinet in the streets of London. It was shelved. He also hoped to kidnap President Woodrow Wilson, who was in London during 1919, in order to force him to give ear to Ireland's case. This, too, failed to happen, and Collins resorted to action nearer home: he ordered the murder of most of the police detectives in Dublin, and when, by 1920, most of them had been shot, he extended his interests to the dispatch of military intelligence officers.

The war itself was nominally conducted under orders from the central headquarters of the Volunteers and the I.R.B., but local direction usually predominated. The shootings and ambushes did not originate with the Dáil government. The Dáil, in fact, at no time ever declared a formal state of war with England. The shootings began spontaneously, with Volunteers seeking arms or eliminating 'spies'. A lot of private hatreds, no doubt, were settled on the side. The Dáil expressed no public view of the conflict, but its president did so, although it is uncertain whether he spoke in a private or an official capacity. De Valera went off to America in May 1919, just after the start of the shootings, and did not return to Ireland until the end of December 1920. But in the month preceding his departure he made a violent attack on the police during a Dáil debate, and this had everywhere been interpreted as encouragement to the gunmen. On his return he accepted personal responsibility for the hostilities, which had, of course, considerably increased during the nineteen months of his absence.

The shooting began on 21 January 1919 – the day on which the Dáil held the first meeting – when the 3rd Tipperary Brigade of the Volunteers under Seán Treacy ambushed a consignment of explosives on its way to a quarry at Soloheadbeg. Two policemen were killed. There was an outcry against the extremists, but Brugha, as Chief-of-Staff and acting president of the Dáil, approved of their action. By the summer the Republicans appeared to have become addicted to the shooting of policemen – over twenty were killed during the year. An attempt to assassinate the Viceroy in December failed: the Volunteers threw their bombs into the wrong car and Lord French escaped. Instead, they wrecked the presses of the *Irish Independent*, a paper which had referred to those involved in the outrage as 'assassins' rather than heroes. Things were clearly getting out of hand.

In 1920 the bloodletting continued: 176 policemen were killed and fifty-four soldiers; forty-three Volunteers and Irish civilians died. It was a year of macabre brutality, in which senseless killing vied with calculated assassination – as in March, when an elderly Dublin magistrate called Alan Bell was dragged from a tram in daylight and shot in the street by a party from Collins's 'squad'. The people were by then so terrorized that none of the passengers in the tram did anything to prevent the crime. The most notorious excesses of the year occurred on Sunday, 21 November, when fourteen army officers whose elimination had been ordered by Collins were taken from their beds and shot to death in front of their families. Later in that day troops and police combing a football crowd at Croke Park in Dublin were shot at and returned fire. In the panic twelve people were killed. When the ground was cleared many revolvers were picked up by the police – dropped by Republican extremists seeking to evade arrest. Yet even the carnage of 'Bloody Sunday' could be exceeded, and in the same month Tom Barry's No. 3 Cork Brigade of the Volunteers ambushed a party of auxiliary police at Macroom, killed eighteen of them, and, according to the official report, mutilated their bodies with axes.

In the first half of 1921 – until the Truce – the outrages continued with undiminished ferocity. In the first four months, seventy-three 'informers' were shot and their placarded bodies left in the streets. The I.R.B. headquarters drew up a distinguished execution list, including Lloyd George and Winston Churchill. Most of the action, however, occurred as a result of local initiative – as in May, when Republican gunmen shot down four Unionists at a tennis party near Lough Cutra, Co. Galway. Age and innocence were not barriers to assassination: Sir Arthur Vicars, the old and retired Ulster King-at-Arms, was riddled with bullets after being dragged from his house, which was then burned down as a warning to 'British' residents in Ireland. A Mrs Lindsay, who was seventy, was captured by the Volunteers after she had ventured to tell the police that she had seen some men preparing an ambush. After failing in an attempt to use her as a hostage, the Volunteers shot her to death. In May 1921, the Dáil cabinet authorized the destruction of the Customs House in Dublin. Government records were accordingly destroyed, and the most beautiful building in Ireland was gutted. Official reprisals, on a set tariff, were drawn up by the Volunteer headquarters. Local brigades added unofficial refinements of their own. The graceful country houses of the Irish countryside, which were often the homes of Unionists, were burned down in increasing numbers. Farms, creameries, industrial installations, public utilities, and police barracks were all destroyed whenever it was possible. The Easter of 1920 had been celebrated by burning a hundred tax offices throughout the country. The loss to Ireland from all this destruction was immense.

During most of this time the press denounced the extremists as criminals guilty of murder. The public rather agreed. When, for example, a government security official called Fergus Malloy was shot to death in a Dublin street in March 1920, the crowd turned on the Republican assassins – who were able to get away only by threatening the people with their guns. It was unfortunate that the Catholic Church felt unable to give any sort of lead. Several individual bishops pronounced against the murder of policemen and soldiers. The hierarchy as a corporate body declined either to recognize the Republic or to condemn the hostilities.

Many of the Republicans' excesses, of course, were in response to action taken by the police and troops. Attack was then met with attack; reprisal with counter-reprisal, in a mounting spiral. But it is important to notice that the unprovoked shootings of policemen began in January 1919, and that it was not until September that the government first took systematic action against the Volunteers. Too many policemen had by then been killed to allow the deterioration of order to continue. Exceptional measures were required, and the public demanded them. In August 1920, the Restoration of Order in Ireland Act gave special powers to the military authorities. The members of the Dáil and the I.R.B., of course, had an obvious propagandist interest in representing police or army action in the most barbarous terms which could accommodate belief. De Valera, prior to his departure from New York in December 1920, issued a statement from the Waldorf-Astoria in which the British government was accused of atrocities 'worse than those of the Bashi-Bazouks'. The various evidences of this are now decorated with the accretions of fifty years of oral tradition, and since it has become modish to equate any political expedients considered disagreeable with those of the Third Reich in Germany, Ireland has not been ignored. Sean O'Callaghan, for example, in his personal history of the I.R.A. (*The Easter Lily*, 1956), declares quite unreservedly that 'Britain's secret service in Ireland at the time was similar to the Gestapo;' and of the activities of the police, he writes that 'they read today like a catalogue of the worst excesses committed by the Nazis.' In September 1920, a party of 'Black and Tan' policemen, infuriated by the murder of a local police inspector by the Volunteers, made an unauthorized and lamentable foray into the small industrial town of Balbriggan, Co. Dublin. Some twenty-five houses were gutted, and a factory – owned by an English company – was burned down. Two men, thought to be Volunteer leaders, were killed during the rioting. A disgraceful episode. Mr O'Callaghan, however, has imagined that the sack of

Balbriggan 'very closely parallels the German destruction of Lidice'.

Throughout the period of the hostilities the forces of the Crown in fact demonstrated considerable restraint. Their opponents wore civilian clothes and this made it much easier for misidentification to result in civilian deaths. The Volunteers also used explosive dum-dum bullets of the type forbidden by international convention, and this was, to say the least, resented by the soldiers and the police. Inability to identify the enemy by uniform, and the risk of death at any moment from a sniper's bullet, made the Crown forces more liable to impulsive over-reaction than they would have been in a conventional operation. Unofficial reprisals were frequent, even though these were consistently condemned by the government. They usually took the form of destroying the property of those suspected of having caused the death of a soldier or policeman. Instances of killing as a reprisal are extremely rare, and the authenticity of those recorded are nearly all open to question.

It was, nevertheless, the unofficial reprisals which attracted the attention of British liberals and American Irishmen, who, suspecting the government of conniving at atrocity, as liberals always tend to do, let off an explosion of protest. Asquith and the independent Liberals in the Commons attacked the use of force in Ireland during 1920. The Labour party, unsuccessful in persuading Lloyd George to set up a parliamentary inquiry, sent a committee of their own to Ireland under Arthur Henderson. They produced a report which condemned everything. An American Commission, after being led around the country by Republican couriers on a carefully selected route, employed thousands of words against the British government. The Archbishop of Canterbury, Cosmo Gordon Lang, condemned both the Republican and the Crown forces in a series of speeches in the House of Lords. At least the troops were not arraigned for sexual misconduct. Throughout the conflict no accusations of that sort were sustained.

The number of troops in action was never sufficient to be effective against an enemy which could run to earth in the countryside or hide in a crowded street. At its greatest capacity, in 1921, the army had 35,000 men in Ireland. There were also 10,000 policemen throughout the country, most of them armed. By the middle of 1920, however, intimidation and fear had prompted the resignations of over 500 constables, and this, together with a falling-off in recruitment, had obliged the government to allow non-Irishmen to enter the R.I.C. as special constables for the first time.

In March 1920, the Specials arrived. They were popularly known as 'Black and Tans', a literal description of their temporary uniforms. Though often supposed, as a legacy of Republican propaganda, to have been recruited variously from English slums, English dosshouses, and English prisons, the Specials were mostly ex-servicemen not yet settled in employment after the demobilization of the wartime army. Recruitment was rapid owing to the emergency in Ireland, but no candidates were admitted who did not pass the ordinary R.I.C. prescribed tests of intelligence and fitness. In July, a force of officer-cadets, the Auxiliaries, was also recruited from England. These men were mostly ex-army officers.

To some extent, despite these reinforcements, there was a disengagement in many parts of the countryside. Early in 1920, after numerous attacks on the police, 300 barracks were evacuated, and the R.I.C. thereafter concentrated in key towns. Large areas of the countryside, as a result, were taken over by the I.R.B. and officials of the Dáil government. Republican courts and Republican police superseded the legal administration of justice in those places. The population was obliged to make use of them. From their strongholds in the rural areas the Republican forces developed a new technique of resistance:

flying-columns scouted the countryside ambushing police and military patrols.

The conflict still remained rather sporadic, and for most of the population normal life was uninterrupted. The losses were not especially heavy on either side. Throughout the whole period of the 'Anglo-Irish War' the government executed twenty-four Republicans, in each case for murder. In the Civil War which followed the British withdrawal from Ireland, by comparison, seventy-seven Republicans were executed by the new Free State government. Much larger numbers, however, were killed in action on both sides. The restraint of the Crown forces sometimes broke down. It was in September 1919 that government troops were first involved in a reprisal against the Republicans. Liam Lynch, a young man of twenty-five who worked in an ironmonger's shop, was organizer of the Volunteers at Fermoy, Co. Cork. On Sunday 7 September a group of his men shot down a party of soldiers who had come into Fermoy to attend church; one was killed and four wounded. When the local coroner's jury refused to return a verdict of murder, troops from the Fermoy barracks wrecked the houses of the jurymen. From this point unofficial reprisals were not infrequent. In Belfast, too, private enterprise justice was resorted to by infuriated Unionists from the slums. In September 1920, the murder of a police inspector by Collins's agents led to sectarian rioting in which there were nearly fifty Catholic and Protestant casualties. In the same month the Lord Mayor of Cork, Thomas MacCurtain, was murdered by unidentified masked raiders. The crime, which was popularly attributed to the 'Black and Tans', did nothing to help the popularity of Crown forces.

Other events in the autumn of 1920 withdrew still more popular sympathy. Kevin Barry, a student of eighteen, was executed in September for his part in the murder of three soldiers in a Dublin street. He became 'the boy martyr of

Ireland'. Another symbol of resistance was Terence MacSwiney, MacCurtain's predecessor as Lord Mayor of Cork. His death from starvation in Brixton gaol in October – he had refused food as a gesture of defiance – also stirred the sympathy of the nation, although the Dáil was careful to issue a warning against hunger strikes in future. Finally, in December, special constables burned down the centre of Cork as a reprisal for the massacre of the eighteen auxiliaries at Macroom. Two members of the I.R.B. were killed in mysterious circumstances on the same night, and damage to the value of £3 millions was done to the city. A military inquiry was ordered, and private reprimands handed out.

The Imperial parliament had an obvious interest in restoring the rule of law. The Irish conflict was bad publicity for Britain at the European peace conference, even though Wilson had agreed with Lloyd George that Ireland was not to be included among the list of nations whose self-determination could be determined by the great powers. There can also be little doubt that a considerable majority of the Irish people would still have settled for Home Rule – as the large popular vote in favour of the Dominion Home Rule settlement in the 1923 elections was to indicate. The doctrinaire Republicans had won a measure of sympathy because they had stood up to Britain; but the public were, as was only to be expected, impatient of the conflict and anxious for the return of stability. The southern Unionists, unofficially led by Lord Midleton and Andrew Jameson, the whisky distiller, looked for security. It was not, therefore, absurd that Lloyd George should have attempted a settlement on traditional lines. Early in 1920 a new Home Rule Bill was introduced to parliament. It provided for two governments in Ireland, one at Belfast, the other in Dublin. They were to be linked in a federal 'Council of Ireland', which was intended to administer common services and provide a place of general debate on Irish questions.

The Act passed in December. The north accepted it, the Dáil voted an uncompromising rejection; and when, in May of the following year, a meeting of Craig and de Valera had failed to identify any common ground between north and south, the partition of Ireland became inevitable. The Act was put into effect, but the Council of Ireland was never set up. In the first general election held under its terms, in May 1921, a northern parliament, with a lower house of forty Unionists and twelve Nationalists and Republicans, came into existence unilaterally. King George V travelled to Belfast to open the new parliament in June.

It was in Belfast that the King made a conciliatory speech inspired by General Smuts. 'I appeal to all Irishmen to pause, to stretch out the hand of forbearance and conciliation, to forgive and forget.' It was a signal to the government to begin approaches for an independent settlement with the southern politicians. Lloyd George had already sent Lord Derby off to Ireland disguised as a travelling salesman and charged with the sampling of opinion. Instructions were now hawked about restraining any interference with the Dáil leaders, all of whom were wanted men. In June, when the police stripped the disguise from an arrested suspect only to discover, to their horror, that it was de Valera, a rapid and embarrassed release of the prisoner had to be arranged. In the same month the government invited de Valera to discussions in London.

A ceasefire was also proclaimed later in June. There was to be no surrender of arms by the insurgents, a provision which, unhappily, resulted in rather frequent violations of the Truce by local Republicans. At the end of the month, also, the southern parliament, called under the Act of 1920, assembled in Dublin. Since only fifteen of the sixty-four members of the upper house and only four members of the lower house turned up – the others being Sinn Féin representatives, obliged to boycott the new legislature – the parliament's brief existence terminated after a quarter of an hour. In July, de Valera crossed to London with a group of cabinet colleagues, leaving Collins behind in charge of the Dáil government. Lloyd George, stuck with the problem of finding some sort of proper yet legal designation for his Republican guest, decided to refer to him rather cumbrously as 'Chieftain of the vast majority of the Irish race'.

Lloyd George has gone down in Irish history as a sharp politician with a steady line in deviousness. He was certainly an acute negotiator. He was also the head of a coalition administration which had a Unionist majority, a consideration which makes all the more remarkable the extent to which he was prepared to compromise. There were elements in his career which made him peculiarly suitable – at least among British politicians – to handle the Irish question. He, too, was a Celt, and one who had made his reputation as a young radical by supporting Irish Home Rule and Boer nationalism. De Valera was evidently unmoved by these considerations, and the two leaders did not get on well personally. Lloyd George offered Home Rule with Dominion status to Ireland, but with partition by implication. The 'Chieftain of the vast majority of the Irish race' turned that down flat, an impulse subsequently endorsed by the Dáil. Lloyd George tried again. But an invitation to the Irish leaders to attend a second conference at Inverness had to be withdrawn after a paper dispute over the Dáil's claim to sovereignty. Instead, negotiations were arranged to begin in London early in October.

For reasons which are still unclear, de Valera decided to remain in Dublin, and it was Griffith and Collins who headed the team of plenipotentiaries which travelled to London. With them went Robert Barton, the Minister for Economic Affairs and a former British officer bristling with all the Republican zeal of the convert; Eamon Duggan, a legal expert and a member of the Truce Committee; and George Gavan Duffy, the Dáil envoy in Rome. Erskine Childers acted as secretary to the delegation. For the government there were the Prime Minister, Lord Birkenhead, Austen Chamberlain, Winston Churchill, Sir Laming Worthington Evans (Secretary for War), and Sir Hamar Greenwood (Chief Secretary for Ireland). Lionel Curtis and Thomas Jones were appointed secretaries.

The terms of reference, set by Lloyd George, required the negotiators to consider how best to reconcile Irish national aspirations with membership of the British Commonwealth. It was always clear that the government would never consent to an Irish Republic. The attitude of the Dáil cabinet to this limitation is difficult to assess. Clearly their negotiators were tactically concerned with urging a Republic, but were surely aware that something less would have to be accepted in the end. Lloyd George offered a radical version of Dominion Home Rule. De Valera had worked in solitary and intellectual isolation to compose, apparently without the knowledge of his cabinet, a device described as 'External Association'. Due to the usual incidence of faction fighting within the cabinet a good deal of ambiguity and misunderstanding surrounded the exact powers of the Irish delegation. On the eve of their departure for London, de Valera produced his 'Draft Treaty A', which outlined an independent Ireland, a Republic in all but formal designation, within the Commonwealth. Partition was to end: there was to be, instead, internal devolution, an all-Ireland parliament but with subordinate legislatures – one of which would be for north-east Ulster. No mention was made of the position of the Crown, but de Valera must have known that acceptance of the ultimate sovereignty of the Crown would be the price paid to get 'External Association'. At the London talks, the government rejected 'Draft Treaty A'.

Lloyd George presented his alternative on 1 December: the

'Articles of Agreement'. Ireland was to enjoy the same status as Canada and the other Dominions. The country was to be known as the 'Free State'. Ulster was to remain separate, with her own parliament, under the Government of Ireland Act, 1920. A Boundary Commission was to be appointed to determine the exact area of Ulster's jurisdiction. The north could, alternatively, opt to join the Free State. There were also provisions for the continued British use of certain naval installations in Ireland – the 'Treaty Ports' – and for the payment of land annuities. There was an oath of allegiance to 'the King as Head of State and of the Empire'.

Sir James Craig and the Ulster government were not parties to the London negotiations, and it was because of Lloyd George's undertaking to present them with a settlement by 5 December that an unnecessary urgency was forced upon the discussions. Birkenhead and Churchill encouraged the Irish delegates to suppose that a Boundary Commission would be likely to award areas of the six northern counties with large Catholic populations to the Free State, and that this, by ultimately reducing the control of the Ulster government to a small remainder, would render its survival impossible and solve the question of partition by default. The constitutional centre of the 'Articles', the offer of Dominion status, was very open-ended. It was just at this time that the Dominions were discussing their own status, and it was quite clear that the sovereignty of the Crown, expressed in the universal oath of allegiance, was likely to become something of a legal fiction. Even Lloyd George was unable to give a precise definition of Dominion status.

The Dáil cabinet, meeting on 3 December, required radical modifications of the new offer before it could be entertained. Again, however, confusion and disagreement surrounded the exact extent of the concessions they were prepared to grant. De Valera, Brugha, and Stack wanted to reject the Articles completely. They were in a minority. The delegates returned to London, and after successfully obtaining a few modifications – but not enough to fulfil the Dáil cabinet agreement – they signed the Articles in the early hours of 6 December 1921. None of the signatories had referred back to Dublin. Lloyd George had insisted that unless agreement was reached there would be an immediate resumption of coercion. Collins, who more than anyone on the Republican side knew how ill prepared the Volunteer brigades were to survive a sustained conflict, saw the need for a settlement as well.

De Valera, returned from reviewing the troops in the west, was just slipping into his robes as Chancellor of the National University, in order to preside at a Dante commemoration, when Duggan arrived from London with a copy of the Treaty. De Valera was livid. On the following day, 7 December, he called a cabinet with the intention of sacking the London delegates and repudiating the Treaty. In this he was restrained by his other colleagues. But when, on the next day, the delegation had returned and the Treaty had been considered by a full meeting of the cabinet, de Valera, Brugha, and Stack were outvoted by Griffith, Collins, Cosgrave, and Barton. The delegates, in fact, were lucky to have reached the cabinet table: extreme Republicans in the I.R.B. had wanted to arrest them on their return from London. De Valera, defeated in his own cabinet, issued a proclamation to the Irish people calling upon them to reject the Treaty. The British government, meanwhile, released all the Irishmen detained in prison.

The Dáil assembled to consider the Treaty on 14 December 1921 in University College. After the exclusion of the press, a lengthy debate revealed extremely sharp divisions. De Valera produced 'Document No. 2', drawn up by himself and Childers, and detailing the 'External Association' scheme. It was the first the ordinary members of the Dáil had heard of it. To many, however, the theoretical distinctions upon which the president insisted seemed too finely drawn, too remote from the realities of Ireland's position. Apart from the oath of allegiance, it did not matter in most practical questions whether the country was a Republic or a Free State: independence had been achieved. The question of partition was not particularly important in the debates – only nine of the 338 pages in the official report deal with it, and even de Valera's 'Document No. 2' had no reference to it. The cabinet members tore one another to pieces. Griffith disclosed an admission by de Valera, made during the earlier cabinet consideration of the Articles, that pure Republicanism was an unrealistic aim. De Valera, in reply, charged the signatories of the Treaty with treason. He retreated to uncompromising Republicanism.

After a recess for the Christmas holiday, the Dáil resumed its deliberations in January, and the Treaty was approved by sixty-four votes to fifty-seven. De Valera resigned as its president, and Griffith was elected in his place. The country as a whole was more substantially pro-Treaty than the Dáil. The Catholic Church was sympathetic, and fifteen bishops had already issued a statement supporting the Treaty. The I.R.B. Supreme Council, loyal to Collins as their head, approved it by a large majority – though this produced a split, and the virtual secession of the extreme Republicans led by Sean T. O'Kelly and Liam Lynch. The Irish press was overwhelmingly in favour of the Treaty. Yet an uneasy sense of impending disruption was settling upon the nation as the Republicans flapped their copies of the 1916 Proclamation. At the beginning of 1922 there were too many bodies claiming the allegiance of the Irish people. Collins presided over the Provisional government set up by the terms of the Treaty until the first Free State elections could be held. Griffith was still president of Dáil Éireann, which continued in separate existence, but which was not recognized by Britain or, after its endorsement of the Treaty, by the Republican extremists. The Army Executive under Rory O'Connor and Lynch established effective independence. The anti-Treaty wing of the I.R.B. looked to the continuation of the Irish Republic under de Valera. In Belfast the successful establishment of the parliament of northern Ireland symbolized the permanence of partition. Ireland was truly divided.

11. The Divided Nation

While the Irish politicians and army officers were breathlessly holding themselves back from the logical application of their divided opinions, the evacuation of British troops began, in January 1922. The Treaty was in operation. Dublin Castle was handed over to the Provisional government, and civil service chiefs, still scarcely able to believe what had happened, were introduced to their new ministers. Who were printing apprentices and post-office clerks were now heads of government; who had been unemployed now conducted affairs of state. Throughout the country the old order was rapidly recalled: the Royal Irish Constabulary was disbanded, and a new civic guard recruited in its place. The evacuation of military garrisons was accompanied, in some provincial areas, by unofficial Republican hostilities – columns of troops were fired upon as they marched towards the ports for departure. Beggars' Bush Barracks in Dublin, after its surrender to the Provisional government, became the headquarters of General Richard Mulcahy's national force, now known ambiguously as the 'Irish Republican Army' (I.R.A.). The new dawn was visible in every particular. 'The name plates on the streets were being changed into Irish, with the English of them underneath – otherwise how would folk know where they were going?' as Dominic Behan has written; '"Sraid Talbot

– Talbot Street", "Cul-de-Sac – Cul-de-Sac", Lord, isn't the Gaelic language wondrous beautiful? . . . Thank God the men of '16 had not given their lives in vain. Only one place had its old name: the Labour Exchange.'

Throughout 1922 the difficulties of a dichotomous government made the actual exercise of political authority as unclear to contemporaries as it has seemed to historians. Collins, as head of the Provisional government established by the Treaty, and Griffith, as president of the Dáil (itself the 'Parliament of Southern Ireland' elected under the Act of 1920), shared common cabinet ministers. Their task was formidable. The make-believe departments of the revolutionary government had suddenly to be regularized within the civil service inherited from Britain. A set of ministers who knew only a state of warfare tried to accommodate themselves to the routines of peacetime administration.

Before the new experiment had really begun, civil war broke out. The Republican deputies of the Dáil, consolidated by de Valera into a new political party (Cumann na Poblachta), chose to absent themselves rather than take the oath of allegiance to the Crown. This refusal to recognize the parliamentary institutions of the young Dominion withdrew some credit from its authority, at least as far as the anti-Treaty sections of society were concerned. It was a frightful start.

In February, Collins had set up a committee to draft a constitution for the Free State, with himself as chairman. In straining to reach some understanding with the Republicans, however, he compromised himself on several occasions by hinting that the new constitution would embody Republican institutions. Since the tentative devices in this direction which he sent to London for approval were clearly violations of the Treaty they were rejected. The final agreed version, published on the same day as the general election in June, was scarcely Republican in either tone or structure. The

Free State (Saorstat Éireann) was to have a Senate of thirty elected and thirty nominated members, the latter chosen by the Governor-General. Sovereignty was vested in the Crown, with all legislators and office-holders taking an oath of allegiance. The lower house of the Oireachtas (parliament), the Dáil, was to be elected by universal male and female suffrage on a system of proportional representation. English common law remained, and all unrepealed statute law. Appeals could be directed to the Privy Council in London. The Governor-General, empowered to summon and to dismiss the legislature and to appoint ministers, was the personal representative of the sovereign, with the right to veto legislation. These executive powers, of course, were not exercised by the Crown directly: as in England they were a convenient surviving description of a sovereignty which was popularly controlled. Republican propaganda against the Constitution tended to ignore the fact that the actual powers of the Crown were somewhat diminished since the seventeenth century. The Free State Constitution defined Ireland as 'a co-equal member of the British Commonwealth of Nations'.

The question of partition was unresolved. In January, Collins and Craig, representing the governments of southern and northern Ireland, had signed an agreement of mutual assistance which also involved a review of the Boundary question. They now intended to settle the matter between two representatives, rather than through the more cumbrous machinery of the Boundary Commission provided in the Treaty. The question was, therefore, theoretically removed from the separate consideration of the new constitution. In another overture to the Republicans, Collins had signed a pact with de Valera in May. This attempted to stabilize the existing divisions until order was guaranteed: a panel of candidates, proportionately balanced to preserve the political cleavage, was to be put before the voters at the June elections on the Treaty. If, as was expected, the parties were returned with the same numbers as in the old Dáil, a coalition ministry would be formed. On 16 June 1922, however, the elections went rather less favourably for the panel candidates than these calculations had allowed for, and nearly a quarter of them were defeated. Fifty-eight deputies supporting the Provisional government were elected, and thirty-four other deputies made up of Labour, the Farmers' party, independents, and Unionists – all supporting the Treaty and the Free State Constitution. Since the Republicans managed to return only thirty-six deputies the election heavily endorsed the Treaty policy. The idea of a coalition was dropped.

By then the Republicans had already begun to resort to violence. Some of the more extreme officers in the I.R.A. had refused to recognize the Treaty from the start. 'We have declared for an Irish Republic,' as Liam Lynch said, 'and will not live under any other law.' These were rather young men, unable to readjust to the less exciting prospects of compromise politics. 'They were,' as Frank O'Connor wrote, 'simply high-spirited, generous, adventurous boys, escaped from farms and classrooms.' Before long they had reduced the country to carnage and destruction. When the British troops had begun their evacuation in January, they had handed over the barracks, weapons, and installations to the most authoritative of the local I.R.A. commanders. It was a matter of chance whether these fell into the control of pro- or anti-Treaty forces: the British were naturally unable to discriminate. The Republican officers of the I.R.A., a large number of whom appear to have been generals, then consolidated their gains by seizing arms and barracks from troops loyal to the Provisional government. At the local level, therefore, and without any authority from Dublin headquarters, I.R.A. brigades and divisions were splitting into two opposed forces.

The Republicans were beyond restraint. In February they began a campaign of violence through most of the country. Guerrilla bands raided government posts in Cork and Tipperary. Limerick was occupied when the British left and held for a time before the troops of the provisional government battered it to submission. In Dublin, snipers discharged at the offices of the government in Merrion Square. The sores of conflict were becoming reinfected. The Unionists had been defeated; now Irishmen turned upon one another in the name of political purity. Some of the young Republicans, like Liam Mellows and Rory O'Connor, were frankly out to provoke the intervention of British forces in the belief that it would reunite the nation behind Republicanism. De Valera tendered moral support. 'If the Army [the I.R.A. Republicans] could save the nation from the calamities which are bound to follow the acceptance of these Articles of Agreement,' he told the world's press, 'I think it justifiable for it to use its strength to do so.'

In March 1922, the Republican wing of the I.R.A., led by Rory O'Connor, held a Convention in Dublin. It had been prohibited by the Dáil cabinet, but the government resisted the temptation to intervene – even when one of the delegations turned up in an armoured car. The Convention crackled with militancy. Some of the 200 delegates demanded a military dictatorship to re-establish the Republic; a motion to prevent the elections on the Treaty by the use of force was only narrowly defeated. The Convention did set up an Army Executive of sixteen officers, with Liam Lynch as Chief-of-Staff, and declared its independence of political control. Its forces, known to the government as 'Irregulars', but to its own members as the 'Irish Republican Army', were in action almost at once. The presses of the *Freeman's Journal* were smashed after the paper had given a ruthlessly accurate analysis of the ultimate objectives of the Convention. Rory O'Connor and Liam Mellows then occupied the Four Courts on the quays of the Liffey and held it, from 14 April, as a military headquarters. There were permanent sit-ins at other buildings in the capital. In a reckless pursuit of funds, Irregulars throughout the country raided post offices and branches of the Bank of Ireland. The precipitation of civil war was only prevented by the sustained restraint of Collins and the Provisional government. At Thurles, on 17 April, de Valera spelled out the prospects for the Republicans. 'They would have to wade through Irish blood, through the blood of the soldiers of the Irish Government, and through, perhaps, the blood of some members of the Government, in order to get Irish freedom.' Intellectuals always see the logic of a situation.

Ulster, meanwhile, was far from quiescent. Eight thousand armed members of the I.R.A. had crossed the border to exploit the permanent religious divisions of the Province – divisions which were, anyway, quite capable of independently producing loathsome disorder. In February, Catholics and Protestants rioted in the poorer districts of Belfast and several other towns; Catholic refugee families crossed into the south as the Republican infiltrators passed them going north. Collins and Craig met in London at the end of March and managed to draw up a peace declaration. Collins was in fact being carried along by events over which he appeared to exercise little direction. With Craig he agreed to stop the I.R.A. activity in the north; in the following month, arguing betrayal by the Ulster government, he was plotting with Liam Lynch to contrive a new Republican offensive against Ulster – an aspiration which also violated the Treaty. The north was not incapable of retaliation: the occupation of two border towns by the I.R.A. was expeditiously ended by British troops.

Ulster's eruptions were only capable of bringing the Free Staters and the Republicans into temporary accord, however. As the south moved towards the brink, through its own internal divisions, the violence in the north declined. The Republican subversives travelled south again, to lend their force to the collapse of order, and Ulster was left to its own perpetual feuding. On 23 June, General Sir Henry Wilson, military advisor to the Northern Ireland government and an extremely outspoken Unionist, who had commanded the British forces during the 'Anglo-Irish War', was assassinated on the steps of his London home by two I.R.A. gunmen. In Ireland the Republicans disclaimed responsibility, and it does in fact seem that Wilson's death was ordered by Collins before the Truce in 1921. That he had forgotten to cancel the order scarcely explains a shooting carried out a year later: Wilson was killed by extremists, acting no doubt without direction, in order to precipitate a confrontation. They were successful. The British government was anyway nervously afraid that a Republican *coup* was being prepared in Dublin. Lloyd George and Churchill warned the Irish people that British troops would reoccupy the country should the Treaty be violated; Collins was told that he must take some action to end the three months' occupation of the Four Courts by the Republicans. On 26 June, to make matters worse, the Republicans had captured the Assistant Chief-of-Staff of the government forces, General O'Connell, and were holding him in the Four Courts. The situation was not allowed to continue. On 27 June, Free State troops were ordered to surround the Courts, and guns from across the river fired shells through the superb dome of the building. This was the first government action, after months of provocation, against the Republicans. The Civil War had begun.

The fighting in Dublin uncannily reproduced the conditions of 1916. It was almost equally short-lived. After three days of bombardment, the Four Courts fell to the government, and a hundred prisoners, including O'Connor and Mellows, were taken. Before evacuating the building the Republicans blew it up. The Public Records of Ireland, comprising thousands of priceless medieval and other documents, were destroyed. Oscar Traynor, as Commander of the Dublin brigades of the Irregulars, set up Republican headquarters in a series of fashionable hotels in Sackville Street. To these buildings resorted a sort of shadow government – de Valera, Brugha, Stack, the Countess Markievicz, and Barton (who had repudiated his own signature on the Treaty). As the Free State forces moved in to flush the Republicans out, Sackville Street was once again, as in 1916, pounded to rubble. Most of the Republican leaders, and many Irregulars, filtered through alleys and back-streets to a precarious safety. Cathal Brugha, refusing to surrender, emerged from his headquarters firing two revolvers simultaneously. This unusual feat was his last. He was shot down. Harry Boland was later shot while trying to escape from a hospital where he was detained. Sixty men were killed in the Dublin rising. De Valera went into hiding. Occasionally he dressed himself as an American tourist; at other times he disguised himself in a trench-coat, wore a false beard, and pulled his hat over his eyes. Incredibly, he remained undetected. During August, other centres held by the Republicans fell to Free State troops. Cork City, a Republican stronghold, was abandoned. The conflict was thereafter removed to the countryside; especially in Cork, Kerry, Tipperary, and Waterford, the Irregulars' flying-columns were, in view of their perpetual shortages of ammunition and equipment, extraordinarily successful. The war, as a result, lasted for a year.

The government was not encouraged in the distasteful task of hunting down former colleagues in arms by the unexpected death of its two leaders. In August 1922 Arthur Griffith died suddenly after a stroke. Michael Collins was surviving head of state for only three days. He was shot to death in a Republican ambush near Macroom in Co. Cork, near the place where he had been born. 'Whatever happens to me,' Collins had ventured to remark shortly before his death, 'my own countrymen won't kill me.' William Cosgrave, the Minister of Local Government and a veteran of the Easter Rising, succeeded to the headship both of the Dáil and of the Provisional government. On 6 December 1922, the first anniversary of the signing of the Treaty, the Irish Free State came officially into existence. The Constitution had been enacted as a British statute, passed through parliament at Westminster. Tim Healy, the old Home Rule politician, was appointed by the Crown as the first Governor-General and removed himself, no doubt to his own surprise, to the vice-regal lodge in Phoenix Park.

The Republicans had formed a rival administration in October, when the Army Executive commissioned de Valera to appoint a cabinet of supporters gathered in from the secrecy of hedgerows and ditches. The Free State government was then moved with even greater determination to extirpate the Republicans from Ireland. Military courts were empowered by emergency legislation to deal summarily with arrested suspects. When consolidated in January 1923, these measures allowed the special courts to pass death sentences for any 'purpose prejudicial to the safety of the state'. Britain, during all her administrations of Ireland, had never imposed so open-ended a measure of coercion. By the start of 1923 there were over 12,000 Republicans in gaol. The barbarities imputed to the Free State prison officials by Republicans rivalled even those attributed to the Black and Tans. Seventy-seven Republicans were executed. Erskine Childers was put to death in November 1922, while his case was still pending before the court of appeal. O'Connor, Mellows, and two other leaders of the Four Courts garrison were executed in the following month; their deaths being something of a reprisal – Republicans had chosen the official inauguration of the Free State to gun down two members of the Dáil. One of them had died.

In the Civil War itself the mortality – for which there are no reliable estimates – was very considerable. Atrocity stories clung to both sides. The destruction of private property at least equalled that of the 'Anglo-Irish War', and the deliberate wrecking of railways, wireless stations, bridges, and police-barracks rather considerably exceeded it. In the last months of the war, the Republicans destroyed almost everything which might be of use to the government. They also burned down the homes of Free State senators. As early as October 1922, the Catholic hierarchy had issued a Pastoral condemning the Irregulars for having 'done more damage in three months than could be laid to the charge of British rule in three decades'. The government was obliged to deploy 60,000 men in hunting down the Republicans, and the war cost £17 millions.

De Valera was ready for peace talks by March 1923. Early attempts to get enough agreement among the Republicans to be able to present a single front to the Free State govern-ment were defeated by the intransigence of Lynch. He was killed in action during April, and his successor as Chief-of-Staff, Frank Aiken, was more sympathetic to a settlement. At the end of April the Irregulars declared a truce, and in May de Valera agreed to a surrender without winning any of his demands. The Republicans buried their arms and those who had the good fortune to avoid capture dispersed to their homes. The Civil War had ended, and the Republicans had been crushed, as General Macready said, 'by means far more drastic than any which the British Government dared to impose during the worst period of the rebellion'.

In August a general election endorsed the government's actions. Cosgrave's party, now called Cumann na nGaedheal, were returned with sixty-three seats, which, together with the other pro-Treaty groups' total of forty-six, gave a large mandate to the Free State. The Republicans were returned for forty-four seats. De Valera had broken his cover in order to address the electors in his own constituency at Ennis, Co. Clare. He was arrested as he stood on the platform. 'Good-bye now, boys,' he said to the crowd as the troops led him away, 'maintain the Republic.' He was in prison for almost a year, during which time, it is recorded, he read nothing but the works of Einstein. His release must have been especially pleasurable, and the crowds who gathered at the gates of the gaol pressed forward to touch his coat as he passed.

The fortunes of the Republicans seemed low indeed, especially as the Free State government went on to endorse partition in 1924. After the northern and southern governments had failed to agree, a Boundary Commission had finally been set up under Justice Feetham of the South African Supreme Court. But Ulster refused to appoint a representative, and MacNeill, for the south, resigned in November 1924 when it became clear that no concessions of territory were likely to be forthcoming. In 1925 Cosgrave signed an agreement with Britain in which he recognized the integrity of the six northern counties under separate jurisdiction. The division of Ireland has remained ever since.

For its first ten years of existence, the destinies of the Free State were guided by Cosgrave as President of the Executive Council. He was, in this period, able to show that Ireland's Dominion status was quite compatible, as the advocates of the Treaty had predicted, with a practical autonomy. During this period, and during the succeeding ministries of de Valera, Ireland's constitutional relations with the British Commonwealth were always somewhat anomalous; yet the readjustments of the Treaty settlement, which continued until 1948, offered a canvass of opinion within which many of the most crucial redefinitions of general imperial relationships were first sketched. The effective independence of the country was evident in almost everything. Even de Valera was obliged in 1932 to confess that a great deal had been achieved since the Treaty. 'There have been advances made,' he then said, 'that I did not believe would be made at the time.' Most southern Unionists also managed to come to terms with the Free State. They were well represented in the senate.

But in Irish domestic politics the bitterness of the Civil War divisions continued, perpetuated in party alignments to the present time. The tradition of lawlessness was only marginally contained as well. There was a lot of disillusionment. 'When we look back on the days when we were oppressed by England,' said John Dillon in 1925, 'it would look like paradise if we could get the same sort of oppression now.' His view was not especially widespread, but there were many who, never having really unwound with enthusiasm for Gaelic culture in the early years of the century, were puzzled by it still. The introduction of compulsory Irish in the schools was not merely an intellectual undertaking. It was promoted for moral and political purposes; 'for the establishment of the Gaelic outlook in the minds of the pupils', as an official instruction of 1922 suggested. Catholic puritanism had also come into its own. In 1925 the Dáil had managed to prevent legislation providing for divorce. The opposition of the upper house was more easily overcome when W. B. Yeats, now a senator, made a ridiculous speech in which he vilified the personal lives of O'Connell and Parnell, and cast witty doubts upon the authenticity of the Gospels. In 1929 a Censorship of Publications Act inspired the first of many lists of banned books. The Irish public were thenceforth excluded from the wisdom of, among others, Bernard Shaw, Aldous Huxley, Wyndham Lewis, Malcolm Muggeridge, Maxim Gorki, Somerset Maugham, Daphne du Maurier, Bertrand Russell, H. G. Wells, D. H. Lawrence, and Godfrey Winn. Two home critics of Irish society were also on the list: Liam O'Flaherty and Sean O'Faolain. Censorship was, on the whole, popular.

The Cosgrave administration experienced a steady electoral erosion. In 1927 the entry of de Valera's followers to the Dáil provided a real opposition presence for the first time. The occasion was a sad one. In July, Kevin O'Higgins, the vice-President of the Free State, was assassinated in Dublin by Republican extremists. Cosgrave responded with the introduction of emergency legislation. From this point Ireland was, as in the nineteenth century, more or less continuously subject to coercion acts. Trial by jury was suspended, the possession of firearms was made a capital crime. A Bill was also brought forward to oblige candidates in parliamentary elections to promise in advance that they would take the oath of allegiance to the king if elected. De Valera's party was faced with the unattractive alternatives of decimation or perjury. They chose the latter. In 1926 de Valera had founded Fianna Fail ('Soldiers of Destiny'), but the deputies elected to the Dáil had always refused the oath and had therefore been excluded from the chamber. Now they duly signed their names to the oath. In the autumn general election of 1927 Cosgrave's Cumann na nGaedheal (later known as Fine Gael or 'Tribe of Gaels') failed to retain an overall majority. They governed for another five years with the support of the minority parties, most of whom were still alarmed by de Valera's doctrinaire Republicanism. In 1931 a new Public Safety Act was passed, despite the night-time visits of gunmen to the homes of deputies with promises of frightful personal consequences for those who voted once more for coercion.

In the 1932 elections, however, Fianna Fail won seventy-two seats and Cumann na nGaedheal fifty-seven. The nine independents and Farmers' party representatives supported Cosgrave, but Labour held the balance with seven seats. They used it to support the election of de Valera to the Presidency of the Executive Council. After ten years in the wilderness, de Valera was in office. Fianna Fail, indeed, has remained in power ever since, with only brief intermissions between 1948 and 1951, and 1954 and 1957. De Valera was a little more moderate. Since 1927 he had been drawing away from the physical force Republicanism of the I.R.A.; in 1934 he replied to those who demanded an immediate declaration of the Republic with the simple formula: 'the time has not yet come.' In practice he believed that the formal constitutional structure of the Free State was the only realistic means of attracting the six northern counties back into a united Ireland. During his long tenure of office he worked for the establishment of his favourite device of 'External Association'. But in his polemical criticisms of Cosgrave's administration he had provided a thesis which Republican extremists have employed ever since: that Ireland was still, in practice, subject to British rule, despite her formal independence. At the annual *Ardfheis* of Sinn Féin in 1968, for example, President Thomas MacGiolla referred to 'British control, direct in the north and indirect in the south'. When political evidences have failed, it is always possible to fall back on the supposition that the mutually beneficial trade and investment relationship between England and Ireland amount to British 'economic imperialism'.

Although one of the most paradoxical features of de Valera's government after 1932 was his attempt to extinguish his Republican opponents, the administration could scarcely be mistaken for one of national reconciliation with the pro-Treaty parties. It was frankly partisan. Those who had followed de Valera on to the hillsides in 1922 were now invested with the long-promised rewards of their faithfulness. Nor did the new president of the Executive Council reserve himself solely for the people of Ireland. In 1923 the Free State had been admitted to the League of Nations, and in 1932 it fell to de Valera to preside at its Council in Geneva.

The astonished delegates saw him lay aside the customary address of international courtesies prepared for him by League officials and listened, instead, to a passionate and intricate denunciation of the partition of Ireland. It was very extraordinary. At home, the new administration began by releasing the Republicans still detained under the coercion acts. They at once plotted to overthrow the government which had released them.

De Valera, meanwhile, pressed ahead with an attempt to fulfil his election programme. It had two essential points: to end the payment of land annuities to Britain – the sums owing as a result of state loans made for tenants to purchase their land, and guaranteed both by the Treaty and by a secret agreement of 1923 between Cosgrave and the British Treasury – and the abolition of the oath of allegiance to the Crown. In 1932, accordingly, the annuities were frozen in Dublin. De Valera refused to lay the matter before a Commonwealth tribunal, and Britain rejected his alternative of an international appeal. Ramsay MacDonald's government, dismayed at this breaking of previous agreements, and no doubt at de Valera's publicized innocence of the 1923 arrangement, retaliated by excluding Ireland from the benefits of imperial preference. The resulting tariff war between the two countries did immeasurable harm to the Irish economy. De Valera had once again put doctrine before welfare: Irish exports had fallen by £26 millions by 1934; there was severe distress among the small farmers and bread queues in the streets of cities. The effects in Britain, of course, were negligible. De Valera acclaimed the economic isolation of his country as the consummation of the Sinn Féin ideal of self-sufficiency, and in a way it was.

In 1933 a Bill was introduced to the Dáil disposing of the oath of allegiance. It was rejected by the Senate, only to become law automatically, by the terms of the constitution, within two years. The right of appeal to the Privy Council was also

303

removed from the Constitution. De Valera, furious with the Senate for opposing him, blasted out at the upper house; in 1936 its sittings were terminated for good. In further elaboration of his campaign against the British survivals in the Free State constitution, de Valera went on to humiliate the Governor-General, James McNeill. Ministers walked out of official gatherings at which the personal representative of the king was present; he was not even invited to the state reception for the reverend delegates to the Eucharistic Congress held that year in Dublin. McNeill was then dismissed at de Valera's initiative and replaced by an unknown shop-keeper from Co. Kildare gazetted as 'Domhuall Ua Buachalla Esq.' (Daniel Buckley Esq.). From this obscure personage most of the remaining powers of the head of state were removed. Having destroyed the Senate and subordinated the Governor-General, de Valera had contrived a position of extreme personal rule. In 1935 Dáil legislation purported to deprive Irish citizens of British nationality, and Ireland also gave up attendance, maintained under Cosgrave, at the periodic Imperial Conferences in London. De Valera also realized the advantages latent in the Statute of Westminster, passed by the British parliament in 1931. As Churchill had pointed out in the Commons debate, it was now possible for Ireland to repudiate the Treaty without illegality. De Valera employed his spare energies, which appear to have been considerable, in composing a new constitution to replace the Free State. The abdication crisis in 1936 supplied a providential oppor-tunity for removing the king from the constitution, anyway, and in 1937 the Dáil adopted de Valera's new instrument of government after a ruthless guillotining of debates.

The Free State was ended; Éire replaced it. The office of Governor-General was abolished and its functions taken over by a President (An Uachteran). The first holder was Douglas Hyde, and on his retirement in 1945 the office passed to Sean

T. O'Kelly. Most of the presidential duties were ceremonial. The Prime Minister (An Taoiseach) was de Valera, with powers comparable to those of his English counterpart. The Senate was restored, and the system of proportional representation for elections to the Dáil retained. The most obvious feature of the Éire Constitution was the achievement of 'External Association'. The king was now excluded entirely from any sovereignty inside Ireland, and was authorized to act only in his capacity as head of the Commonwealth, and only, therefore, over foreign relations. The Roman Catholic Church was explicitly given legal recognition as the religion of the great majority, and the Constitution also included a provision that 'no law shall be enacted providing for the grant of a dissolution of marriage'.

At the 1937 general election Fianna Fail lost seats, but the new Constitution was narrowly approved. Britain patiently gave legal recognition to the changes. For the next ten years, Éire was an undeclared Republic. By an agreement of 1938, made in London between de Valera and Neville Chamberlain, the land annuities question was settled with Ireland undertaking to pay one tenth of the amount owing to Britain. Tariff warfare then came to an end, and the resulting popularity for Fianna Fail gave the party its first clear majority in the general election of 1938. The 'Treaty Ports' were also handed over to the Irish government, who, in return, promised to refuse their facilities to foreign powers in the event of war. It was, of course, the threat of war in Europe which had presented the urgency of neutrality to de Valera's administration. Only the surrender to Irish control of the ports held by the British navy could prevent Éire being included involuntarily in the European conflict which, through succeeding months, seemed inevitable. Ireland was the only nation in the Commonwealth not to declare war on Germany in 1939.

Ireland was also stuck with grave problems of internal

security. Now totally disenchanted with de Valera, the I.R.A. began a new campaign of terror in 1932. Old comrades in arms once again found themselves in civil conflict. Much of the enthusiasm for the I.R.A. among working men was no doubt generated by the suffering of the years of depression caused in large measure by the government's prosecution of the economic warfare with Britain. But there were ponderous ideological differences. Some of the Republicans were attracted to international Communism. Six members of the Executive Council of the I.R.A. had gone to Moscow to study revolutionary tactics at Lenin College. The Irish section of the 'Friends of Soviet Russia', with superlative taste, had even presented a portrait of the Countess Markievicz to the Museum of Revolution in Moscow. These, however, were fringe enthusiasms. The new I.R.A. terror campaign was cast in a rather more traditionally Irish mould. There were shootings, burnings, intimidation, and arms-raiding. In 1936 Admiral Somerville, an Irish sympathizer of seventy-two years of age living in retirement, was shot to death in his drawing-room by an I.R.A. execution squad as an example to other British officers living in the country. The disgusting round of atrocities had begun again.

In August 1932 right-wing supporters of the Free State settlement organized in opposition to the new I.R.A. offensive. Known variously as the 'White Army', the 'National Guard', and the 'Blue-shirts', the counter-revolutionaries found a *duce* in General Eoin O'Duffy, Police Commissioner of the Irish Free State. They announced the futility of party politics and described a future nation–state of military dictatorship and dead Jews. In Ireland, too, therefore, the weighty international conflict of communism and fascism produced an unlikely expression. De Valera's government, even less in sympathy with the militant supporters of the Free State than with the I.R.A. – who were, at least, former colleagues

– picked up, as usual in Ireland, the weary instruments of coercion. O'Duffy was dismissed from his post, and in 1934 a national ban of public parades was enforced – at first only against the Blue-shirts, then supposed to number about 100,000 men. The movement was reduced as a result. Local outrages between the opposing armies had by then brought death and division to most parts of the country, and all the old wounds of the Civil War discharged again. De Valera, in desperation, banned the I.R.A. in 1936, and stuffed its leaders into prison. A branch of special police was formed to investigate political organizations. Local conflict had scarcely diminished when the Civil War in Spain redefined the sharp ideological cleavage in Ireland. Three hundred I.R.A. men joined the International Brigade. The Irish Catholic hierarchy supported Franco, and so did the Blue-shirts. Groups of the latter also set out for Spain. Some were picked off by I.R.A. sympathizers before they even reached the ports of departure.

The neutrality of Éire during the Second World War was, in effect, a dispensation by Britain – under whose potential protection the luxury of non-combatant status was possible. Thousands of Irishmen crossed to England to enlist in the British forces, and de Valera, wise to the reality of Ireland's position, did nothing to stop them. Neutrality did not win friends on either side. A German air raid on Dublin in 1941 caused a number of deaths, but the government was not to be provoked into joining the Allies. In 1944 de Valera offended the Americans by refusing a request to expel the German and Japanese ambassadors from Dublin.

He did, however, take action against the I.R.A., who, in 1938, had declared war on Britain for failing to deliver the people of Ulster to the control of the southern government. Throughout the earlier years of the war, the I.R.A. stretched its resources to sabotage the British war effort. The wrecking campaign was directed by Sean Russell, Chief-of-Staff. Bombs exploded in English railway stations, cathedrals, and hotels. Marker-flares were dropped in the streets of Belfast to guide the *Luftwaffe* towards the shipyards. The Belfast cross-channel steamer was sunk by an I.R.A. bomb off Liverpool. Several people were killed. In 1939 the mortality resulting from an explosion in a crowded shopping street in Coventry especially shocked the public of both England and Ireland. De Valera saw a threat to neutrality in these outrages; they also provided a splendid chance to apply strong coercive measures against the I.R.A. By 1940, 600 men had been sent to prison for political crimes. The Republicans retaliated: a bomb exploded in Dublin Castle.

The I.R.A. analysis of the war was, in fact, romanticized and historical. The old doctrine that 'England's difficulty was Ireland's opportunity' presented itself with austere simplicity to men whose hatred was directed as much against the puppet regime in Dublin, as they supposed it, as against the Imperial parliament in London. It was all rather unreal. Sean Russell intrigued with German agents and even went so far in emulation of Casement as to slip away to Germany in 1939 to persuade the High Command of the advantages of invading Ireland. He was returning in a submarine in 1940, intending to land in exactly the same place in Tralee Bay as his notable predecessor, when he died from a perforated stomach ulcer. In both Éire and Ulster I.R.A. arms raids, and random killings, continued.

When the war was over, Sean MacBride organized a new Republican opposition party, Clann na Poblachta ('Children of the Republic'), to continue the struggle constitutionally, and this did manage to divert some sections of the I.R.A. into less savage political activity.

In 1948 Fianna Fail was defeated in a general election, and de Valera was obliged to give way to an inter-party coalition administration under Fine Gael control. It was this government which, paradoxically, passed the legislation which converted Éire into a Republic. The era of legal fiction had drawn to a close. Britain gave statutory recognition to the new status of Ireland and at the same time guaranteed the independence of Ulster so long as its people should elect for self-government. Now outside the Commonwealth, the Republic demonstrated its continued neutrality by declining to join the North Atlantic Treaty Organization.

Fianna Fail resumed the functions of government after the 1951 election, and has continued, with the exception of the second coalition administration of 1954–7, to exercise them ever since. The 1950s were a period of relative disillusionment. Irish nationalism was insufficient to sustain political enthusiasm once the last obstacles to its free expression had been removed. New generations of younger men were restless with a political society which owed its definition to a civil conflict which had ended thirty years before. Economic development, as elsewhere in Western society, began to reorder some of the national priorities of Ireland in the later fifties. De Valera retired to the presidency of his country in 1959, and his old colleague, Sean Lemass, who became Prime Minister, was more acutely aware of the possibilities of the Irish economy than his predecessor.

Political advance was less evident. In 1954 the I.R.A. began yet another terror campaign on the Border, and the government replied with yet more coercion. Two hundred Republican extremists were gaoled. Attempts to readopt the British machinery of parliamentary elections in place of proportional representation have twice been defeated. The Republic of Ireland, despite its constitutional separation from the United Kingdom, is in fact indelibly English in its institutions. It is a slightly old-fashioned England, however, lacking most of the components of a welfare society and lagging considerably behind economically. The failure of the language revival movement, although it had received official support for nearly fifty years, will preserve the similarities with Britain for the future as well. The experience of national independence in Southern Ireland has revealed to its people, and to the people of Britain, who are no doubt equally surprised, that the heritage they have enjoyed in common cannot be disposed of by the writing of constitutions and the staffing of customs-posts. It is a salutary awakening.

Whereas partition left the south with a reasonably homo-geneous society, the north was isolated with the main burden of traditional Irish divisions. The Ulster government had the double disadvantage of administering an artificial political unit whose majority would rather have stayed united with England, and of presiding over an area which constituted a museum of all the religious, political, racial, and social divisions which had created the disruptions of the past. The three north-eastern counties were overwhelmingly Protestant; the others were mixed, with many areas containing a Catholic majority which looked south across the border for political sympathy. Belfast and Londonderry are divided cities, with Catholic and Protestant districts jealously defined. Many of the ordinary stresses germane to an industrial society produce, in those cities, chronic sectarian unrest. Northern Ireland offers the unusual example of a Protestant working class which votes solidly for a Tory government.

It is remarkable that this small province, born out of the defiance of an unofficial army, and sustaining a large minority who for so long sought only the overthrow of its institutions, should have developed, not into a species of fascism, but into a liberal democracy with an advanced level of public welfare. In some senses the result is an indication of the failure of the Irish people to apply the logic of their own politics. When the Stormont parliament came into existence the Protestants voted Unionist, the Catholics Nationalist, and the Republican extremists voted for Sinn Féin. It is easy, therefore, to suppose that it is religious rather than political beliefs which provide the substance of northern views about government. But in Northern Ireland the two are inseparably conjoined. The politics of the province, as a result, are defined in practice by the local balances between the two populations who happen to find themselves living in the same geographical area. To an external observer, the political behaviour of Ulster can sometimes seem extraordinarily volatile, and the basis of society much less secure than in fact it has become. When, for example, the world's press arrived to cover the general election of February 1969 they expected to report an Irish manifestation of an international political trend – Ulster, they had heard, was a copy-book instance of a right-wing government denying the essential elements of 'civil rights', just like the southern states in America. What in fact they discovered, to their evident annoyance, was a complexity of local squabbles. It was, in short, a typical Irish election. The world's press impatiently took the Ulster people to task for not treating their own politics with the ponderous solemnity currently considered proper. The psephological predictions all went wrong as well. Religious opinion and protest-voting wobbled round the edge of the charts; but the size of the Unionist vote remained roughly constant despite the split within the Unionist party. The *annus mirabilis* held its surprises in suspension, and political issues continued to filtrate through the screen of religious sectarianism. How many of the 33,000 rural voters who supported Miss Bernadette Devlin, aged 21, in the mid-Ulster by-election of April 1969 really subscribed to her brand of Trotskyite anarchism? They voted for her because she is a Catholic.

Northern Ireland continued, after partition, to be subject to the 1920 Government of Ireland Act. There was a Senate and a House of Commons in the parliament at Stormont, with the Governor-General as personal representative of the Crown. The Imperial parliament reserved some quite important questions for its own control – including foreign affairs, financial contributions towards imperial expenses, and the right to revise the 1920 Act. By the Act of 1948 the people of Northern Ireland were guaranteed an autonomous existence so long as they should continue to desire it.

The province has remained an integral part of the United Kingdom with representation in the Westminster parliament. Initially large annual sums were paid to London for the common Imperial services, but these diminished in the 1930s, and Ulster has, since that time, received frequent financial assistance from the British Treasury – subvention made necessary because the 1920 Act allowed financial powers to Stormont which were inadequate to enable Northern Ireland to raise sufficient revenue for itself.

The politics of the province have a simple history. In the first general election, in 1921, forty Unionists, six Nationalists, and six Sinn Féin members were returned. Lord Carson had retired from Ulster public life, and Sir James Craig (Lord Craigavon) formed a Unionist administration which, under the subsequent leadership of Andrews, Brookborough, O'Neill, and Chichester Clark, has continued in office ever since. Unionist government was at first unequivocally sectarian. In 1932 Craigavon declared that 'Ours is a Protestant Government and I am an Orangeman.' Since party officials and cabinet ministers were also not infrequently members of the Orange Order, party government was unmistakable in its loyalties.

The opposition parties have always been weak, for two thirds of the people of Ulster have consistently voted for the government, and a high proportion of seats, until quite recent times, remained uncontested at elections. The Nationalists could only bring themselves to espouse a single policy anyway: reunion with the south, to be prepared tactically by an initial restoration of direct rule from London. In 1928 their members of parliament, after a good deal of hesitation, took their seats at Stormont for the first time and formed a proper opposition. Sinn Féin became a physical-force party, as in the south. Its members declined to take their seats, sometimes for the involuntary reason that they were in gaol. Labour has rarely managed to achieve a political foothold. There have been few constitutional changes. In 1927 the device of proportional representation was dropped, and this helped to consolidate the opposition behind the Nationalist party. The old tradition of Ulster Liberalism, which had vanished in the Home Rule crisis, did not return. Liberal elements merged into the Unionist party, and this has, with time, given Ulster Unionism some of the characteristics of a Liberal–Tory coalition.

The establishment of the welfare state has had the most decisive influence on the political orientation of the province. Its components, as in England, were anyway evident during the early years of the present century. In 1930 Craigavon announced the intention of his government to advance 'step by step' with the social reforms to be introduced by Ramsay Macdonald's Labour administration in London, and this policy has been adhered to with consistency ever since. Ulster's economic depression in the thirties was more terrible than England's – by 1938, thirty per cent of the working population were unemployed. Disturbances inspired by the prevailing distress, as in the rioting of 1935, appeared in the guise of religious confrontation. During the war unemployment dropped to four per cent, and the later diversification of industry, assisted by state aid under the New Industries Development Act of 1945, has prevented a recurrence of real distress. But Ulster's unemployment rate remains higher than that of the rest of the United Kingdom.

Legislation introduced by post-war governments created the modern machinery of welfare administration, a consolidation of earlier developments and the addition of a lot more. State aid to local authorities for housing was provided in a measure of 1945. A separate Ministry of Health emerged from the Home Department. The Education Act of 1947 raised state financial grants to Catholic and other voluntary schools to sixty-five per cent. In 1948 the nationalization of transport was completed. The Catholic hierarchy cast a critical gaze upon those aspects of state intervention which might in theory conflict with the rights of the family. The Church's insistence on separate denominational schools for Catholic children has been one of the most divisive aspects of Ulster society: the state schools, as a result are largely identified with Protestantism, and children are obliged to recognize separate development from an early age. The Catholic population, however, are the chief beneficiaries of large family allowances and socialized medicine. The advent of the welfare state has persuaded many of them to vote Unionist. It has also tended to diminish the priority of the Border issue in Catholic politics. To join the south, at the present time, would involve the dismantling of the welfare state.

Ireland, therefore, seems to be set for a divided future. The good relations informally established in the early 1960s between Lemass and O'Neill, the southern and northern premiers, have unhappily failed to survive the recurrence of sectarian rioting in Ulster after 1968. Old issues once again intervened, and old Ireland showed that her scars still bisect the barriers of partition. 'Men and women of Ireland,' as General Mulcahy had predicted with histrionic but accurate vision at the graveside of Michael Collins in 1922, 'we are all mariners on the deep, bound for a port still seen only through storm and spray, sailing still on a sea full of dangers and bitter toil.' And that, after all, is not so good.

Note on Further Reading

The following suggestions do not comprise an exhaustive analysis of works on the history of the period. Those books are listed which ought to be easily available to the reader in most libraries; and those which seem merely to duplicate information are left out. Sources which might be useful only for research purposes – articles in periodical journals, primary printed materials, and documents – are also omitted. The recommendations are grouped according to the chapter headings in the present study.

I. IRISH QUESTIONS AND ENGLISH ANSWERS

The best general surveys of the period are J. C. Beckett, *The Making of Modern Ireland, 1603–1923* (London, 1966), and Oliver MacDonagh, *Ireland* (Spectrum, 1968). L. J. McCaffrey, *The Irish Question, 1800–1922* (Kentucky, 1968), is a very traditional interpretation, sympathetic to Irish nationalism; and G. Locker Lampson, *A Consideration of the State of Ireland in the Nineteenth Century* (London, 1907), though still extremely useful for its detailed information, is full of doctrinaire Liberalism. Nicholas Mansergh, *The Irish Question, 1840–1921* (London, 1965), which is a revision of the earlier work published as *Ireland in the Age of Reform and Revolution* in 1940, has extremely interesting comment on the European implications of Irish nationalism. The best works on Irish emigration are A. Shrier, *Ireland and the American Emigration, 1850–1900* (Minneapolis, 1958); J. A. Jackson, *The Irish in Great Britain* (London,

1963); and J.F.Hogan, *The Irish in Australia* (London, 1888). For social and economic analysis, there are G. A. T. O'Brien, *Economic History of Ireland from the Union to the Famine* (Dublin, 1921); R.D.Collison Black, *Economic Thought and the Irish Question, 1817–70* (Cambridge, 1960); K.H.Connell's *The Population of Ireland, 1750–1845* (Oxford, 1950) and *Irish Peasant Society* (London, 1969); J.E.Pomfret, *The Struggle for Land in Ireland* (Princeton, 1930); J.Dunsmore Clarkson, *Labor and Nationalism in Ireland* (New York, 1925); and J.J.Auchmuty, *Irish Education: An Historical Survey* (Dublin, 1937). R.B.McDowell, *The Irish Administration, 1801–1914* (London, 1964), is an admirable introduction to the departments of government, but there is no satisfactory parliamentary history for the nineteenth century – it is perhaps best still to use R.B.O'Brien's *Fifty Years of Concessions to Ireland, 1831–1881* (London, 1883), which at least has the merit of generous quotation from *Hansard*. Religious history is also badly served. The relevant chapters in James McCaffrey, *History of the Catholic Church in the Nineteenth Century* (Dublin, 1902), and James Byrne (ed.), *Essays on the Irish Church* (Oxford, 1866), are the most useful.

2. THE UNION

W.E.A.Lecky, *History of Ireland in the Eighteenth Century* (London, 1892), remains impressive in the grandeur of its detail and judgement. Maureen Wall, *The Penal Laws, 1691–1760* (Dundalk, 1961), is essential to a comprehension of Catholic sentiment. Thomas Pakenham's recent study, *The Year of Liberty. The Great Irish Rebellion of 1798* (London, 1969), is vivid and accurate. Three recent works of critical scholarship have done much to clear away misconceptions about the Union and its political background: E.M. Johnston, *Great Britain and Ireland, 1760–1800* (Edinburgh, 1963); Hereward Senior, *Orangeism in Ireland and Britain, 1795–1836* (London, 1966); and G.C.Bolton, *The Passing of the Irish Act of Union* (Oxford, 1966). Further background information can be tumbled out of J.T.Gilbert (ed.), *Documents Relating to Ireland, 1795–1804* (Dublin, 1893); T.H.D.Mahoney, *Edmund Burke and Ireland* (Harvard, 1960); H.M.Hyde, *The Rise of Castlereagh* (London,

1933); and R.B.McDowell, *Irish Public Opinion, 1750–1800* (London, 1944). Those in need of diversion will doubtless find it in *The Autobiography of Theobald Wolfe Tone*, edited by R.B.O'Brien (London, 1893). D.A.Chart, *Ireland from the Union to Catholic Emancipation* (London, 1910), is still the only version of the first years of the new century. Norman Gash, *Mr Secretary Peel* (London, 1961), contains an excellent account of the Irish administration during Peel's period of office as Chief Secretary in the Liverpool ministry. E.R.R. Green, *The Lagan Valley, 1800–50. A Local History of the Industrial Revolution* (London, 1949), is a good economic survey of the peculiar circumstances of north-east Ulster in the period.

3. O'CONNELL AND RADICALISM, AND
4. RADICALISM AND REFORM

For the Repeal agitation, most earlier works have been superseded by Angus MacIntyre, *The Liberator, Daniel O'Connell and the Irish Party, 1830–1847* (London, 1965). But for the Emancipation campaign, see J.A.Reynolds, *The Catholic Emancipation Crisis in Ireland, 1823–1829* (Yale, 1954), and Denis Gwynn, *Daniel O'Connell* (Cork, 1947). Specialized aspects of the Repeal agitation are very well treated in Kevin B. Nowlan, *The Politics of Repeal. A Study in the Relations between Great Britain and Ireland, 1840–50* (London, 1965), and J.F.Broderick, *The Holy See and the Irish Movement for the Repeal of the Union with England, 1829–1847* (Rome, 1951). The Maynooth question is described in E.R.Norman, *Anti-Catholicism in Victorian England* (London, 1968). R.B.McDowell's *Public Opinion and Government Policy in Ireland, 1801–46* is the best general survey of these years. There are old, but usefully documented biographies of the three great ecclesiastics of the period: J.F.Maguire, *Father Matthew* (London, 1863); Bernard O'Reilly, *John MacHale, His Life, Times, and Correspondence* (New York, 1890); and W.J.Fitzpatrick, *The Life, Times, and Correspondence of the Rt Revd Dr Doyle* (Dublin, 1861). Fitzpatrick's *Correspondence of Daniel O'Connell* (London, 1888) is also a good source for agitations which O'Connell engineered.

Three great works by Sir Charles Gavan Duffy are still the main source: *Young Ireland, 1840–45* (London, 1880); *Four Years of Irish History, 1845–49* (London, 1883); and *Thomas Davis* (London, 1890). M. J. MacManus (ed.), *Thomas Davis and Young Ireland* (Dublin, 1945), contains some informative if sometimes rather uncritical contributions. Works by two contemporaries convey some of the leading ideas of the nationalists: John Mitchel, *Jail Journal* (Dublin, 1914); and the *Collected Writings of James Fintan Lalor*, edited by L. Fogarty (Dublin, revised edn., 1947). The only really adequate accounts of the famine are in Dudley Edwards and Desmond Williams (eds.), *The Great Famine. Studies in Irish History, 1845–52* (Dublin, 1956); and Cecil Woodham-Smith, *The Great Hunger* (London, 1962), which is emotionally satisfying.

6. EXPERIMENT AND REBELLION

The politics of the period are discussed with balance and critical insight in J. H. Whyte, *The Independent Irish Party, 1850–59* (Oxford, 1958), a book which in some, but not all, things has replaced the older study by Sir Charles Gavan Duffy, *The League of North and South* (London, 1886). On Fenianism there is Desmond Ryan, *The Phoenix Flame. A Study of Fenianism and John Devoy* (London, 1939), which is well intentioned but uncritical, T. W. Moody (ed.), *The Fenian Movement* (Cork, 1968), which is well intentioned and critical, and John O'Leary, *Recollections of Fenians and Fenianism* (London, 1896), an interesting account by a Fenian polemicist.

7. THE FAILURE OF THE LIBERAL ALLIANCE

J. L. Hammond, *Gladstone and the Irish Nation* (London, 1938), is really very informative but irritatingly Gladstonian. Lord Eversley, *Gladstone and Ireland. The Irish Policy of Parliament, 1850–94* (London, 1912), is an older work but with some useful information on English questions. E. R. Norman, *The Catholic Church and Ireland in the Age of Rebellion, 1859–1873* is an attempt at a definitive study of the political agitations of the period, reduced for the general reader in *The*

Catholic Church and Irish Politics in the Eighteen-Sixties (Dundalk, 1965). The early years of the Home Rule movement are well described in David Thornley, *Isaac Butt and Home Rule* (London, 1964). T. de Vere White, *The Road of Excess* (Dublin, 1945), is a sensitive and at times perceptive biography of Butt. F.H. O'Donnell, *A History of the Irish Parliamentary Party* (London, 1910), written with stimulating rancour and patent prejudice, contains useful documentation and surprisingly reliable detail.

8. PARNELLISM

R.B.O'Brien's *Life of Charles Stewart Parnell* (London, 1899) is still the standard biography. Two scholarly works of considerable distinction illuminate particular aspects of Parnell's political career: Conor Cruise O'Brien, *Parnell and his Party, 1880–90* (Oxford, 1957), is an extraordinarily impressive analysis of the composition of the parliamentarians; F.S.L. Lyons, *The Fall of Parnell, 1890–91*, is essential for an understanding of the division of the party. Henry Harrison, *Parnell Vindicated* (London, 1931), is also a useful account of the last years. Tom Corfe, *The Phoenix Park Murders* (London, 1968), is a competent survey of the position in Ireland between 1879 and 1882. L.P.Curtis, *Coercion and Conciliation in Ireland, 1880–1892* (Princeton, 1963), which is about coercion and conciliation, is full of interesting perspectives. The American background of support is usefully, and at times originally, discussed in Thomas N.Brown, *Irish–American Nationalism* (Philadelphia, 1966); and the best source for the part played by Fenianism is *Devoy's Post-bag*, edited by W.O'Brien and D.Ryan (Dublin, 1948 and 1953). A.V.Dicey, *England's Case Against Home Rule* (London, 1886), should be read if only to show that the opponents of devolution were not the absurd reactionaries the Liberal tradition has subsequently suggested.

9. CONSOLIDATION AND DISSENT

Two books by F.S.L.Lyons provide a solid and trustworthy guide to the politics of the period between 1891 and 1914: *The Irish*

Parliamentary Party, 1890–1910 (London, 1951), and *John Dillon* (London, 1968). Denis Gwynn, *The Life of John Redmond* (London, 1932), written with the author's usual enthusiasm and partiality, contains competent details. Liam O'Flaherty, *The Life of Tim Healy* (London, 1927), is similarly prejudiced in conception, but then so are the other political biographies of the leading figures of the period. Diarmid O'Cobhthaigh, *Douglas Hyde* (Dublin, 1917), is informative about the Gaelic League, and some of the less esoteric cultural reflections of the time went into *Ideals in Ireland* (London, 1901), edited by Lady Gregory. Padraic Colum, *Arthur Griffith* (Dublin, 1959), has realistic moments, but Sean O'Faolain, *Constance Markievicz* (London, 1934), to be read for its staggering if unconscious psychological revelations, is rather far from objectivity of judgement. Margaret Digby, *Horace Plunkett* (Oxford, 1949), is, in contrast, scholarly and historical, a balanced assessment of the social and economic schemes of the period. Labour politics are well described in Emmet Larkin, *James Larkin, Irish Labour Leader* (London, 1965), and C. Desmond Greaves, *Life and Times of James Connolly* (London, 1961). James Connolly's own work, *Labour in Irish History* (Dublin, 1910), offers the Marxist interpretation of Ireland's troubles. R. M. Henry, *The Evolution of Sinn Féin* (Dublin, 1920), is surprisingly critical. On the Ulster question there are A. T. Q. Stewart, *The Ulster Crisis* (London, 1967), A. P. Ryan, *Mutiny at the Curragh* (London, 1956), and *The Life of Lord Carson*, by E. Marjoribanks and I. Colvin (London, 1932). The southern response is rather inadequately treated in *The Irish Volunteers, 1913–1915* (Dublin, 1963), edited by F. X. Martin. L. Paul Dubois, *Contemporary Ireland* (Dublin, 1908), is a not unfair, though personal account of aspects of Irish life in the early years of the century. But the best general survey of the period is *The Shaping of Modern Ireland* (London, 1960), edited by C. C. O'Brien.

10. THE REVOLUTION

Most of the books about the revolutionary disturbances are merely propagandist attempts at justification. Among the most useful, because of their narrative selections, are Max Caulfield, *The Easter*

Rebellion (London, 1964), which has frequent lapses into actual fiction; James Stephen, *The Insurrection in Dublin* (Dublin, 1966), a contemporary account; and L. O'Brien, *Dublin Castle and the 1916 Rising* (Dublin, 1966). Dorothy Macardle, *The Irish Republic* (London, 1937), though a standard work, is in large measure Republican polemicism. W. A. Phillips, *The Revolution in Ireland 1906–23* (London, second ed., 1926), though less obviously biased, gives a moderate Unionist view. Edgar Holt, *Protest in Arms. The Irish Troubles, 1916–1923* (London, 1960), is refreshingly impatient with everybody. Denis Gwynn, *The History of Partition, 1912–1925* (Dublin, 1950), and the much more distinguished *Peace by Ordeal* by Frank Pakenham (London, 1935) are the best sources for the Treaty negotiations. Richard Bennett, *The Black and Tans* (London, 1959), reproduces a lot of old legends. *The Irish Struggle, 1916–1926*, edited by Desmond Williams (London, 1966), is a both informative and stimulating collection of essays. Biographical works wander into hagiography: Frank O'Connor, *The Big Fellow, Michael Collins and the Irish Revolution* (London, 1937) – Rex Taylor, *Michael Collins* (London, 1958), is much better. M. J. MacManus, *Eamon de Valera* (Dublin, 1944), and Mary C. Bromage, *De Valera and the March of a Nation* (London, 1956), are generous to their subject. So is *Eamon de Valera* by Lord Longford and T. P. O'Neill (London, 1970). Hedley McCay, *Padraic Pearse* (Cork, 1966), includes some extraordinary revelations. The revelations in René McColl's *Roger Casement* (London, 1956) on the other hand, are very much what one would expect.

II. THE DIVIDED NATION

The political history of the early struggle is best dealt with in Carlton Younger, *Ireland's Civil War* (London, 1968), which, though not a scholarly work, is all there is in the direction of a specialized study of a subject which most Irishmen would rather forget. The author is Australian. Leo Kohn, *The Constitution of the Irish Free State* (London, 1932), Nicholas Mansergh, *The Irish Free State; its Government and Politics* (London, 1934), J. L. McCracken, *Representative Government in Ireland: a Study of Dáil Éireann, 1919–1948* (London,

1958), and Donal O'Sullivan, *The Irish Free State and its Senate* (London, 1940) are all trustworthy and authoritative. D. W. Harkness, *The Restless Dominion. The Irish Free State and the British Commonwealth, 1921–31* (London, 1969), is an extremely good survey of constitutional relations. Denis Gwynn, *The Irish Free State, 1922–7* (London, 1928), and Francis MacManus (ed.), *The Years of the Great Test, 1926–39* (Cork, 1967 edition), give useful narrative outlines. T. P. Coogan, *Ireland Since the Rising* (London, 1966), is also a useful outline account. T. Mahoney, *The Irish Economy* (Cork, 1962), and Sean O'Callaghan, *The Easter Lily. The Story of the I.R.A.* (London, 1956), are competent and absurd respectively. On the history and institutions of Ulster there are Nicholas Mansergh, *The Government of Northern Ireland* (London, 1936); R. J. Lawrence, *The Government of Northern Ireland: Public Finance and Public Services, 1921–64* (Oxford, 1965); and D. G. Neill (ed.), *Devolution of Government, The Experiment in Northern Ireland* (London, 1953): all of which are generally reliable. Hugh Shearman, *Not an Inch: A Study of Northern Ireland and Lord Craigavon* (London, 1943), sustains the interest with lively comment.

Index

A Penguin Special

Ulster

The Sunday Times Insight Team

This is a revised and extended version of two
remarkable articles on Ulster which were published in
the *Sunday Times* in November 1971. The report,
written by the famous Insight team, was internationally
acclaimed and the entire text was read into the United
States Congressional Record as 'an extremely valuable
record of the development of the tragedy in Ulster'.

The team spent four months on intensive investigation
and interviewed generals, civil servants, IRA leaders
and ordinary people. From the first stirrings of the Civil
Rights protest to the rebirth of the IRA and its bloody
aftermath, their story dispassionately follows the
sequence of events in Ulster and fearlessly exposes the
facts of discrimination against Catholics and the
ill-defined motives of the Provisional IRA.

Apart from details of the 'hooding' techniques used in
interrogation – and first revealed by Insight – many new
facts emerge in this Penguin Special, which contains
additional material about the reform programme, the
role of Whitehall, the effects of internment and the
Compton report. But its main purpose is to analyse
how social, military and political pressures have built
up the most violent post-war crisis in Britain.

Divided Ulster

Liam de Paor

The violence which erupted in Northern Ireland in 1969 and has been continuing sporadically since then was, in Liam de Paor's opinion, easily predictable from the turbulent history of the region.

The issue of civil rights for the Roman Catholic minority produced widespread sympathy, but this is basically more than just a religious dispute. Almost equally deprived in Ulster are the poor Protestants, yet they oppose the Catholics with as much ferocity as the Paisleyite extremists.

Liam de Paor is the author of several books on Ireland and is a lecturer at University College, Dublin. In this skilful and perceptive analysis he takes us through the long and difficult history of Ireland since the great settlement of the seventeenth century and through the struggle for independence. He shows how the Six Counties came to be treated separately and how the religious divisions of the north have been used as an instrument of policy.

In this Pelican edition Liam de Paor has added an introduction and revised his final chapter to cover the more recent events down to the resignation of Major Chichester-Clark.

'By far the most comprehensive, best written and most rewarding book yet published on the Northern Ireland situation and its full background' –*New Statesman*

'The best short summary of the Ulster problem to appear so far' – *Guardian*

The Irish

Sean O'Faolain

'A creative history of the growth of a racial mind' – this is Sean O'Faolain's own description of a book in which he has no truck with political events, wars, or rebellions and rejects the popular Irish notion of 'seven hundred years of slavery'.

Many racial, religious, social, and intellectual strands have, over the centuries, been woven into the cloth of Irish genius, and it is Sean O'Faolain's achievement to have disentangled these in a study which first appeared as a Pelican over twenty years ago and has now been largely re-written. The wild, imaginative, disunited Ireland of the Celts, which for years was the fountainhead of Christianity; the intrusion of Danes and Normans, who defied the Irish horror of towns and began to urbanize the island; the years of English ascendancy, when new populations and a new language were planted; the upsurge of Irish nationalism and Irish letters after 1800 – all these Sean O'Faolain records, critically and engagingly.

Finally he distinguishes six representative types which have branched from the Tree of Liberty – the new peasantry, the Anglo-Irish, the rebels, the priests, the writers, and the politicians.

Not for sale in the U.S.A.

Agony at Easter

The 1916 Irish Uprising

Thomas M. Coffey

This is an account of the uprising that led eventually to the independence of Ireland. The pitiful band of revolutionaries, scorned by most of their fellow Irishmen, were convinced that through their defeat and deaths they would arouse the Irish people to a victorious fight.

From the first day, when belief in a dream outweighed all military considerations, to the seventh day, when the overwhelmed insurgents were finally defeated, this is the dramatic minute-by-minute story of the uprising in and around the Post Office during the week of siege, vividly reconstructed by Thomas Coffey from personal interviews and painstaking research.

'An extraordinarily readable book and a most moving one' – J. H. Plumb in the *Saturday Review*

'While he sticks to the facts and never allows himself any flights of fancy, his account still reads like a good novel' – Benedict Kiely in the *New York Times*